Research
Writing
Revisited

A SOURCEBOOK

FOR TEACHERS

Edited by

PAVEL ZEMLIANSKY
WENDY BISHOP

Boynton/Cook
HEINEMANN
Portsmouth, NH

Boynton/Cook Publishers, Inc.
A subsidiary of Reed Elsevier Inc.
361 Hanover Street
Portsmouth, NH 03801–3912
www.boyntoncook.com

Offices and agents throughout the world

Companion website material can be found at: *www.boyntoncook.com/ researchwritingrevisited*

Library of Congress Cataloging-in-Publication Data
Research writing revisited : a sourcebook for teachers / edited by Pavel Zemliansky and Wendy Bishop.
    p. cm.
  ISBN 0-86709-555-5 (alk. paper)
  1. Report writing—Study and teaching (Secondary)—Handbooks, manuals, etc.
2. Report writing—Study and teaching (Higher)—Handbooks, manuals, etc. 3. Research—Methodology—Study and teaching (Secondary)—Handbooks, manuals, etc. 4. Research—Methodology—Study and teaching (Higher)—Handbooks, manuals, etc. I. Zemliansky, Pavel. II. Bishop, Wendy.
  LB1047.3.R47 2003   2004010433
  808'.02—dc22

Editors: Jim Strickland and Lisa Luedeke
Production editor: Sonja S. Chapman
Cover design: Night & Day Design
Compositor: Valerie Levy / Drawing Board Studios
Manufacturing: Steve Bernier

Printed in the United States of America on acid-free paper
08   07   06   05   04   VP   1   2   3   4   5

Contents

Acknowledgments

We thank Boynton/Cook editors Lisa Luedeke and James Strickland for supporting this project and helping to make it happen. We also thank the editorial and production staff at Boynton/Cook Heinemann for their expertise and assistance.

Most of all, we want to thank the talented and expert teachers who contributed to this collection. Thank you for sharing your passion for teaching and writing and for your generosity.

Finally, we thank our families, friends, and colleagues for their help and support.

Introduction

As the work on this collection neared completion, we learned that Wendy Bishop had passed away. I was very lucky to know Wendy and work with her. Our relationship, which began as one of a professor and graduate student, evolved into one of collaboration and friendship. I was a student in Wendy's classes, she directed my dissertation, and we coedited two books. But we also had many conversations about teaching and writing. Wendy inspired me to be a teacher and a scholar, and I am very grateful for that. She was a great teacher, mentor, and friend, and we will miss her sorely.

When we began working on this project, we had two ideas in mind: that research is important for all kinds of writing; and that the traditional research paper assignment that has been a staple in many writing curricula for over eighty years does not reflect either the importance of research for all writers or the true nature of research as rhetorical inquiry.

Guided by these two principles, in this book we wanted to gather a broad range of approaches to teaching research writing. All the chapters in this collection treat research as a rhetorical and active process, and not merely as a matter of information-gathering.

Research Writing Revisited consists of two parts: a book and a website. The book is divided into five parts, each part dealing with different kinds of research writing assignments and different aspects of the research-writing process. Part I of the collection presents the fundamentals of the rhetorically based approach to the teaching and learning of research writing. The essays in this part challenge the traditional research paper assignment's emphasis on information-gathering and form and instead present useful alternatives. Their authors ask readers to approach research rhetorically and actively, seeking not to repeat old knowledge but build new understanding of their topics. We feel that Part I will be welcomed in particular by those teachers who work with more traditional forms of academic argumentation with their students. The chapters in Part II show how to use research for creativity and for self-expression. They continue to reinforce the idea that research is essential for all writers, regardless of the genre in which they work. The authors of the chapters in Part II also work to debunk the myth that research writing must be completely objective and not show the writer's personality. Essays in Part III are designed to help teachers with research-writing instruction across different genres, settings, and disciplines. Part IV promotes the idea that research writing is a vehicle for collaboration and community action. Finally, Part V contains four chapters dedicated to the teaching of research writing as a process.

We wanted to make the website an integral part of the project; it contains one essay as well as diverse classroom materials. We join the contributors to this collection, who generously shared these materials, in inviting you to use them with your students. The URL for the companion website is: ***www.boyntoncook.com/researchwritingrevisited.***

Let this book not only help us to teach writing, but also remind us of Wendy Bishop—a kind and generous person, a friend, and a valued colleague.

PART I

Research as Empowerment

1

Developing
"Interesting Thoughts"
Reading for Research

Janette Martin

In *Narrative of the Life of Frederick Douglass, an American Slave*, readers are struck by a pivotal moment when Douglass (2002) describes his reading of two essays in *The Columbian Orator*. One is a dialogue between a master and slave that results in the slave's emancipation, and the other is an argument by Richard Brinsley Sheridan in favor of Catholic emancipation. Douglass writes,

> These were choice documents to me. I read them over and over again with unabated interest. They gave tongue to interesting thoughts of my own soul, which had frequently flashed through my mind, and died away for want of utterance. . . . What I got from Sheridan was a bold denunciation of slavery, and a powerful vindication of human rights. The reading of these documents enabled me to utter my thoughts, and to meet the arguments brought forward to sustain slavery. (1840–1841)

Douglass' impassioned narrative frames that "conversation" between reader and writer that educators encourage students to engage in as they embark on challenging reading and writing tasks, including reading for research writing. As Douglass synthesizes the "conversation" between master and slave with Sheridan's rhetoric for an emancipated Catholicism, he finds his own voice and enters into a Burkean "parlor" of "interesting thoughts" crucial to his time and formative of his own identity, and he does this at twelve years of age!

In our hearts, we long for our students to have the kind of reading experience that Douglass rehearses. We hope their opinions will be influenced, extended, provoked, and shaped by encounters with the ideas of others. Yes, teaching research writing provides students with practical researching skills. However, whether teaching a first-year composition course, a history course, or any other course in which we require research writing, we try to craft assignments requiring critical thinking and fostering intellectual growth ("interesting thoughts"). I agree with Doug Brent's (1992) argument that research is

> the main mode of developing thought in academic disciplines.... "[R]esearch" simply means making contact with other human beings by reading the texts they have produced, and then updating one's own system of beliefs with reference to those texts. It represents a particular social form of inquiry. . . . It is, in fact, the classroom version of the way in which virtually all human knowledge is rhetorically developed. (xiv)

Yet for many of us, fostering a Douglass-like epiphany through a "social form of inquiry" may seem near to impossible when we head into the library stacks with college students who often have little reading experience and whose reading abilities vary at least as much as their writing abilities. However, we try hard to provide our students with the best possible tutelage in reading for research that we can. In this chapter, I share some of the methods that have served my classes best through years of teaching research in a variety of class settings. And, like Douglass and his sources, my methods and way of thinking about reading for research come from a synthesis of conversations with teachers, students, and readings on the topic. The following practices at times follow a sequence and at times go on concurrently.

Foregrounding Context and Purpose
for Research Work

Research assigned in various classes may be unique to the class context and instructor's purpose. Discussing student experiences with research along with their assumptions about what they'll do in my class and my assumptions about what they already know about reading and research is a first step in clarifying context and purpose. First-year, first-semester students may or may not have ever been invited to offer their opinions or theories in high school research work. In this case, sending them off to read sources and synthesize the ideas they discover on their own may cause some bewilderment. Moreover, many of my upper-level students read sources and write reports in their majors, not thesis-driven papers. Just as we emphasize the different contexts and purposes for writing, we need to emphasize differences in reading for research.

Different contexts and purposes may lead students into particular patterns of dealing with sources. I like to address this by assigning a class reading of Patrick J. Slattery's (1991) essay, "The Argumentative, Multi-Source Paper: College Students Reading, Thinking, and Writing About Divergent Points of View." Slattery describes what he calls "dogmatic," "noncommittal," and "analytical" approaches to reading and using sources. These approaches reflect simple to more complex engagement with sources. In a dogmatic approach students use only sources that fit their own ideas and opinions. Here, the student might even write the research paper and then go look for citations to "throw" into the paper. Sources aren't "read" so much as they are transcribed into the student's writing. My own students who tend to use the dogmatic approach have often written reviews and opinion papers in high school with little if any synthesis or analysis of source materials. The dogmatic approach is also easy, offering the path of least resistance through an assignment because it requires little synthesis or managing of a "conversation" between student and sources. It's helpful to let student discover that the disjunction between the student's voice and citations can make the dogmatic approach a rough ride for the reader. Few "interesting thoughts" are likely to emerge as the student chooses voices of sources to simply echo his or her ideas.

The "noncommittal" approach includes various sources and diverse opinions but without synthesis, evaluation, or the student's own ideas. If in the dogmatic approach the student's voice eclipses that of the sources, in the noncommittal approach the student is not so much a participant in the conversation in the "parlor" as she is a servant in the background silently moving from guest to guest. Doug Brent's early teaching of research writing, which I have been guilty of too, facilitated this noncommittal pattern. He explains,

> My students learned how to use quotations, more or less: that is, they learned how many spaces to indent and on which side of the quotation marks to place the period. . . . But their research papers . . . remained hollow imitations of research, collections of information gleaned from sources with little evaluation, synthesis, or original thought. They approached research as they would gathering shells at the beach, picking up ideas with interesting colors or unusual shapes and putting them in a bucket without regard for overall pattern. (xiii)

Many of my students regularly practice this sort of "noncommittal" collecting of citations for research papers in classes where reporting is emphasized and analyzing or evaluating is forbidden. Students fresh from high school may also practice this collage approach if their research work has primarily involved cutting and pasting from Internet sources. In such cases, work with sources is an afterthought and "getting" the conventions of documentation becomes the goal of the work. Unfortunately, the only "interesting thoughts" that arise from the reading are those attributable to the sources.

Slattery's final approach demonstrates a level of reading sources that many of us strive for in teaching reading for research. Here, some of Slattery's students "demonstrated an analytical approach [and] not only understood but also successfully analyzed and evaluated sources" (373). This approach is most promising for generating those "interesting thoughts" that arise from a real conversation with sources, and it is also the approach, like any good conversation, that calls for the most work.

Students in my upper-level rhetoric classes who read Slattery's essay explained that they use these approaches individually or in combination for different contexts and purposes, for example according to their energy level, or with an eye to the grading criteria in the class. I ask students to provide specific examples of how Slattery's approaches fit their own practices, and I offer examples of my own approaches to research. These examples can be seen on this volume's companion website. Bringing students' awareness to these approaches is quite useful in helping students as they begin to read for research.

Encouraging Students to Assume an Attitude of Curiosity

From the onset of the course, I like to openly discuss the attitudes that students assume toward their work. If a student is uninterested in a topic or bored with the assignment, the reading will hardly spark "interesting thoughts." In class, students can share concerns that they have about the research work that might be affecting their attitudes. If they fear reading difficult sources and trying to synthesize them in papers, if they've written dozens of research papers that have drawn a letter grade but no comments from the teacher, if they view research as busywork, students may well need some persuasion to open up to the assignment. My practice includes helping students find their way into a topic to stay within the context of the class but to suit the student's particular interests. Students might believe that they are not interested in the research topic; however, with some class and group discussions, students will generally find a narrow topic that relates to their interests.

If we're working on a shared topic, I try to give students the opportunity to choose their own narrow topics within the context of our course materials. For instance, one composition student was frustrated when confronted with a research assignment that was to be inspired by Michel Foucault's "Panopticism," a chapter from Foucault's book *Discipline and Punish*, a history of how Western society has evolved into a highly disciplined system of social institutions and relations (see Chapter 1 of the companion website). What, she resisted, did she know about Foucault or the history of discipline? She had read Foucault quite literally, as an examination of prisons and institutions and their systems of discipline and as having no relevance to her own life. But with some help from the instructor and her group, she realized that as an athlete, she followed a rigid, prescribed disciplinary routine. This research topic attracted and maintained her interest while opening up a new way for her to see herself as a part of a larger disciplinary mechanism that had not previously occurred to her. Once she saw this, her reading of Foucault had more resonance with her life, and her mind opened to the voices of others (her sources) who had nothing to do with Foucault. In classes where the topic is much more open, I use a "research prep form" to help students identify areas of interest they may not think would be relevant for a research paper but in fact are. The form can be seen in Chapter 1 of the companion website.

Reading Challenging Texts Throughout the Semester

Once we've talked about the purpose and context for the research we'll be doing, and we've explored ways to make the work meaningful and interesting, we begin reading and discussing shared texts that offer students challenging reading. I've experienced the uncomfortable situation of having assigned easy-to-read, mass-audience articles throughout the semester only to then present students with extremely challenging reading, for example of refereed publications, near the end of the semester when they embark on the high-stakes research project. This pitfall is easily avoided by introducing a variety of challenging sources from the beginning of the semester. Students are often alert and willing to do whatever we ask at this early moment, and they haven't yet figured out what they can safely omit from assigned reading!

In first-year composition courses, I've been using a particularly challenging reader, *Ways of Reading: An Anthology for Writers*, edited by David Bartholomae and Anthony Petrosky (2002). The reader includes John Wideman, Walter Benjamin, Jane Tompkins, Michel Foucault, Gloria Anzaldua, and others. Bartholomae and Petrosky argue, "Reading involves a fair measure of push and shove. You make your mark on a book and it makes its mark on you. . . . We'd like you to imagine that when you read the works we've collected here, somebody is saying something to you, and we'd like you to imagine that you are in a position to speak back, to say something of your own in turn" (1). The book's introduction repeatedly underscores the "hard" readings and the "work" that will be involved. While I was skeptical of presenting freshmen with difficult readings, after my first semester with the text students convinced me that they will rise to the occasion of tackling difficult texts that have meaningful messages for them, that draw them into conversations worth having.

From the beginning and throughout the semester, I also like to assign reading of a few refereed publications, taking one at a time and doing a thorough analysis of each. We can discuss samples of these often difficult texts together, and many are now available online for easy access by all class members.

Modeling the Reading

While working with shared texts, I model reading for students. Inspired by a colleague's tip, I show students my own annotations of readings in our class text. I was surprised to learn that most students had never thought of extracting key words or phrases from paragraphs and writing them in the margins. We may think that students who read assigned handbook chapters on note-taking and annotating "get" this, but showing them seems to be a more effective way to demonstrate how this technique looks and works. This practice helps students index long or difficult readings so that they can locate important points they wish to return to for their responses or papers. In addition, we can talk about how we find key ideas in a text, and we can debate what seems important in the text during initial and subsequent readings.

Another way of modeling critical reading is to assign group work on tough readings. In groups, students share their experience and expertise with difficult reading, and they also compete with one another, which helps energize their responses to texts.

Moreover, to help students avoid a "dogmatic" approach where they select only those sources whose ideas support their own opinions, we need to demonstrate through models how and why sources contradict each other. Students may want to simplify their reading by ignoring these valuable contradictions. Reading discussions and assignments might guide students through evaluation of sources to detect bias or to trace contradictions. We might ask whether the researcher should try to "reconcile" contradictions or not, and we can draw attention to the nature of the contradictions, emphasizing that they're natural and should not be suppressed from writing. After all, the contradictions and biases make the "conversation" students are constructing vital and allow the space needed for the student's own opinions and new knowledge. M. Linda Miller (2001) advises students about this process in "Revisiting the Library":

> I may not quote all of the voices I've heard in my final paper, but I can include the relevant ones as citations in the reference list. Or I may quote some of them to rebut them. Or, some of them may make me rethink and modify my initial position in some way, and I'll want to let my readers know about the influence these authors have had on my view. (67)

Teasing out subtle biases, bringing to light the contradictions and multiple perspectives evident in credible sources, questioning, and evaluating are core to the production of "interesting thoughts" our students will discover as they find their own voices and enter them into the conversation. As Cindy Moore (2001) puts it in "Finding the Voices of Others Without Losing Your Own":

> Of all the critical reading activities, analyzing and evaluating are especially crucial for maintaining your voice, because they help you see that the power in texts isn't necessarily a given, but that it comes from the relationship between reader and writer. That is, there is no quality inherent in a book, article, or Internet site that should cause you to immediately drop all of your own views in favor of what the author says—to surrender your voice to his. (123)

I love to see students argue with a text or take sides when discussing two or more texts with conflicting biases. *CQ Researcher*, a database of information on issues of topical relevance published by *Congressional Quarterly* and available online through many libraries, offers short "pro/con" articles that provide excellent examples of ways in which "authorities" disagree or interpret facts differently according to bias. These samples provide a model for reading that helps students maintain their own voices rather than relinquish them to their sources.

Assigning Reading Responses Throughout the Semester

Modeling reading and asking students to work through difficult shared readings in class can be reinforced through weekly assignments. I assign brief critical thinking responses that move students' thinking through careful analyses of sources. Prompts ask them to seek patterns, to identify sections within a large piece of writing, to work out confusing or difficult passages, even to go to the dictionary to decode unfamiliar words and phrases. To use the Foucault example, I ask first-year composition students to read the selection twice, first to get a general idea of the point of the essay, and second to track recurring words, ideas, and images, particularly those that have meaning for them. For samples of such reading responses, visit Chapter 1 of the companion website. This practice of asking students to follow an idea or image in a reading that seems somehow to relate to them ensures their reading of the material and is useful later during class discussion or should they need to write a paper that incorporates the reading.

Starting Small and Incorporating Reading for Research from Early On

Even while we are working with shared readings in class, I like to assign the reading and inclusion of source material from the beginning of the semester. We often begin reading for research by writing short papers that incorporate citations from the shared text. A description of such an assignment can be found in Chapter 1 of the companion website. We can look at samples of these citations in papers to see how effectively the student is engaging in a conversation with the source. Because we share the text and thus familiarity with the material, we can also disagree with one another about the knowledge produced from the engagement with the text. That "social form of inquiry" Brent articulates becomes manifest in the classroom discussion. Assigning the Slattery piece prior to a first assignment that asks students to read and cite a source is a good way to set up a discussion of the dogmatic, noncommittal, and analytical approaches. In fact, one assignment might ask students to try out each of these approaches to reading and incorporating source materials in the writing. Soon after this initial exercise, we move to more difficult shared readings, such as those from refereed journals accessible online. Students seem to enjoy reading and discussing excerpts from each other's papers. Like detectives, they ferret out disjointed lines of thought, gaps between the source's and student's voices, unsynthesized contradictions of ideas, and other areas where the reader is closed out of the "conversation." This practice helps them become better readers of their own writing as well. Starting the reading of outside sources in a small way and expanding—looking at one, then two, then multiple sources—can give students time to grow into the more complex reading.

Helping Students Find Promising Sources to Read

Once students set off on their high-stakes research work, I encourage them to explore their topics by surveying general reference tools first. These reference tools introduce key terms and figures and open up myriad avenues of exploration for narrower topics while giving students a quick and easy reading of the topic at the onset of their project. When possible, I arrange for an orientation to relevant reference tools by a reference librarian who is far more knowledgeable and up to date on library resources for particular disciplines than I am. For instance, while teaching classes in American literature, I take my students to the reference section, where a librarian walks students through an exercise in which they locate appropriate sources useful to their upcoming research projects. She also gives them a handout that helps guide many of them through the initial stages of research for their project.

Guiding students to sources that are not general reference is another part of my process. Earlier, we've searched for and read sources, including selected refereed publications, in a shared setting. As I move toward more individual work with nonshared sources, I hold a one-class tutorial in a computer lab to demonstrate using online search tools, and I lead a one-class tour of the library to demonstrate locating sources. While I prepare a hands-on assignment for library work, our institution provides an online tutorial for locating sources. Databases, online catalogues, and other standard computing concepts may not need to be included in instruction since high schools are more and more involving students in use of these tools. It's a good idea, however, to find out exactly what students know.

Depending on the context and purpose of the course and assignment, instructors define the requirements for reading sources. My own preference is to set minimum requirements for the number and kinds of sources students need to read and include in their research writing.

Because we begin with a shared text and move through the semester to a variety of sources in the culminating research paper, students are prepared to tackle the challenging conversation that results from following a topic across a range of media. What they've learned about audience becomes quite clear when they compare a mass-audience publication's article to one printed in a trade journal. They see the benefits and limitations of a book's coverage of a topic when compared to an Internet article of the same. I like them to discover radio as a means of information, not just entertainment. A good part of my reasoning for assigning a number and variety of sources is to expose students to a broad conversation held in a number of voices. However, contexts and purposes vary. Some instructors introduce a variety of sources and then let students choose which and how many they feel they need to read and include. When I've tried this, I find students gravitate to Internet sites geared toward mass audiences.

Showing How Sources Might Provide "Indirect" Information

Students often begin their research by looking for sources that directly connect to their narrowed topics. One student of mine ran into a snag when confronted with the requirement to include information from a book for a paper he was writing about immigrants' rights and the Patriot Act. Frustrated and about to give up on his topic, he complained that no book existed on his specific topic. But we can encourage students to look for sources to help define, contextualize, and provide history on their topics rather than reproduce the specific paper topic. In this case, he was able to use books to build a section in his paper on the history of U.S. laws and immigrants, which then provided context for what he was learning from other sources about the current situation. We can also help students read sources for analogous examples rather than examples that fit the specific topics of their papers. Scholars use this way of reading sources all the time and often with effective results.

Assigning an Annotated Bibliography

If time permits, at about mid-semester I like to assign an annotated bibliography that reflects a good part of the reading for research students have performed up to this point. This means giving the multiple-source research paper assignment early, even if it isn't due until the end of the semester. The annotated bibliography ensures that work on the research project is in motion and that students are reading a variety of sources. It also encourages students to summarize sources and helps identify areas of common interest among sources. In this latter respect, students may start to see the "conversation" about the topic emerging from sources. Many students, even those in upper levels, are unfamiliar with annotated bibliographies, or confuse them with lists of works cited, so it's a good idea to provide models of this form (see Chapter 1 of the companion website).

Keeping a Conversation Going Throughout the Reading

Asking students to share their reading progress and describe how that reading is shaping their own ideas helps students clarify their experiences and map the course of their research as it progresses. In my teaching writing class for education students, class members regularly shared their research. One student in my teaching writing course was researching homeschooling. As a future public school educator, her own bias was that public school education has more advantages for children than homeschooling, but she was frustrated when she could not find sources that criticized homeschooling in the ways she expected. Pavel Zemliansky (2001) encourages students to track the evolution of their thinking as they process sources' ideas as my student was doing.

> Listen to what other voices say and have said about your topic. Read other opinions and evaluate their credibility. And always come back to what you began with—your previous knowledge. It is important to think about what you knew before as you expand your knowledge because it lets you see how your understanding of your topic changes based on new information and insights. (114)

This student indeed followed this process. She came out of the project with a new understanding and appreciation of homeschooling along with many advantages of public schooling drawn from her own experiences as a public school student and teen swimming counselor working with homeschooled children. It was exciting to see the resourcefulness with which she read her sources. Rather than reject them in favor of a dogmatic approach to the research project, she allowed them into a conversation, a give-and-take, and this was far more interesting than a one-sided argument. Being able to share her reading experiences while in the process of researching encouraged her to be inventive and participate in this conversation. It allowed her to hang onto a topic that was exciting and meaningful to her. In this case, the reading sparked "interesting thoughts" which led to the kind of growth and opening of the mind that we hope all of our students will undergo in their research.

Conclusion: From "Interesting Thoughts" to Action

I'd like to leave this chapter as I began it, with the words of Frederick Douglass. Douglass' elation at finding voice for "interesting thoughts" is quickly followed by his realization that his sources did something else too. They set him on a course of action, first to learn also to write, second to enter the fight for abolition. "The silver trump of freedom had roused my soul to eternal wakefulness. Freedom now appeared, to disappear no more forever. It was heard in every sound, and seen in every thing" (1842). Douglass' struggle to literacy and then freedom was solitary and lonely. We are fortunate to be on hand to assist our students, to facilitate their reading, their "social form of inquiry," and to witness their "wakefulness" arise. And we know that for our students, as for Douglass, the meaningful conversations they craft through their reading of sources just might take them far beyond learning the conventions of a style or developing "interesting thoughts." They can inspire the choices and actions of a lifetime.

Works Cited

Bartholomae, David, and Anthony Petrosky, eds. 2002. " Introduction." In *Ways of Reading: An Anthology for Writers*, 1–18. Boston: Bedford/ St. Martin's.

Brent, Doug. 1992. *Reading as Rhetorical Invention: Knowledge, Persuasion, and the Teaching of Research-Based Writing*. Urbana, IL: NCTE.

Douglass, Frederick. 2002. *Narrative of the Life of Frederick Douglass, an American Slave*. In *The Heath Anthology of American Literature* 4th ed., Volume 1, 1817–1880, edited by Paul Lauter et al. Boston: Houghton Mifflin. (Note: Douglass' narrative is dated 1845.)

Miller, M. Linda. 2001. "Revisiting the Library: Old and New Technologies for Effective Research." In *The Subject Is Research: Processes and Practices*, edited by Wendy Bishop and Pavel Zemliansky, 60–68. Portsmouth, NH: Boynton/Cook.

Moore, Cindy. 2001. "Finding the Voices of Others Without Losing Your Own." In *The Subject Is Research: Processes and Practices*, edited by Wendy Bishop and Pavel Zemliansky, 119–28. Portsmouth, NH: Boynton/Cook.

Slattery, Patrick J. 2002. "The Argumentative, Multi-Source Paper: College Students Reading, Thinking, and Writing About Divergent Points of View." In *Teaching Argument in the Composition Course: Background Readings*, edited by Timothy Barnett, 361–77. Boston: Bedford/St. Martin's. (Note: Slattery's article was originally published in 1991.)

Zemliansky, Pavel. 2001. "Using Your Preexisting Knowledge During Research." In *The Subject Is Research: Processes and Practices*, edited by Wendy Bishop and Pavel Zemliansky, 111–18. Portsmouth, NH: Boynton/Cook.

2

Rhetorically Writing and Reading Researched Arguments

Maureen Daly Goggin and Duane Roen

> There cannot be one set of standards or skills that constitutes the
> ends of literacy learning. . . . Gone are the days when learning a
> single, standard version of the language was sufficient. . . . No
> longer do the old pedagogies of a formal, standard, written national
> language hold the utility they once possessed.
> —Cope and Kalantzis (2000a, 6)

We open our chapter with Bill Cope and Mary Kalantzis' powerful observation to signal that we are interested in tackling complex questions concerning
the learning and teaching of research, reading, and writing, and to suggest that
our treatment of these questions offers but one of numerous possible pedagogical approaches to literacy learning. The other pieces in this volume offer
other valuable methodologies that, when taken together, go a long way toward
answering Cope and Kalantzis' (2000a) implicit call for multiple pedagogies.
However, while Cope and Kalantzis note that the old pedagogies no longer
"hold the utility they once possessed" (6), we may reasonably question
whether they ever were as effectual as implied by their observation. Our goal
here is not to quibble with Cope and Kalantzis. Rather because the notion and
treatment of literacy as an independent skill that transcends social, cultural,
and contextual forces remains stubbornly in place, particularly as evidenced
by the plethora of writing textbooks that continue to support this dubious and
indefensible view, we find it important to situate our discussion of teaching research writing within some of the scholarship that makes clear why there
never could be a "one set of standards or skills that constitutes the ends of literacy learning" (6).[1]

Shirley Brice Heath's (1983) landmark study *Ways with Words* problematizes in extremely fruitful ways conceptions of reading and writing as neutral, natural, acontextual, universal, developmental skills. Her (1982) theoretical construct of *literacy event* as "any occasion in which a piece of writing is integral to the nature of participants' interactions and their interpretive processes" (50) broadens notions concerning *what* counts as a literate *object*; *what* counts as literate *practice*; and *who* counts in the production, circulation, and consumption of reading/writing materials. This construct thus contributes to rethinking how reading and writing are learned and conducted in different social spaces. In short, Heath's research and that of other ethnographers following in her wake provide the grist for challenging what Brian Street (1984) first termed *autonomous models* of literacy. These models assume a one-size-fits-all literacy independent of those who engage in it, absent the purposes for which it is invoked, apart from the times and places it occurs, and irrelevant to the materiality of the practice. Such views construct, and perpetuate, a binary (literate/illiterate) that is not only meaningless but is culturally and socially debilitating (Street 1995). Those who do not read and write in recognizable and privileged ways are deemed abnormal and defective either intellectually or morally. The myth of a monolithic literacy has been so powerful that it generates periodic outcries of literacy crises from media, educators, politicians, parents, and other public groups (Varnum 1986).

The assumption that there is one way of reading and writing has been exploded by scholars coming from all sorts of different perspectives: historical (Clanchy 1993; Graff 1991), theoretical (Bazerman 2000; Gee 1996; Street 1984), and ethnographic (Barton, Hamilton, and Ivanic 1999; Journet 1999; Street 1995, 2001). Various scholarly inquiries have clearly demonstrated that research, reading, and writing are interdependent practices that vary greatly not only *across* different sociocultural contexts but *within* specific contexts. That is, inquiry, reading, and writing do not take place in a vacuum; these take place within communities of practice and are adjudicated by those communities.[2] What counts as topic, inquiry, evidence, preferred genres, and purposes for the discourse are among the discursive aspects that are both shaped by and shape a community. These discourse practices are learned by participating in the given community (Gee 1996; Street 1995). As Vicki Carrington (2001) so well puts it, "literacy is neither one definitive concept nor one specifiable practice. Rather, it can more profitably be conceived of as families of literate practices, all of which are representative of cultural arbitraries, and which may or may not gain social advantage for those who manifest them" (265). Thus, inquiry, reading, and writing are best understood as multiple, social practices.

As if this situation were not complicated enough, the seismic shift from an industry-based to a knowledge- and information-based society (fostering and being fostered by rapid globalization) means that our students are confronted with, and must learn to participate in, increasingly multilingual and

polydiscursive practices. Under the rising demands of the emerging new social order, the need for teaching and learning diverse practices in critical inquiry, reading, and writing in a variety of print and digital media is becoming
all the more pressing. Further, in many ways, information technology and information literacy are raising awareness of this need.

These observations raise an important question for teachers: if literate practices are so variable, and if radical societal changes are demanding more, and increasingly differentiated, literate practices, how then do we teach students ways
of participating in so many disparate rhetorical contexts? We argue here that
flexible rhetorical strategies for critical inquiry, reading, and writing provide a
scaffold that helps students learn to assess and participate in a variety of literate
arenas (Fleming 1998; Petraglia 2000; Young 2003). Learning and practicing
flexible rhetorical strategies should, in other words, enable students to grapple
successfully and effectively with a multiple range of (and situationally different)
personal, professional, civic, and academic literate tasks.

Our chapter is divided into two major sections. We begin by explicating
the theoretical framework that has informed our concepts of literacy, pedagogy, classroom activities and assignments. We discuss this framework in detail because as T. R. Johnson and Shirley Morahan (2002) so rightfully point
out: "every choice you make as a writing instructor is informed by some philosophy of composition and of teaching composition, even if you're not fully
aware of the philosophy you hold. The more aware you become of your assumptions and premises, the more you can rethink and improve your teaching"
(1). Different philosophies of writing and teaching writing lead to different
pedagogical approaches. To our mind, what is important is that as writing
teachers we act as "reflective practitioners," to use George Hillocks' (1995)
term, so that we recognize not only how the theories we hold privilege certain
pedagogical practices but also limit others. In the second section, we then describe a methodology for guiding students to construct researched historical
arguments and to respond effectively to their peers' emerging researched arguments.[3] Our approach is informed by literature in collaborative/cooperative
learning that theorizes conditions that lead to more effective peer collaboration: positive interdependence, individual accountability, equal participation,
the role of the teacher as a guide, and attention to interpersonal skill building
(e.g., Bruffee 1993; Gere 1987; Johnson, Johnson, and Smith 1991; Kagan
1992; LeFevre 1987). More specifically, we provide an eleven-day sequence
of activities in which students working with other students respond to a series
of heuristics and develop questions to guide critical inquiry into a specific historical issue of their choosing, and respond to peers' researched arguments as
they emerge. At the companion website for this collection, we include in an
appendix specific handouts for the assignment, a series of heuristics that aid
student in their inquiry, writing, and reading, as well as peer response and critical reflection activities.

New Sociocultural Dynamics: Intersections Among Work, Communication, and Epistemology

Our post-Fordist world is spawning what Brian Street (2001) terms the "'New Orders'—the New Work Order, the New Communicative Order and the New Epistemological Order" (2). Taken together, these new orders have enormous implications for how we prepare students for the world. The New Work Order is emerging as a result of expanding globalization of material and knowledge production and distribution. As James Gee (1996) points out, "there is now a great deal more attention paid to the selling environment at every level of production, from design to distribution. So while the old work order stressed issues of costs and revenue, the new work order emphasizes asset building and market share" (viii). In contrast to the regimented Taylorist principles of organization, the new order calls for "flexibility and adaptation to change" (Street 2001, 3). Further, while the old work order focused on the individual operating within a rigid hierarchy, the new order calls for teamwork within ostensibly flattened organizations. This new order requires complex New Communicative systems that take place in a variety of media. Thus, in addition to alphabetic literacy, competencies (differentially defined) in reading and writing visual, verbal, and digital signs of all sorts will determine who is "literate" within the new order. Finally, the New Epistemological Order emerges as a critique of modernism and Enlightenment philosophies and science. It values the local over the universal, the reflective over the objective, and the social over the individual (see Scollon and Scollon 2002, esp. 106–34). These three interdependent facets of the New Order require new ways of conceptualizing, teaching, and measuring literate practices. In short, they require a "New Literacy."

Brian Street coined the term "New Literacy" to describe current theories and approaches to reading and writing that challenge traditional models of literacy as merely a technical, decontextualized skill that is imposed from above. As he points out, "the 'autonomous' model of literacy works from the assumption that literacy in itself—autonomously—will have effects on other social and cognitive practices. The model, however, disguises the cultural and ideological assumptions that underpin it and that can then be presented as though they are neutral and universal" (2001, 7; also see Gee 1996; Scollon and Scollon 2002). By contrast, an alternative model—what Street terms the "ideological model"—"offers a more culturally sensitive view of literacy practices as they vary from one context to another" (7). It is worth quoting Street at some length:

> [An ideological model of literacy] starts from different premises than the autonomous model—it posits instead that literacy is a social practice, not simply a technical and neutral skill; that it is always embedded in socially-constructed epistemological principles. It is about knowledge: the ways in which people address reading and writing are themselves rooted in conceptions of knowl-

edge, identity, being. Literacy, in this sense, is always contested, both its meaning and its practices, hence particular versions of it are always "ideological,"
they are always rooted in a particular world-view and a desire for that view of
literacy to dominate and to marginalize others. (2001, 7–8)

Within the ideological model, any individual must be understood as be-
longing to multiple literate systems, some of which overlap and some of which
are competing and contradictory. In any given situation, these systems interact
with each other. Thus, discursive systems are never stable; "any discourse
system is constantly in the process of evolution and change" (Scollon and
Scollon 2002, 206). The challenge for our students then is to develop strategies
for figuring out what counts as a topic, a question, a method, acceptable evidence, and approved ways of discoursing within particular contexts. In short,
our students must learn not only to control multiple practices but also to develop strategies for confronting new and changing literate situations.

New Pedagogies to Accommodate the New Orders

Teaching within the context of the New Order demands new pedagogical strategies. Based on research conducted by New London Group (2000) on literacy
learning, we advocate the following five pedagogical tenets:

1. *Situated Practice*: the concept that students learn best when immersed in
   the contexts in which literate practices take place—when, in short, they experience meaning making in real contexts and through a variety of media.
   Literate *practices* are acquired through enculturation (Gee 1996; Goggin
   1995; Street 2001; Scollon and Scollon 2002).
2. *Overt Instruction*: the concept that students who develop metacognitive
   skills through studying theory achieve competency in choosing and using
   appropriate literate strategies. In other words, students need more than just
   practice; they also need to understand *why* they are being asked to engage
   in particular activities.
3. *Critical Framing*: the concept that when students learn to interpret social
   and institutional contexts in terms of diverse purposes and audiences, they
   discern the most effective ways to communicate.
4. *Contextual Design*: the concept of student-consultants who learn to think
   simultaneously as consumers and designers of rhetorical texts (cf. Kaufer
   and Butler 1996, 2000).
5. *Transformed Practice*: the concept of students as meaning makers who become the designers or builders of relevant kinds of texts by transforming
   rhetorical strategies they already control (New London Group 2000, 9ff;
   also see Cope and Kalantzis 2000b; Goggin 1995; Street 2001).

Since inquiry, design, and consumption of arguments are situationally based and interdependent, we focus on ways to help students engage and develop flexible heuristics for research, reading, and writing in specific contexts and across various discursive media. Our approach, and the assumptions underlying it, departs significantly from other (especially more traditional) approaches to teaching research and what is often ubiquitously dubbed the "research paper."

Unlike approaches that treat library or bibliographic research as if it were the only method of conducting scholarly inquiry, we help students to understand that critical inquiry varies depending on the rhetorical task. Further, we help students understand that the different kinds of critical inquiry lead to different kinds of genres with the essay as one of many available genres. This is important because essay-text literacy is often privileged in the writing classroom (especially as presented in many textbooks) as the *only* literate practice. As James Gee (1989) points out, "essay-text literacy, with its attendant emphasis on the syntactic mode and explicitness, while only one cultural expression of literacy among many, is connected with the form of consciousness and interests of the powerful in our society" (59). This connection explains in part the hegemony of the research essay in education. Paradoxically, however, it threatens to disenfranchise students and keep those already at the margins firmly in place. As Harvey Graff (1991) argues, "an inflexible view of literacy, without attention to contextual needs and uses, results only in disappointment" (393). More than mere disappointment, such a view masks the political, cultural, and social implications of narrow notions of literacy—masks, in short, the social inscription of what counts as a literate act and who counts in its production. In particular, the ubiquitous research essay (that exists only as a school-based genre but is often treated as if it were the sole conduit of scholarly activity) may be best understood as *antirhetorical* (Scollon and Scollon 2002, 119–20). As Scollon and Scollon (2002) note, the *antirhetorical* characteristic of the school-based research essay is that it "should appear as to give nothing but information, that [it] should appear to be making no attempt to influence the listener or reader except through his or her exercise of rational judgment" (120). Authority under this view rests with the text, which tends to foster a formalist approach to teaching.

Our approach also departs significantly from what has been dubbed a "process approach" (an umbrella term that covers lots of competing theoretical positions).[4] Although there is much to value in a process approach, it often treats composing processes in a lock-step, generic fashion. As Joseph Harris (1997) argues: "[T]he advocates of process did not redirect attention to what students had to say so much as they simply argued for what seems to me a new sort of formalism—one centered no longer on textual structures but instead on various algorithms, heuristics, and guidelines for composing" (56). While we argue for teaching heuristics as valuable strategies within composing, we frame these as flexible strategies that vary dramatically depending on the rhetorical context, the literate task, and the writer. We do not advocate asking students to march through the same sets of generic process activities but rather we argue that students be taught that different kinds of heuristics serve different inquiry, reading, and writing ends. And most important is that the heuristics serve to engage them in the kinds of critical inquiry processes that will permit students to develop their own strategies for posing the kinds of rhetorical questions that will help them participate in any given rhetorical context.

The five tenets we described earlier, namely, situated practice, overt instruction, critical framing, contextual design, and transformed practice, offer a pedagogical model for accomplishing these goals. To demonstrate our approach and how we incorporate these five tenets into our teaching, next we describe in detail one unit on teaching literate practices in history.

Enculturation and Socialization: Writers Working with Peers

In the remaining pages of this chapter, we describe a flexible eleven-session sequence of activities in which students engage in a series of heuristics, develop questions to guide critical inquiry, work through analyzing historical data of different kinds, and establish rhetorical situations to guide them in drafting a history. The sequence represents but one of many possible ways to guide students as they respond to peers' researched histories as they emerge. The sequence could occur in eleven consecutive face-to-face classroom meetings, but teachers can easily modify the sequence for students working synchronously or asynchronously in online environments or in face-to-face groups outside of class. Further, teachers can adapt the sequence for other kinds of writing assignments. We have also prepared appendixes with specific handouts of heuristics to aid students in their inquiry, writing, and reading. They appear on the companion website for this collection.

In preparing this sequence, we considered the following questions to guide us:

1. How does the following sequence of peer collaboration and responses relate to course learning goals?
2. How does the sequence address the five tenets: situated practice, overt instruction, critical framing, contextual design, and transformed practice?
3. What are the teacher's roles and responsibilities as students engage in this sequence?
4. What are the students' roles and responsibilities?
5. What is the effect of offering student writers these kinds of activities and differing kinds of feedback over an extended period of time?
6. What sort of classroom climate will enhance the effectiveness of this sequence?
7. How does this sequence affect the classroom climate?

A Brief Version of the Assignment

For this project, each student writer selects a sociocultural community (e.g., professional group, academic discipline, community group, public or government group, company) to do an historical analysis. (A full description of and rationale for this project appears in Chapter 2 on the companion website for this collection.) The project is designed to engage students in critical framing—our third tenet—one family of methods (i.e., historical) for interpreting social and institutional contexts. Because there are any number of aspects the writer might select, a focused selection is crucial. A key for a writer is to identify an aspect related to the social organization (e.g., an event, a person, a trend) that the writer *wants* to learn more about either because she or he already participates in the community of practice or wishes to enter it in the future. The second key is to set limits on the history. Students are advised to limit their historical study by time frame (e.g., one decade), place, and object of inquiry (activity, event[s], person/people, and so on).

As students engage in this project, they read and discuss in class several articles on historiography that overtly tackle different ways historians conduct research and write.[5] They then apply these concepts to several historical articles, examining them for the kinds of inquiry, data, and genres used. These activities contribute to our second tenet, overt instruction. Reading about and in history is meant to help students develop meta-awareness of the different kinds of literate practices that operate in various contexts. Throughout the eleven sessions, students work together, not only giving them practice with teamwork—crucial to the New Work Order—but also helping them gain valuable critical reading/writing skills by helping each other work through various inquiry, writing, and reading practices relevant to the histories they are conducting.

For this assignment, each student writes a paper historicizing an event, activity, or phenomenon that is related in some way to the sociocultural community that interests him or her most. Histories typically are chronologically ordered—or in Hayden White's (1978) term, "plotted" like a story. The idea is to reconstruct the phenomenon in ways to help readers (and ultimately the writer) better understand it. As with virtually all writing, the student writer will need to construct a clear rhetorical situation (the target audience, the purposes, the role[s] as writer, the context) to help the writer decide which details to include and what the most effective organization will be.

For an elaborated student version of this assignment, please visit the companion website for this collection and see Chapter 2.

A Brief Conclusion

We end our chapter by returning to our opening as a symbolic gesture to enact what to our minds is the most important thing we as teachers of writing can do—*reflective practice*. As we indicated at the beginning of our chapter, a one-size-fits-all writing pedagogy and a one-size-fits-all view of writing no longer suffice, if they ever did. Thus, we delineate a unit design and pedagogical approach not as *the* way but as one of many available ways of teaching research, reading, and writing. This collection provides additional available means. As reflective practitioners, we need flexible strategies to guide us in designing writing classroom activities and assignments. Richard Young's (2003) recent call for a new pedagogy describes our goals well:

> [W]e need a new art of rhetoric that encourages inquiry and discussion; the present art . . . while valuable for many purposes, does not do this well. It emphasizes abstract principle, the self-evident, and the axiomatic in contrast to the particular, the practical, and the probabilistic; and it emphasizes technical knowledge and craft in contrast to effective action. It tends to devalue shared experience, communal belief, the situational and contingent, and the prudential. . . . Because our students bring this [former] tradition with them into the classroom, any alternative to it needs to be taught explicitly: we cannot assume that it too is part of their rhetorical inheritance even though it is part of rhetorical history. (166)

In explicating a pedagogical approach to rhetorically reading and writing researched arguments, we focus on ways to encourage multiple critical inquiry, reading, and writing practices that value "shared experience, communal belief, the situational and contingent, and the prudential." The five tenets—situated practice, overt instruction, critical framing, contextual design, and transformed practice—that guide our pedagogy go a long way toward answering Young's (2003) call and toward equipping our students with flexible rhetorical strategies that will prepare them for actively participating in diverse literate situations.

Notes

[1] For cogent discussions of the modernist ideology that has sustained impoverished concepts of literacy, see Scollon and Scollon 2002, Gee 1996, and Street 1995. Also see Bullock and Smith (1998), whose national study of writing programs found that contrary to proclamations by many in rhetoric and composition about changes in the field, virtually all of the programs they analyzed were firmly rooted in current-traditional practices. They argue that composition's narrative of the victory of process over formalist pedagogies needs to be challenged, for it does not hold up under a close scrutiny of the current state of writing programs.

[2] We prefer the term "communities of practice" over the terms "discourse community" and "speech community" since these terms have been so heavily, and rightfully, critiqued. Discursive practices are at the center of any community (whether academic, professional, social, familial), signaling both group member and claims to that group. See Johnstone (2002) for a good discussion on this point, especially 115–16.

[3] Our pedagogical strategies may be adapted for a variety of critical literate tasks; we focus on history because it draws on multiple kinds of inquiry

practices. In addition to traditional library research, historians analyze a wide range of different kinds of textual, visual, and material artifacts; further, those who conduct oral histories also engage in empirical research, primarily through interviews and observations. Hence, history offers a particularly rich—but by no means the only—area for guiding students through a variety of inquiry, reading, and writing tasks.

[4] For a cogent overview of various competing writing pedagogies, see Tate, Rupiper, and Schick (2001).

[5] Some rhetoric textbooks do overtly discuss historiography, such as Diana George and John Trimbur's (2001) *Reading Culture: Contexts for Critical Reading and Writing*. 4th ed. New York: Longman. However, teachers may also wish to put together their own packet of readings, selecting from history scholars such as Gene Wise (1980), Albert Cook (1989), Dominick LaCapra (1983), Peter Novick (1988), Paul Thompson (1988), and Hayden White (1978), to name a few. Finally, there are good websites devoted to historiography. Since Web addresses can change rapidly, rather than provide URLs, we recommend a Web search on the key term "historiography."

Works Cited

Barton, David, Mary Hamilton, and Roz Ivanic, eds. 1999. *Situated Literacies: Reading and Writing in Context*. London: Routledge.

Bazerman, Charles. 2000. "A Rhetoric for Literate Society: The Tension Between Expanding Practices and Restricted Theories." In *Inventing a Discipline: Rhetoric Scholarship in Honor of Richard E. Young*, edited by Maureen Daly Goggin, 5–28. Urbana, IL: NCTE.

Bruffee, Kenneth A. 1993. *Collaborative Learning: Higher Education, Interdependence, and the Authority of Knowledge*. Baltimore, MD: Johns Hopkins University Press.

Bullock, Richard, and William E. Smith. 1998. *Doing the WPA Straddle: Gaps in First-Year Composition and WPAs' Perceptions of It*. Paper presented at the Writing Program Administrators Conference, 18 July in Tucson, AZ.

Carrington, Vicki. 2001. "Literacy Instruction: A Bourdieuian Perspective." In *Difference, Silence, and Textual Practice: Studies in Critical Literacy*, edited by Peter Freebody, Sandy Muspratt, and Bronwyn Dwyer, 265–86. Cresskill, NJ: Hampton Press.

Clanchy, M. T. 1993. *From Memory to Written Record, England 1066–1307*. 2nd ed. Oxford: Blackwell.

Cook, Albert. 1989. *History/Writing*. Cambridge: Cambridge University Press.

Cope, Bill, and Mary Kalantzis. 2000a. "Multiliteracies: The Beginnings of an Idea." In *Multiliteracies: Literacy Learning and the Design of*

Social Futures, edited by Bill Cope and Mary Kalantzis, 3–8. London: Routledge.

———, eds. 2000b. *Multiliteracies: Literacy Learning and the Design of Social Futures*. London: Routledge.

Fleming, David. 1998. "Rhetoric as a Course of Study." *College English* 61: 169–91.

Gee, James Paul. 1989. "Orality and Literacy: From the Savage Mind to Ways with Words." *Journal of Education* 171: 39–60.

———. 1996. *Social Linguistics and Literacies: Ideology in Discourses*. 2nd ed. London: Taylor and Francis.

Gere, Anne Ruggles. 1987. *Writing Groups: History, Theory, and Implications*. Carbondale: Southern Illinois University Press.

Goggin, Maureen Daly. 1995. "Situating the Teaching and Learning of Argumentation within Historical Contexts." In *Competing and Consensual Voices: The Theory and Practice of Argument,* edited by Patrick J. M. Costello and Sally Mitchell, 10–22. Clevedon, England: Multilingual Matters Ltd.

Graff, Harvey J. 1991. *The Legacies of Literacy: Continuities and Contradictions in Western Culture and Society*. Bloomington: Indiana University Press.

Harris, Joseph. 1997. *A Teaching Subject: Composition Since 1966*. Upper Saddle River, NJ: Prentice Hall.

Heath, Shirley Brice. 1982. "What No Bedtime Story Means: Narrative Skills at Home and School." *Language and Society* 11: 49–76.

———. 1983. *Ways with Words: Language, Life and Work in Communities and Classrooms*. Cambridge: Cambridge University Press.

Hillocks, George Jr. 1995. *Teaching Writing as a Reflective Practice*. New York: Teachers College Press.

Johnson, David, Roger Johnson, and Karl A. Smith. 1991. *Cooperative Learning: Increasing College Faculty Instructional Productivity*. Washington, D.C.: ASHE/ERIC Higher Education.

Johnson, T. R., and Shirley Morahan, eds. 2002. *Teaching Composition: Background Readings*. Boston: Bedford/St. Martin's.

Johnstone, Barbara. 2002. *Discourse Analysis*. Malden, MA: Blackwell.

Journet, Debra. 1999. "Writing Within (and Between) Disciplinary Genres." In *Post-Process Theory: Beyond the Writing-Process Paradigm*, edited by Thomas Kent, 96–115. Carbondale: Southern Illinois University Press.

Kagan, Spencer. 1992. *Cooperative Learning*. 2nd ed. San Juan Capistrano, CA: Resources for Teachers.

Kaufer, David S., and Brian S. Butler. 1996. *Rhetoric and the Art of Design*. Mahwah, NJ: Lawrence Erlbaum.

———. 2000. *Designing Interactive Worlds with Words: Principles of Writing as Representational Composition*. Mahwah, NJ: Lawrence Erlbaum.

LaCapra, Dominick. 1983. *Rethinking Intellectual History: Texts, Contexts, Language*. Ithaca, NY: Cornell University Press.

LeFevre, Karen Burke. 1987. *Invention as a Social Act*. Carbondale: Southern Illinois University Press.

New London Group. 2000. "A Pedagogy of Multiliteracies Designing Social Futures." In *Multiliteracies: Literacy Learning and the Design of Social Futures*, edited by Bill Cope and Mary Kalantzis, 9–37. London: Routledge.

Novick, Peter. 1988. *That Noble Dream: The "Objectivity Question" and the American Historical Profession*. Cambridge: Cambridge University Press.

Petraglia, Joseph. 2000. "Shaping Sophisticates: Implications of the Rhetorical Turn for Rhetoric Education." In *Inventing a Discipline: Rhetoric Scholarship in Honor of Richard E. Young*, edited by Maureen Daly Goggin, 80–104. Urbana, IL: NCTE.

Russell, David R. 1995. "Activity Theory and Its Implications for Writing Instruction." In *Reconceiving Writing, Rethinking Writing Instruction*, edited by Joseph Petraglia, 51–78. Mahwah, NJ: Lawrence Erlbaum.

———. 1997. "Rethinking Genre Theory in School and Society: An Activity Theory Analysis." *Written Communication* 14: 504–54.

Scollon, Ron, and Suzanne Wong Scollon. 2002. *Intercultural Communication: A Discourse Approach*. 2nd ed. Malden, MA: Blackwell.

Street, Brian V. 1984. *Literacy in Theory and Practice*. Cambridge: Cambridge University Press.

———. 1995. *Social Literacies: Critical Approaches to Literacy in Development, Ethnography and Education*. London: Longman.

———. 2001. "Introduction: Ethnographic Perspectives on Literacy." In *Literacy and Development: Ethnographic Perspectives*, edited by Brian V. Street, 1–17. Cambridge: Cambridge University Press.

Tate, Gary, Amy Rupiper, and Kurt Schick, eds. 2001. *A Guide to Composition Pedagogies*. New York: Oxford University Press.

Thompson, Paul. 1988. *The Voice of the Past: Oral History*. 2nd ed. Oxford: Oxford University Press.

Varnum, Robin. 1986. "From Crisis to Crisis: The Evolution Toward Higher Standards of Literacy in the United States." *Rhetoric Society Quarterly* 16 (3): 145–65.

White, Hayden. 1978. *Tropics of Discourse: Essays in Cultural Criticism*. Baltimore, MD: Johns Hopkins University Press.

Wise, Gene. 1980. *American Historical Explanations: A Strategy for Grounded Inquiry*. 2nd ed. Minneapolis: University of Minnesota Press.

Young, Richard E. 2003. "Toward an Adequate Pedagogy for Rhetorical Argumentation: A Case Study in Invention." In *Beyond Postprocess and Postmodernism: Essays on the Spaciousness of Rhetoric*, edited by Theresa Enos and Keith D. Miller, 159–70. Mahwah, NJ: Lawrence Erlbaum.

PART II

Research as Art and Self-Expression

3

Creative Research for All Writers

Wendy Bishop

> I'd conveniently forgotten that research is more than just a skill; it's a calling and an obsession that often takes on a life of its own, much like the writing process itself.
> —Catherine Wald, novelist (2000, 60)

The assumption of many undergraduate writers is that the writing world is divided into fact and fiction. Too easily they assume that facts are there to be found (and not subject to interpretation), and that novelists and other storytellers draw primarily on memory in order to newly invent other worlds. Professional authors, on the other hand, often discuss the complicated relationship between fact and fiction and, more realistically, as in this chapter's epigraph, realize that research for creative writers represents a complicated and recursive process. It requires a type of dedication and investment that early in their careers writers struggle to learn, while later in their careers they wouldn't be without. Our classes of course are premised on helping writers move from earlier to later states in their understanding of research, generally after they have developed an understanding of and fluency with writing processes in general.

This sort of growth was illustrated in an upper-level article and essay workshop, as Margaret Steele used research to develop her response to my initial assignment that asked class members to write about something that they had always wanted to write about but hadn't yet. To compose her essay, Margaret turned to a collection of her deceased mother's telegrams and postcards in an effort to piece together a version of her mother's life in the years before Margaret was born. In her process memo, Margaret noted:

> I researched [the history of] telegrams so that I could add a beginning paragraph about telegrams and completed the paper except for the ending. I also

29

added in dates and places that I did not know before. I spoke to my sister to find out some of these missing details. I also worked on different ways to present the telegram. I decided the telegrams should be in a hand-written font since my research told me that the telegraph operator wrote the message as it came across the wire.

Margaret's research required multiple sources—interviews with family members, a study of Western Union telegrams, the Depression, and WWI and II. Learning more about telegrams, she chose script fonts to give a certain verisimilitude to the documents she "invented" via researched reconstruction. After learning more because she herself was interested, Margaret learned, as well, that she might need to search some more in order to answer readers' questions: "I was in a dilemma about how to proceed with my paper in the direction most readers wanted it to go while maintaining a non-fiction format." In order to progress further, Margaret continued to explore her topic and was willing to do so, no doubt, because she had a strong investment in the quality of the final product beyond class requirements, and because I structured class discussions and workshops to emphasize the ways class members had conducted research, sometimes without being aware that these activities could be considered such.

Margaret's process shouldn't stand out, but it does. While it's always seemed evident to me as a writer and a teacher of writing, that authors of every type and every genre regularly conduct research to enrich their texts, this fact is rarely as evident to the creative writing students I work with. Some are relatively unaware that all authors feel a need to ground their work in cultures and communities or that many authors speak most convincingly when they draw from experience, regularize their observations, augment their memories, and draw on the many resources—primary and secondary—available to them: historical accounts, weather reports, encyclopedias, eyewitness accounts, interviews, pictorial dictionaries, site visits, and so on.

While it is possible to write a strong essay, story, or poem without any of these aids or to draft a scene for one's memoir exclusively from memory, it is more likely that the prose or poetry will be enhanced through research, using conventional and unconventional, expected and unexpected methods. Equally, it is likely that the expert writer has internalized research practices and has been noting down details and researching lifelong, accumulating files, articles, daybooks, and journals to return to during the drafting stage of a work. As Melissa Goldthwaite reminds us in "This, Too, Is Research": "We ourselves (our memories and experiences) and the world around us are sources, and it's likely that most anything we write will involve some form of research: research for inspiration, for details, for enriching memories, for learning" (2001, 193–94). The challenge for creative writing teachers, for any writing teacher, is to provide their students with a jump start on acquiring the research habit.

Before sharing a set of exercises for a creative nonfiction course that illustrates the way personal writing is usefully contextualized and supported by research, I want to underline my belief that writers in all genres research by providing an illustration from an upper-level undergraduate course titled Poetic Technique, designed to introduce students to the practices, processes, and products of contemporary poets. I use this exercise because most students, and many general readers of poetry, overlook the amount of research that informs the poems they care about.

Invention and Research in a Poetry Course Begins Day One

To illustrate that poetry writing benefits from research, I begin each technique or workshop class with an exercise that illustrates the range of sources a practicing poet regularly draws upon. As the term begins, I provide the sources in the hope that this quiet initial modeling will take some poets into new territories and so far it always has, though sometimes not until term's end. This exercise serves as a touchstone/illustration/reminder throughout the rest of the course, and while research isn't required, it continues to be highlighted. For those students who do have a yearning to become more professional, the lesson takes, for research can add depth, a range of word choice, and/or a telling detail to a first or subsequent draft.

For this exercise, I ask students to write about a common object. Because I live in Florida, in the fall I use pecans, in the spring camellias, and in the summer gardenias from my yard. I've also used a collection of rocks from the Southwest, shells from the Gulf of Mexico—enough of each for the entire class. (In a pinch I've used multiples of common office objects: staplers, pens, pencils, scissors, paper clips, enough of these for groups of five students each.) I prefer organic objects for two reasons: first, they are similar by species or type yet widely varied and they can be (with care) tasted, touched, deconstructed, or watched over a week to view the processes of decay; second, a surprising number of my technoliterate students have lost touch with the names for common plants and trees and mention (sometimes proudly) being unconnected to the world outside their dorms and classrooms at this point in their lives. I'm concerned with this because I believe writers research because they are curious and interested in learning . . . about everything. A tree name, the history of a small town, how the King James Bible was collaboratively coauthored, the perils of the new drug on the street . . . everything. I want students to get a feel for the same sort of curious excitement that propels an interested poet to learn anything and everything that will enhance a draft. And research aids their reading as well. Without caring about precise definitions, allusions, meanings, and names, how can novice writers appreciate D. H. Lawrence, Gary Snyder, Mary Oliver, Mark Doty, and other fine poets of observation? How can they develop a richer vocabulary of the world? My initial answer is by observation plus doing a research exercise, which is available, in full, on this book's companion website.

That day in class, students struggle with the concept of writing about a flower. I hear "What's this called?" "How do you spell it?" "What does she mean, a myth?" And eventually: "Did you know it was also called a Chinese rose?" as someone begins to consult the research materials. Our first attempts are begun in class on the otherwise chaotic first day of the term, and the handouts allow writers to continue to research, easily in this first instance, when they go home that night.

Based on their freewrites and first drafts, the camellia on these students' desks could be any pink flower, a rose, a camellia, a carnation (just as early love poems could be too song-like, and thus, about *any* love relationship). One such draft begins: "Her flamingo pink petals / She's imperfect but beautiful like a woman, / her floral aromas fill the room with glamour. . . ." There is no evidence the poet has seen either a camellia or a flamingo in person.

As the poets consult the research materials I've provided, as an active few revise after roaming through a local nursery or their neighborhood or the Internet, richer drafts evolve, and I continue to present options for becoming more precise, suggesting writers learn varietal names, Latin names, consider growing conditions, life cycle of the plant, and so on. Poets learn how details can support their meaning—often generated during the in-class invention but not yet embodied in the poem; for instance, the memory of a mother who floated fresh flowers—perhaps camellias?—in a yellow bowl on the dinner table whenever the poet's father came home late from work to welcome him at the end of a draining day. What details will help us see this scene from the poet's point of view?

Through this exercise, poets explore the fundamental challenge every author faces, including those working in prose, to represent, approximate, characterize: "I want to know what things looked like, what they smelled like, what colors they were, what they felt like, what they sounded like," explains Patricia O'Toole in an interview with Catherine Wald (2000). To meet those needs, O'Toole suggests writers could consult "voice recordings or museum exhibits . . . multimedia sources . . . venture beyond standard online services and search engines to proprietary databases that are available thorough big research institutions and libraries . . . good old-fashioned newspaper clips" (62–63).

By the end of the camellia sequence, twenty-five poems have been posted on the Web-board, demonstrating a wide range of options. Slowly, a poet's experiences are embodied in more exact and resonant language: "Elfin green, ovate leaves with little green teeth that don't really bite / Press a finger on the edge to see for yourself. / Chinese rose, your life is so short. / Protective petals brown before you grow from bud to blossom. . . ." At this point, with luck, a student who knew nothing about ovate leaves rolls the word around in her mouth, tries it on a page for other students to discuss and emulate and critique. In the shadow of an initial lesson in research, the term continues.

Research to Explore Options in a Nonfiction Course

To illustrate research in a similar vein for writers of nonfiction or memoir, I'll share current versions of three assignments (which are available, as well, in different versions, in Ostrom, Bishop, and Haake 2001; Bishop 2003).

1. The basic assignment for "Reading Your Own Times: When You Came to Be" (Ostrom et al. 2001, 9) suggests writers can tap primary and secondary sources to investigate personal, local, and global events in order to create an essay that illuminates or refers to the year they were born. To discuss a time in their past for which they *can't* rely on personal memory, writers must consult family members, magazines, newspapers, and historical documents from that time period. With this assignment, there are also useful chances for collaboration (several members of the class may have been born in the same year) and cross-generational education (some members of the class may have been born in entirely different decades).

   For her essay, Rachel Herrington's focus for 1978, the year of her birth, was not a cult suicide or details of the Carter administration but a snowstorm in Iowa: "Since we basically were given the freedom to take this paper in any direction, I wanted to narrow my paper down to facts and research that parallels my birth and is fascinating to me: weather patterns, specifically winters in Iowa." While some class members wrote about the music scene at the time of their birth, recreated their parents' early years, or considered a year of world headlines, Rachel chose to focus on weather, on snow, after years of living in the warmer south. (See Bishop 2004 for Rachel's essay and complete process memo.)

2. The assignment called "The Power of Names" (Ostrom et al. 2001, 70–71) asks writers to tell the story of how they were named—which may require family interviews or, in some cases, making up a "reasonable" story to explain why the name might have been chosen if family can't be contacted in the time available. Writers investigate what the name means, not only its historical derivation but also the author's lifetime sense of the name, classmates' reaction to the name, and they perhaps speculate about or research generational naming (why Shirley and Ophelia in one decade and Jennifer and Tanya in another decade?). Like all the assignments discussed in this chapter, this project asks the writers to connect the individual to the community and culture. One student, Sarah, organized her essay in four sections, investigating all three of her names, first, middle, last, and then considering her fiancé's name and the naming of their future children. She found her essay subheads and organization in the process.

3. The assignment for "Writing About Ordinary Objects" (Bishop 2003, 98–105) grew from a desire to illustrate the wealth of topics that surrounds every writer. It suggests that the most overlooked items or elements of our lives could prove of interest to—and the subject for—the essayist. After brainstorming a list of commonplace objects that we might find ourselves

curious about (playing cards, tarot cards, dice, scissors, spoons, sewing machine, mirrors, makeup, toothbrush, Band-Aids, zipper, bathing suit, brassiere, condoms, ice cream, marbles, firecrackers, roller skates, and so on), class members are encouraged to choose their own "ordinary object" for a paper sequence.

These exercises work well as a modified I-Search: write what you know on the subject; interview classmates; find someone who relies on/works with this object and interview them; conduct secondary, historical research; tell us what you've learned in an old-fashioned contemplative (think Montaigne) essay—"On Scissors" or "On Brassieres" (a subject one of my students self-selected and handled well). Debbie Olander's essay, "The Practical and Romantic Paperclip," opens this way: "Johan Vaaler, a Norwegian wizard of invention who had degrees in electronics, science, and mathematics, created the humble paperclip in 1899." Her final draft included sections on what the state of files and filing was like before this invention (people used pins, ribbons, wax), includes a diagram of the complicated machine that makes this simple product, and also relays the fact that Office Depot's inventory has "no fewer than forty-five kinds of paperclips available for purchase." Teachers can readily see how such an assignment would benefit from being translated into a hypertext.

I have several goals for the products of such research: to illustrate how it is possible to prepare a formal researched paper that has benefited from exploratory invention and experiment with forms; and to encourage some students to stick with alternately styled texts because they have had less success with a traditional reporting format but are engaged with this new way of researching. For both sorts of students, I hope the reasons for researching and the sources where writers find their data are broadened and made clear through our discussions so that new research tools are added to their writing repertoire.

In addition, I use the ordinary object project to illustrate how research is used in different genres of writing, both personal and academic. For this sequence, I ask students to undertake primary and secondary research on their chosen object and to share the results in *two* sorts of essays: one using first-person voice and few to no internal citations—an essay that might appear in a magazine they like to read; and the other as a more formal, historical and/or scholarly essay (although first-person is still a possibility) that features MLA-style citation. The two versions are developed in either order and each is shared in class workshops using the format appropriate to the version. By drawing on the same sources for two strikingly differently structured works, the author investigates citation systems for his own purposes by analyzing the rhetorical effects of each set of choices. In her process memo, Margaret Steele comments on this sequence:

A few days later, I searched the Internet for information on safety pins or bobby pins. There was not enough information for even a one-page report.

I'm sure if I had weeks to research, I would eventually find enough information for a decent essay but that was not the case. . . . I have a small collection of bells and decided to do that. I searched the Internet again and found lots of information on bells. After over an hour of searching and printing out information, I was already getting bored. I thought about perfume. There was plenty of information on that but I wasn't hooked on the subject. I looked around my living room at other objects. My mirrored wall that gives the illusion of a larger room caught my attention. There were a lot of Internet sites about mirrors. Still undecided, I asked my teenage daughter whether she would prefer to read an essay about perfume or mirrors. I was surprised when she immediately said mirrors. So, mirrors it was.

Margaret wrote a brief history of the mirror for one essay and then a satire on the TV show *Survivor* in which she suggests that (and explains why) a *Survivor* team member might decide to choose a mirror as a must-bring-along item. (Both of Margaret's essays and a complete process memo are available in Bishop 2004; in addition, consult Chapter 3 of the companion website for a sample class syllabus that encourages these sorts of assignments.)

I use these exercises and student writing examples to build my case that research should be considered more broadly: no matter the genre, it is one of any writer's most important creative tools. As your students begin to engage in this sort of invested, even passionate research, issues arise. We all want our students to become involved, but involvement can lead to certain sorts of excess. That's certainly not a problem if we take time to use these situations as discussion points, moments to share minilessons on research practice. The companion website contains some advice to help you achieve those goals. I wish the best, most creative, most passionate research possible to you and yours.

Works Cited

Bishop P., Wendy. 2000. *Thirteen Ways of Looking for a Poem: A Guide to Writing Poetry*. New York: Longman.

———. 2003. *Reading into Writing—A Guide to Composing*. New York: Addison Wesley Longman.

———. 2004. *On Writing: A Process Reader*. Boston: McGraw-Hill.

Goldthwaite, Melissa. 2001. "This, Too, Is Research." In *The Subject Is Research: Process and Practices*, edited by Wendy Bishop and Pavel Zemliansky, 193–201. Portsmouth, NH: Boynton/Cook.

Ostrom, Hans, Wendy Bishop, and Katharine Haake. 2001. *Metro: Journeys in Writing Creatively*. New York: Longman.

Wald, Catherine. 2000. "Research and the Fiction Writer." *Poets and Writers* Sept./Oct.: 60–65.

4

Scratching a "Marvelously Itchy" Itch
Teaching the I-Search Paper

Tom Reigstad

What I Knew

This is an excerpt from a paper I wrote on rise-fall imagery in Alexander Pope's "Essay on Man" as an undergraduate English major thirty-five years ago:

> The two principles of man which, according to Pope, must be understood before man can come to grips with his condition, are self-love and reason. The pursuit of these two principles is directed toward a common goal—man's happiness. A constructive step toward happiness is to expand self-love, which consists of loving fellow men and animals. The "chain of love" combines "all below and all above" (III ll. 7–8). This is the first way in which rise-fall imagery is resolved by Pope. However, the operation of man's pride often destroys the communion of love among beings on the great chain. The man whose pride elevates him to a feeling of superiority over fellow men and animals "*falls* short of reason."

Yawn. Where in the text am *I*, the thinker and the writer, amidst those frozen pronouncements and nominalizations? I can't remember why I chose this topic and I certainly can't find any evidence of personal investment anywhere in my piece. Yet, I apparently performed well enough in this eighteenth-century British Literature course offered by a highly regarded English department at a large state university. The professor, who chaired the undergraduate division, wrote "good" in the margin next to the above passage, gave me an "A-," and added in a summative comment: "This is an intelligent and well-executed essay.

Your writing is generally lucid, but it could use a little polishing." A year later I loaned him this paper to refer to when he wrote a favorable letter of reference to enhance my chances of getting into a grad school.

Fast-forward eight years to the spring of 1976. I am in my fourth year of teaching English and am enrolled as a part-time doctoral student in a composition/ rhetoric program. In an evening class called Advanced Composition for Teachers my professor, Lee Odell, distributes a reprint of the first chapter of Ken Macrorie's 1970 book, *Telling Writing*, in which Macrorie labels the voiceless prose of academic essays, "the phony, pretentious language of the schools," as "Engfish" (1). Engfish is what most English teachers require and it is what most English teachers get. It is writing that relies on an objective, third-person point of view and passive-voice constructions, and it is a lifeless presentation of facts and information. Engfish, in other words, was Tom Reigstad on Alexander Pope.

In that grad course we learned much more about voice by reading Walker Gibson and Peter Elbow and by experimenting with our own styles. But I remained hooked by Macrorie's suggestion that an alternative exists to "the official language of the school," that there is a way for teachers to invite a student to "express truths that count for him" (4). I was piqued by Macrorie's promise in the closing lines of the reprint: "In this empty circle teacher and student wander around boring each other. But there is a way out" (4).

It took me four more years to discover exactly what Macrorie was talking about. Once I found out, there was no going back.

My teaching epiphany occurred on November 7, 1980. I was a new PhD just three months into my first tenure-track assistant professorship in English. As part of my duties, I was supposed to coordinate an annual gathering of area English teachers, the Drake Conference in Composition and Communication Skills, hosted by my department at Drake University in Des Moines, Iowa. Luckily for me (and for the success of the event), a department colleague, David Foster, bailed me out by taking charge of the conference, which involved a dinner and keynote speaker—none other than Ken Macrorie. In a banquet room packed with a couple of hundred well-fed, attentive English teachers, Macrorie described the I-Search paper.

I recall how this casually dressed, low-key educator and writer stepped down from the stage, away from the podium, and addressed the crowd from the floor. He spoke passionately about how the I-Search paper is an alternative to the conventional, lifeless academic research report.

I was inspired. This was the "way out."

When Dave Foster asked if I would give Macrorie a lift to the Des Moines airport after his talk, I jumped at the chance. During the twenty-minute drive, Macrorie chatted about his current project—he was writing a book about twenty extraordinary teachers (*Twenty Teachers* was published in 1984). He told me that these special teachers were "enablers," that is, teachers who cultivate humane classrooms that encourage learners to seek surprise and explore the power of storytelling, among many other activities.

Well, that did it. Macrorie had given me a professional itch to scratch. I wanted to be an enabler. I wanted to teach the I-Search paper.

In the ensuing years, I have incorporated the I-Search paper as a unique and staple assignment in a wide variety of writing and literature courses. My students have written I-Search papers to follow leads on Mark Twain in undergraduate and graduate seminars. They have used I-Search papers to explore questions about writing pedagogy in undergraduate and graduate methods courses on teaching writing. I have read outstanding I-Search papers on various authors and works in a survey course on American literature. And I have enjoyed I-Search stories on an amazing assortment of subjects composed by writers in my freshman composition and creative nonfiction courses. Portfolio assessment is an essential element of the freshman writing program at my university. One piece of the portfolio evaluation scheme, a program I instituted and coordinated for three years, is that every freshman writer must include a significant research report. As a faculty we welcome samples of traditional research papers, but encourage alternatives such as the I-Search paper or multigenre research projects. I have found that my writers almost always choose the I-Search path on subjects that matter to them: building a backyard greenhouse, Love Canal, stuttering, and vegetarianism for children (an important topic for one of my students, who was creating a meatless diet for her daughter). I am pleased to say that none of the papers even remotely resembled my stuffy effort on Alexander Pope.

The Search

Before jumping in to revolutionize the idea of research reporting in my courses, I needed to flesh out a fuller picture of this strange, unorthodox animal, the I-Search paper. Macrorie first described this alternative research/writing technique in *The New York Times* in 1979 and in the same year—1980— that I heard him speak in Iowa, he published *Searching Writing*, which was later reprinted by Boynton/Cook as *The I-Search Paper* in 1984 and 1988 editions. *The I-Search Paper* and a videotape of Macrorie speaking to teachers at Radford University in 1984 (*Searching Writing: Making Knowledge Personal*) have been my most indispensable primary resources. Macrorie's book is a detailed account of the I-Search paper process and I have borrowed from it and adapted it extensively. The videotape is of a talk very similar to Macrorie's presentation at Drake University and has complemented his book nicely for me.

In the first weeks of class I spend a fair amount of time introducing the I-Search paper requirement as an exciting opportunity for students to dig into and enjoy a topic that captivates them. I often place Macrorie's videotape and book on reserve in the campus library in case students want to find out more about the task. Macrorie's *The I-Search Paper* reprints five sample I-Search papers by his students, two written by college freshmen, which my students frequently consult for ideas on the form and content of I-Search papers. I also give students time to browse through a folder of sample exemplary I-Search papers from past classes to serve as models. They find, for example, how one of my former students got a wealth of information for an I-Search paper on school literary magazines by talking to the traffic coordinator of *Merlyn's Pen* over the phone. These supplemental I-Search materials relax some anxious students who seem overwhelmed at first by the unusual features of this kind of thinking and researching and need a nudge to become liberated from the "official language" formula. As part of my duty to make students comfortable with "breaking out," I cover the basics of the I-Search paper process. In Chapter 6 of *The I-Search Paper*, Macrorie provides a useful overview of the assignment and what makes it unique. He lists eight suggestions for undertaking research and recommends a reporting framework.

I tell students that unlike the typical academic paper, which focuses mostly on reporting *just the results* of research from an analytical, objective point of view, the I-Search paper requires them to carefully document their *research and writing processes* as well as their ultimate findings and to tell the story of their entire search in an engaging, personable, first-person voice. I stress that as writers they will be accounting for the complex twists and turns that they took as data collectors. Early on I also share a copy of the scoring rubric I have developed to grade the papers. (Chapter 4 of the companion website describes the rubric for the I-Search paper in my Methods of Teaching Writing course). I have found that knowing the features, expectations, and standards of the I-Search paper ahead of time helps clarify the assignment for students. One last tidbit of information that I distribute in the first couple weeks of each term is a fact sheet, a kind of "Everything You Always Wanted to Know About I-Search Papers," designed to anticipate student questions about the nature of the task and to suggest deadlines for completing phases of it. (See the companion website for an example of such a tip sheet for my senior honors course on Mark Twain.)

I reinforce the difference between the traditional research report format and the I-Search paper by telling students that their determination as researchers will be rewarded. I promote researcher traits such as "enterprise," "resourcefulness," doggedness," "originality," "ingenuity," "intrepidness," "risk taking," "legwork," "initiative," and "open-mindedness" to plant seeds of the joy they will experience as they embark on their I-Search journey and to inspire them to go the extra mile to connect with a live source of information, to follow up on a lead, or to nail down an obscure fact.

Once the I-Search paper is somewhat demystified, the next challenge is for students to find a topic. All I ask is that it be course specific. That is, Survey of American Literature students must pursue a subject centered on an author or work that we are studying; Teaching and Evaluating Writing students must pick some facet of teaching or assessing composition to explore; Twain students must look into a corner of Twain studies; the creative nonfiction writers have a universe of topics to investigate.

I love using Macrorie's "itch" metaphor. In *The I-Search Paper* he says that an ideal topic is one that makes a writer so curious to delve into that she can't be satisfied until it's done in depth, much like the pleasurable prolonged scratching of an itch: "original searches in which persons scratch an itch they feel, one so marvelously itchy that they begin rubbing a finger tip against it and the rubbing feels so good that they dig in with a fingernail" (14). In his videotape, Macrorie (1985) puts it another, less colorful, way, but still emphasizes how vital it is that students have a personal investment in their I-Search topic: "I've always felt in teaching the I-Search paper that the essential thing is that the students search after something that they feel they need to know. Students should be writing out of a need."

By the end of the first month of the course, students complete two brainstorming activities aimed at narrowing their I-Search paper topic. First, I poll each student in class, along the lines of the "status of the class" technique described by Nancie Atwell (1998), to uncover potentially scratchable itches. At the beginning of her writing workshop sessions, Atwell quickly surveys each writer—and takes notes on a chart—for an update on their progress on a current writing project. As my students vocalize their most likely topic idea in front of the group, their classmates and I often suggest additional resources for the writer to chase. Another brainstorming aid is to require students to plot out on paper what they know and don't know, what sources they have already looked into, and what sources they plan to consult. This prewriting act forces students to jot down early notes and plan a course of action, rather than waiting until the end of the semester to identify a topic and commence their search. I have designed a graphic organizer for this purpose (see Chapter 4 of the website). Students submit either the filled-in graphic organizer or a brief prose description of their activities so that I can monitor their progress and intervene with suggestions of my own. Susan's informal update four weeks into a graduate seminar on Twain charted the moves she had made in arriving at her topic:

> Once we got rolling with Twain, I began keeping my eyes, ears, and thoughts open for interesting I-Search ideas. A few things piqued my interest initially. I was very interested in Twain's impact while he stayed in Buffalo, working at the Express. I disregarded that idea, however. I became sick of it after awhile. The next idea that kept creeping up was the angelfish. I must say I really became obsessed with this. I never heard about this strange affinity Twain had. The fact that this great literary American mind could find his only intellectual stimulation with children toward the end of his life . . . this both irked me tremendously and intrigued me to find out more. My journal group, however, kept telling me that I was obsessing. After some thought, I began to agree with them. On went the search. The next idea was: where and when was it decided that Twain was the genius American writer? Was it immediate? Was it the opinion of the masses? Of

the critics? And more importantly, what makes him such a genius? I'm still thinking about this idea a bit, but I am also interested in the wild popularity of Huck Finn. I settled on this idea because I taught the book to eleventh graders last year and that question kept popping up in my head. Practically every school (that hasn't decided to ban the book) has a class set. I think it's an interesting story, don't get me wrong. I do, however, think it is inappropriate for high school. . . . This is where I am now. The search has begun. Any thoughts or pointers?

Susan's preliminary reflection gives her a jump start on the project and provided me with a glimpse into her search so that I could steer her toward a couple sources; it also formed a discovery draft for the opening page of the I-Search paper she eventually completed, "Huck: Controversial from Birth."

Macrorie (1988) recommends that the opening segments of I-Search papers begin in a natural way, telling readers *What I Knew (or Didn't Know) and What I Wanted to Know*—in story form" (100). He says this is the point of departure for a voyage of discovery, much like Homer's *Odyssey*. In fact, one of my graduate students (a classics minor as an undergraduate) in a composition/rhetoric pedagogy course once wrote an I-Search paper about the I-Search paper in Homeric terms. She interviewed fellow students about their composing processes, examined Macrorie's writings and video, and included this line in her lead paragraph: "My faithful Penelope, this is the story of my quest, not to learn what the I-Search paper is, but to experience what the I-Search paper becomes."

Other openings of I-Search papers chronicle in innovative, stylish, reader-friendly voices the unexpected ways that the itches, or topics, present themselves to writers. Paul, like Susan, writing about *Adventures of Huckleberry Finn* in the classroom, began his paper this way:

> It's funny how life works out. Once you get a chance to look back on it, little random acts that seem unconnected at the time start to fall into place in a pattern. Serendipity seems to push a person in just the right direction and good fortune seems to turn into fate. Such was the case with me when it comes to Mark Twain and his 1885 novel, *Adventures of Huckleberry Finn*.

Paul recalls the origins of his researchable idea by telling how he first read *Huck Finn* in high school but didn't encounter it again until last year, when a colleague at the high school where he teaches suggested that the novel is overrated. At that point, my summer seminar came along and the book was required reading; Paul seized the opportunity to investigate. Paul rounds out the opening of his I-Search paper with this insightful articulation of his itch:

> I knew about Twain's novel being banned in several academic settings, but I also knew that I wanted to teach the novel someday (when I was prepared for both it and its accompanying controversy), so over the years I cut out and

put in my Twain file any newspaper stories that had to do with HF and censorship. (I'm the type of pack-rat teacher who cuts out and saves anything that might be useful someday.) I should also mention that I'm sort of a civil libertarian who despises state censorship and anything that infringes on my intellectual freedom as a teacher. So my goal in this I-Search project is to find out if *Adventures of Huckleberry Finn* is indeed an American classic worthy of its exalted place in the canon and is it suitable for teaching in America's public high schools, including my own. I basically want to be the best teacher I possibly can be, so I want to be as prepared and knowledgeable as possible on both the novel and the firestorm it often stirs up.

Another graduate student, Wynnie, started her I-Search paper for my composition pedagogy course by describing a remarkable string of coincidences that eventually led her to her topic. After reading Nancie Atwell's *In the Middle*, she was inspired to try the reading/writing workshop method in her middle school English classes. Then, just a week before taking my graduate course, Wynnie attended a presentation that Atwell gave in Buffalo. She discovered afterward that Atwell had started her teaching career in the same school and department where Wynnie works. Wynnie was curious about what Atwell was like as a young teacher and the legacy Atwell may have left at Tonawanda Middle School. She knew that Atwell had coauthored a piece about their middle school writing curriculum in a 1976 issue of *English Journal*. Wynnie tenaciously tracked down local teachers who had supervised Atwell as a student teacher, interviewed colleagues who had known Atwell twenty years earlier, and retrieved relevant archival documents such as yearbooks and student records. Wynnie began her I-Search paper, "The Search for Nancie Atwell," with an engaging story tracing the evolution of her topic:

> Eleanor Roosevelt said, "When you are genuinely interested in one thing, it will always lead to something else." This was the case with me and Nancie Atwell. A name synonymous with the writing workshop scenario, her ideals have become a common buzzword throughout my five years of teaching. Little did I know what an impact Nancie Atwell would have on my life.
>
> After completing *In the Middle*, I went to my principal and told him I wanted to go strictly "writing-reading workshop" for the next school year.
>
> Soon, a new idea dawned on me. Due to class discussion and sharing of ideas in the writing course that I am currently taking, the idea that Nancie Atwell is a former English teacher at my school sparked my interest. Suddenly, my curiosity over the early Atwell years caught my attention.

Wynnie's saga of one source leading to another is a consistent theme in I-Search papers. In his video Macrorie (1985) urges students to venture out into the world and talk to authorities on their subject. These experts, in turn, can provide further avenues for the researcher to follow: "Go to experts in the flesh first. Phone them, make an appointment, be nice to them, bring them whiskey or candy or whatever they like. Ask them to recommend someone else or a reading you can go to." Macrorie (1988) suggests additional tips to help students conduct field interviews, such as preparing a list of questions before the interview. I share these and other interviewing strategies with students when they are ready to locate live sources. One handy interviewing technique, Gilleland's GOSS formula, is outlined by Peter Anderson (1974). The GOSS method is a memory aid enabling interviewers to center questions around Goal, Obstacle, Solution and Start. I find the chapter on interviewing by William Zinsser (2001) in *On Writing Well* to be loaded with practical advice to share with students. Perhaps the most indispensable resource, though, for training I-Searchers to be comfortable with interviewing is John Brady's (1976) *The Craft of Interviewing*, particularly his sections on avoiding pitfalls and alternatives to the face-to-face interview. A listing of works that I have pulled interviewing nuggets from for my students may be found in Chapter 4 on the companion website.

I have read some amazing stories by students who zealously pursued their topics. In an American literature survey course, a student wanted to find out more about Ogden Nash. After summoning up enough courage, she made two early morning phone calls trying to reach a woman she assumed to be Nash's daughter. She never connected, but the account of her failed attempts was riveting. Macrorie (1985), again on video, reminds us that the ups and the downs of the search need to be told: "Odysseus went out there and all those things happened—some of them were good, some of them were bad." Another literature student tried stubbornly to reach author Mark Harris, but gave up after several polite phone conversations and emails with staff at Arizona State University, where Harris is a professor emeritus. These dead ends comprise a vital part of the I-Search story and chronicle the industriousness and hard work involved in exploring a topic.

Other students have had phenomenal success in locating "live" sources. Distinguished Mark Twain scholars, such as Vic Doyno and Shelley Fisher Fishkin, have been extremely generous in responding to email inquiries, phone calls, and requests for face-to-face interviews by my Twain students. William Least Heat-Moon's secretary courteously relayed email questions about *Blue Highways* from students in my creative nonfiction class to the author. He patiently responded, again through his secretary.

And students in Teaching and Evaluating Writing have spoken by phone to a very gracious Tom Romano to elicit his impressions about writing assessment and tasks that motivate young writers. One student in the methods class became extremely interested in alternative writing assignments. To research her I-Search paper, she read Romano's *Writing with Passion* (one of our course textbooks) and phoned him—a conversation that translated into two pages of Q and A in her paper. She also bought and read Wendy Bishop's *Elements of Alternate Style: Essays on Writing and Revision*. But her coup de grâce was a spirited effort, with her father's assistance, to locate and contact Winston Weathers. In the fall of 1997, before emailing and Internet fact-finding were as widespread and sophisticated as they are now, she and her father found two men named Winston Weathers in two different parts of the United States. They deduced, correctly, that their man was the one in Oklahoma. She emailed Weathers, a retired University of Tulsa professor, asking for more information on his notion of "Grammar B" as an alternative to traditional styles of writing. Over a two-week period, Weathers responded in detail to her series of questions. His interview filled four pages of my student's authoritative I-Search paper, which was entitled "To 'B' or Not to 'B'?" Searches like these make thrilling and gratifying reading.

As with the aforementioned pun on Hamlet's line, I-Search writers often enjoy playing with language in their titles. (Incidentally, the title of my old paper on rise-fall imagery in Pope's "Essay on Man" was simply: "Rise-Fall Imagery in 'Essay on Man.'") A truly superb I-Search paper written by a methods student, Madonna, was cleverly called "Start the Presses: High School Journalism as a Tool for Teaching Writing." To creatively frame her paper Madonna used a personal anecdote about confronting censorship as student editor of her sixth-grade newspaper. She also reported on multiple perspectives eloquently: she interviewed a local high school English teacher and newspaper advisor; she read articles on scholastic journalism in journals such as *Editor & Publisher*; she traveled about ninety miles to her alma mater, St. Bonaventure University, to interview the dean of the school of journalism; she cited relevant court cases; she designed and administered a survey to area journalism teachers/newspaper advisors; she interviewed high school students; and she conducted an extensive phone interview with the director of the Western New York High School Press Association. Madonna's energy and initiative enabled her to thoroughly explore her ambitious central question: "My I-Search set out to examine the current state of high school journalism as a means of encouraging students' free expression as writers, and as a tool for providing the 'real work' experience many communities are demanding schools provide."

Rachel conducted another remarkable investigation in my American literature survey course. That semester the entire class had subscribed to *The New Yorker* magazine to study its weekly fiction and poetry. Early in October of 1999, we discussed a short story, "Nilda" by Junot Diaz, a young Dominican-American writer. Rachel was intrigued by Diaz and by the end of the month eagerly planned an I-Search paper about him. Her extensive preliminary groundwork was impressive. On October 29 she submitted a graphic organizer with these notes on it:

What I already know: Junot Diaz—short story author—writes w/ethnic slant
   Places searched so far/Information gathered so far: New York magazine interview. In college, got into competitive writing program @ Cornell; Influenced by Toni Morrison; Still lives in Brooklyn. Internet NYS Writers Inst.

Writer's Online/Cites Joyce's "Dubliners" (characters) as a major influence on his work; 1st book of short stories, *Drown*, published in 1996—Diaz 28 yrs. old. *Austin Chronicle* (Review)/Earned 6-figure advance for *Drown* & an unnamed, unfinished novel (*In the City of Boys?*); Does *not* hang in literary circles; Believes his childhood as a "normal kid" allows him to write w/ a real perspective of youth

 Interesting related facts: How did Diaz become such a success at such a young age? Does he have anything published outside of his Latino genre? What's next? Can I contact him, e-mail, internet?

 Key words: Diaz, *Drown*, Dubliners

 What's next in my search: short stories to read: The Sun, the Moon, the Stars (*N Yorker* 2/2/98); (got it) Otravida, Ottavez (*N Yorker* 6/21-28/99); (got it) How to Date a Brown Girl (*N Yorker* 12/25/95) *published before *Drown* (1st one?); Still ck: *N.Y. Times* Book Review, *People* Weekly

Clearly, Rachel had launched a meaningful search to know more about Diaz. My small role was to mention a couple of additional Diaz stories for Rachel to read. But Rachel had plenty of self-motivation as a researcher. During her search she read as much of Diaz's fiction as she could get her hands on. Along the way, she even submitted a bid through Amazon.com to purchase an uncorrected proof of *Drown*. Rachel soon learned that Diaz taught creative writing at Syracuse University, an easy drive down the New York State Thruway from Buffalo. But after emails and phone calls, she discovered that he was on academic leave for the 1999–2000 year, temporarily living and writing somewhere in Manhattan. Undeterred (or as she wrote in her paper: "I chalked up the e-mail as a dead-end, and turned my attention in another direction."), Rachel turned next to Diaz's recent alma mater, Cornell University, "banking on the fact that people there, such as professors, would remember him." Her email to the director of Cornell's creative writing program met with a prompt reply steering Rachel to a couple of avenues: Diaz's master's thesis and his graduate advisor. Rachel tried mightily, but unsuccessfully, to borrow Diaz's thesis. However, she did manage to get fascinating insights into Diaz by emailing his Cornell master's advisor and one of Diaz's Syracuse University students. She closed the inquiry into her new-found favorite author with these contagiously enthusiastic lines, statements that allow the reader to feel the author's burning love of literature:

> Perhaps I'll acquire a proof of *Drown* soon, and that is exciting. My small but selective home library will benefit greatly! In the meantime, though, I will continue to keep my eyes open for news of Junot Diaz, and will be among the first to read his upcoming novel. Like other readers, I will be looking for a new angle from him. He is a man with much to say, and only time can tell if he will be able to say it in new and interesting ways. Go Junot!

What I Discovered

One thing I've learned in teaching the I-Search paper is that inventive and entertaining products like Paul's, Wynnie's, Madonna's, and Rachel's don't magically appear on my desk at the end of the semester. I have found that a formative evaluation step is very helpful. Macrorie (1988) describes an "editing day" for authors to exchange drafts and respond to them before the due date. I, too, ask authors to bring in a working draft of their I-Search paper—a substantial but unfinished chunk—for peer review. Students meet in small groups, circulate their drafts, and write down reactions for the authors on a form that I designed (see Chapter 4, Response Sheet, on the companion website). I also deliver feedback to drafts either via the form or in one-to-one conferences before the final deadline for papers.

Much to my delight, I-Search papers often take on a life of their own, beyond the scope of a fifteen-week semester or the space of a twelve-page paper. Months after he completed his I-Search paper on *Huckleberry Finn*, Paul emailed me an update about having taught the novel uneventfully in his classes. Several months after finishing her I-Search paper, I received a note from Wynnie asking for a letter of recommendation for teaching abroad in a summer program, with this postscript: "By the way—off the subject—I attended the New York State English Council Conference in Albany last October and got to interview Nancie Atwell. I'll keep you posted on my project." Some of my students have developed their I-Search papers into master's theses. Maureen, a graduate student who teaches high school English, wrote that she intends to teach I-Search papers to her own students and to require them to use a nifty research gimmick that helped her keep track of her complicated search:

> I think one of the most difficult aspects of completing this paper was that I never knew where the search would take me. Staying in one place was unheard of! One site would take me to another and then to another, and, before long, I would forget why and how I got there. Early on, I found it necessary to keep a journal of sites visited . . . I feel that it is important to note that I was diligent in my record keeping. When I use the I-Search paper in my teaching next year, I will require my students to keep a written log as they search.

The I-Search paper might be messy, it might consist of unfinished business, and might raise more questions than it answers. It might inspire more reading, thinking, writing, and research after the paper itself has been signed, sealed, and delivered. Its itch can be so marvelous, so tantalizing that you don't really want to stop scratching. The *search* is the thing and so is what you learn from it. Unlike the standard academic research paper, posing a hypothesis and collecting information to prove or disprove it, the I-Search paper may not necessarily have immediate closure. The I-Search paper is capable of being the Energizer bunny of alternative research methods—it keeps going and going and going. Who knows, maybe someday I'll revisit Alexander Pope, but not before developing an appropriately marvelous itch.

Works Cited

Anderson, Peter J. 1974. *Research Guide in Journalism.* Morristown, NJ: General Learning Press.

Atwell, Nancie. 1998. *In the Middle.* Portsmouth, NH: Heinemann.

Brady, John. 1976. *The Craft of Interviewing.* New York: Randon House.

Gibson, Walker. 1969. *Persona.* New York: Random House.

Macrorie, Ken. 1970. *Telling Writing.* Rochelle Park, NJ: Hayden Books.

———. 1985. *Searching Writing: Making Writing Personal.* Portsmouth, NH: Heinemann.

———. 1988. *The I-Search Paper.* Portsmouth, NH: Heinemann.

Zinsser, William. 2001. *On Writing Well.* New York: Harper.

5

Researching Like a Writer
The Personal Essay as Research Paper

Paul Heilker, Sarah Allen, and Emily L. Sewall

Thinking back to the first time we taught "the research paper" assignment in our courses, we have to wonder if our students were as frightened by it as we were. We are guessing they were—and for the same reasons: our profession sets up research writing as an alien and exceedingly difficult endeavor. Even writing programs that offer their faculty and students substantial individual autonomy to develop distinctive reading and writing sequences can be counted upon to nonetheless require and police a universal and highly specified research assignment at the end of their curricula as a way of maintaining programmatic integrity and "disciplining" students for work in their majors. The research assignment always comes last in our courses because "we have to build up to it"; it is almost always 100 percent longer than any other paper written before it; we generally devote twice as much time to it as any other assignment in the semester; we give it inordinately heavy weighting in our percentages for the semester (indeed, students can often fail for the term by failing on this one assignment).

Moreover, this assignment embodies and enacts a ludicrously complex perspective on the collaborative nature of writing. On the one hand, we make it abundantly clear that this is the one assignment in the semester that students definitely cannot do on their own (thereby implicitly contradicting anything we have said earlier about how *all* writing is collaborative in nature); on the other hand, this assignment, more than any other, makes us harp on issues of plagiarism and collusion (thereby insisting that students had better be original and produce their own work even as they are forced to work extensively with other people's ideas and words for the first time all year). Furthermore, we require students to engage in a new and vastly different process to produce this paper. They are now required to compose research notebooks, explicit search strategies, time-management outlines, note cards or their electronic equivalents, and paper proposals; to master a host of new technologies (databases, indexes, search engines); and to work with a panoply of new textual forms (bibliographies, articles from scholarly journals, government documents, scholarly websites, newsgroup postings), each of which must be read in a distinctly new way (looking for bias, authoritativeness, currency, whether it is a primary or secondary source) and documented according to an impossibly arbitrary, arcane, and ephemeral system of documentation. In something very much like a quintessential heroic quest, students are required to leave their home cultures, go on long and arduous journeys alone, do battle with strange and daunting beasts, and return home with their treasures, no doubt deeply transformed by the process. No wonder we dreaded the research paper; no wonder students are still frightened by it.

But the fact is that research writing is not some new and scary alien; we just set it up that way. *All writing is research writing*. This is something we should stress in our teaching and impress upon students from the outset. They have been doing research writing all their lives. Every text they write is a research paper. A *grocery list* is a research paper. If you are writing a grocery list, your research involves looking in the pantry, the refrigerator, and the freezer to find out what you have and what you need. An *email message* is a research paper. If you are writing an email to a friend about what happened last week, your research involves accessing that database of gray matter between your ears to call up the appropriate events to discuss. And since grocery lists and friendly emails are research writing, every essay our students have ever written is research writing, too.

We think the personal essay is an excellent vehicle for teaching research writing. It is a genre most students have great familiarity with, so they are comfortable with its rhetoric, audience, purpose, process, and structures. Indeed, students are so comfortable with the personal essay, they very often write the drafts of their "research papers" in this format anyway, no matter what strictures or constraints we might put on the assignment. When they are beginning their research, we can frequently hear students ask, "If I can't find any sources on my topic, is it OK to put my own ideas in the paper?" Likewise, in workshops and conferences, it is common to observe notations on a student's draft indicating where she plans to "go back and plug in the quotations" to fill out her own text. While we used to sigh when we heard this question, or wince when we saw these notations, we now realize that students' efforts to write research papers this way are hardly a problem, but rather a great strength, one we should take greater advantage of as writing instructors.

We are not alone in suggesting that the essay is a useful vehicle for teaching research writing, of course. Bruce Ballenger (2001), for instance, argues that the essay serves to put *inquiry* at the heart of a research-based writing course. The essay, he contends, works to overturn students' "mistaken assumptions about the nature of inquiry," including the erroneous notion that academic writers always set out "to *prove* rather than *to find out*," that they are "more concerned with answers than questions." He thus recommends that students think of their work as a "research *essay*, a potentially more subjective, less formal, often more exploratory mode than the formal argumentative research paper" (xxii–xxiii). But whereas Ballenger uses the essay as a more accessible means of helping students through the traditional, externally directed research paper process (including developing a research timeline, improving notetaking skills, and the like), we prefer to emphasize the personal, even idiosyncratic aspects of essay writing as an effective way into research writing.

The greatest difficulty facing student writers in "research" assignments is how to use their research without being used *by* it, how to make the sources they cite serve *their* purposes as authors rather than dominate their papers, how to use the sources they find to supplement and support *their* ideas rather than substitute for them, how to research like *writers* rather than like students. The personal essay as research writing begins with a topic and an approach to that topic that are *personally meaningful*. We don't think we can overstate the importance of this fact. Rather than choosing from a list of preapproved topics *someone else* cares about, students select a subject *they* are personally interested in. Rather than going through the motions of research, engaging in a yet another simulacrum to satisfy the arbitrary requirements of a teacher-driven assignment, the student engages in research because she *wants to*, because she cares about the topic and wants to know more about it. This kind of personal, intrinsic motivation urges students to become *independent* researchers, and it will sustain their efforts over several weeks. Indeed, personally motivated research prepares students for the kind of independent research they will need to grapple with in their lives outside of our courses, whether in their college majors, in their workplaces, or in their functioning as citizens in a participatory democracy.

While we can hardly discount the power of extrinsic motivators (in the form of grades and the like) in students' performance, we have found that extrinsic motivators alone are simply not enough to fuel and support a long-term research project by themselves. But deadlines and grades are not the only kind—and hardly the most powerful kind—of extrinsic motivation and validation available to student writers who work with personally meaningful topics in their research assignments: a far more effective motivator is a series of formative responses from *interested readers*, from teachers and peers who invoke the student writer as the local authority on a topic they want to know more about. We have found that students' personally meaningful topics are frequently compelling reading, far more interesting than the tried, true, safe, and boring lists of research topics from which students often get to work. Hence, students composing personal essays as research writing benefit from a strong synergy of internal and external motivations to write effectively.

Besides being a more familiar and personally meaningful genre within which to produce research writing, the personal essay is also a more challenging one than the traditional research paper, actually putting greater intellectual and rhetorical demands upon the writer. Utilizing the personal essay to teach essay writing is hardly a step backward. Rather, it decidedly raises the bar when compared to traditional research papers. As Gary Tate (1989) has argued, writing textbooks have it exactly backward. Almost every writing textbook on the market begins by asking students to write personal, narrative essays, since they are assumed to be the easiest kind of paper to write, and concludes by asking them to write "research papers," since they are assumed to be the most difficult. But as Tate pointed out, writing about yourself without being utterly self-involved, writing about yourself in a way that makes it meaningful and worthwhile for *other* people to read and care about is, in fact, the *hardest* kind of writing to do. Working objectively with other people's ideas and materials and keeping yourself out of the text is actually quite a bit easier to manage, Tate contended, so we might do better by having students do "research papers" first and personal essays last (Tate 1989). Curricular quandaries aside, using research material in personal essays is a most effective way to show how the writer's idiosyncratic thoughts and experiences dovetail with the larger commonalities of human experience all readers share and value. Using research in personal essays will help prevent students from being solipsistic.

But this is hardly news, of course: since Montaigne's invention of the essay, writers in the genre have sought to repair the scholastic fragmentation of experience into mutually exclusive disciplines and discourses by combining in a single text both the subjective and the objective, both the inner and the outer, both art and science, both the high and the low, both the language of the court and the language of the street (see Spellmeyer 1989, 262–63). The personal essay as research paper is but an arch example of this effort to fuse the intrinsic and extrinsic, to bridge the personal versus academic divide. A quick glance at any of Montaigne's essays (1958), for instance, reveals how aggressively and relentlessly he cites a wide diversity of other authors' views while developing his very personal topics. In "Of Friendship," for instance, he cites Horace (four times), La Boétie, Aristotle (three times), Aristippus, Plutarch, Catallus (twice), Ariosto, Cicero (three times), Laelius, Chilo, Diogenes, Terence (twice), and Virgil, to name but one essay example (134–44). In the preface to his collected essays, Aldous Huxley (1959) offers a tremendously useful schematic on this point: the very best essays, he says, work toward three different poles of development at the same time, simultaneously driving toward the personal/autobiographical, the objective/factual, and the abstract/universal. Arguing that the discourse of "professional sages . . . is apt, in a tight corner, to reveal itself as ludicrously inappropriate to the facts of life as it is really and tragically lived" (viii), Huxley contends that the essay counters this weakness by trying to merge all kinds of discourse, all areas of knowledge, into a single text. The "most richly satisfying essays," he says, are

> those which make the best not of one, not of two, but of all three worlds in which it is possible for the essay to exist. Freely, effortlessly, thought and feeling move in these consummate works of art, hither and thither between the essay's three poles—from the personal to the universal, from the abstract to the concrete, from the objective datum to the inner experience. (vii)

In sum, in its attempts to weave together as many varied voices, textures, and discourses as possible, the personal essay is, perhaps, the perfect vehicle for teaching research writing.

Some Suggested Pedagogy

Our suggestions for using the personal essay as a vehicle for teaching research writing are pretty simple, really. After choosing topics they are personally interested in, that they find personally *meaningful,* students should be asked to produce a first draft that is all about them, that is unapologetically personal and autobiographical in nature. Some useful options for prewriting on this first draft include asking students to

- freewrite in cycles about their topics, taking a surprising or intriguing aspect that emerges in each cycle as the focus for the next cycle of freewriting;
- tell a story or stories about their topics from their own pasts;
- do a sensory inventory of one experience they had with their topics, cataloging everything they saw, heard, smelled, tasted, and felt at that time;
- do a "memory dump," rapidly rendering everything they know about their topics, feel about them, have heard about them, and wonder about them.

We try to remind students that even this utterly subjective discourse on their topic is nonetheless a research paper: they have to research their own histories and experiences, their own biases and values, their own assumptions and ideas by combing through the database between their ears. We also remind them that while researching through their own gray matter may seem simple, it is not necessarily easy. We caution students to remember that this first draft renders only one of the many voices that will eventually be in their texts, so they shouldn't be perfectionists about getting their thoughts and feelings about their subjects onto the page.

When their completely personal drafts are finished, students are now at that "teachable moment" when instruction on how and why to use different search strategies and different information resources becomes personally meaningful. Since most now care about their topics and their approach to their topics (as embodied in their first drafts), we have found students at this point attend effectively to sessions offering information literacy training. *This* is the moment when students should take the "library tour" and meet the reference librarians, learn to use Boolean searches, learn to navigate the local library's electronic catalog and available databases, learn to use Internet search engines effectively, and learn to critically evaluate the quality of websites, because *this* is the moment they care about such things: they know exactly what kind of information *they* are looking for and why it is important for *them* to find it. They become purposeful and strategic in their efforts, researching more like authors than students.

After gathering and processing their sources, two basic options present themselves for incorporating this external research into the students' evolving essays: first, students could use the new material as a springboard, simply adding new externally discovered content at the end of their first drafts; second, students could seek to interweave the externally discovered content throughout their first drafts. Both of these basic moves are represented in the student texts in Chapter 5 of the companion website for this volume. We present these options to students as exactly that—options, which use handouts that graphically represent where the new material might go and example texts that demonstrate each technique. Students are also encouraged to invent their own additional, creative ways of incorporating their research beyond these two basic moves (working with multiple fonts and setting up simultaneous columns of competing/cooperating text are frequent choices in this regard) and to mix various methods in original combinations.

The first model included in Chapter 5 of the companion website for this volume, in which the writer explores the power certain kinds of music have over her, is additive. It simply appends the externally researched content to the end of the internally researched first draft. The writer uses the Internet sources she found to expand upon her first draft, the revision of which constitutes the first three paragraphs of her final paper. She also uses traditional MLA citation format.

In the second example, an examination of the import of kissing, which is also available in Chapter 5 of the website, the writer, rather than using the external research to build upon the end of the personal/subjective first draft, works instead to weave the externally discovered research *into* her personal first draft. She alternates the voices in fairly large blocks and uses obvious signals to indicate where the discourses start and stop, employing what Robert L. Root Jr. calls a "segmented essay," one in which the "chief structural devices" are "stanza-like sections or segments" (2002, 321–22). As Winston Weathers (1980) notes, in these texts, each such stanza or *crot* is an "independent and discrete" block of text, "an autonomous unit, characterized by the absence of any transitional devices that might relate to preceding or subsequent crots," allowing for sharp and rapid changes in perspective (14). Toby Fulwiler (1998) writes that we can "[t]hink of crots as snapshots in words, a photo album, scrapbook, slide show, pictures in an exhibition . . . each separated from the others by white space, numbers, asterisks, or dots, sometimes numbered, sometimes not" (104). But whereas some segmented essays tend toward *collage*, in Peter Elbow's terms, toward associatively ordered fragments "arranged how shall we say?—poetically? intuitively? randomly?" (148), this student's text is better understood as an example of what David W. Chapman (1991) calls a "counterpoint essay." It is schematically organized, orchestrating two alternating styles to render and arrange her internally obtained and externally obtained research on her topic. Chapman maintains that this alternating movement provides "a bridge between what D'Angelo calls syntagmatic and paradigmatic expression in *A Conceptual Theory of Rhetoric* (1975, 79), a bridge between the concrete/particular/unique and the abstract/general/universal" (79). In addition to her more complex structure, this student also chooses not to document her external sources in any formal way, but rather cites sources in the manner of professional essayists.

While both of the texts could easily be revised to incorporate more numerous sources, more scholarly external sources, or more frequent interplay between the author's ideas and the source material (and thus be more "rigorous" in terms of being "research papers"), we think they are indicative of the benefits of teaching the research paper as a personal essay. Both models show students being independent researchers working to find material on specialized topics; both models show students using research to improve their personally meaningful texts, expanding the scope of the discourse and making it worthwhile for others to read and care about; both models show students using research rather than being used by it, using research for *their* purposes and intentions; both models show students weaving together internal and external research to create compositions that develop their topics in complex ways; both models show students researching like writers rather than researching like students.

We share our grading criteria for these texts with our students from the moment we give them the assignment so that there is no confusion about what they are being asked to produce. In many ways, these criteria are identical to the ones we would use in evaluating a traditional research paper: we are looking for

- a narrowly focused topic
- unity of development
- depth and specificity of development
- conscious, strategic organization
- use of strong, appropriate sources
- effective use of sources (sources supplement rather than dominate author's perspective)
- clarity and conciseness in diction and style
- correctness in grammar, mechanics, punctuation, and MLA format

Beyond these traditional criteria, we remind students from the beginning that the personal essay makes its own distinctive demands on their writing. As we noted before, Montaigne and Huxley urge us to value writing that

- crosses disciplinary boundaries
- offers multiple perspectives on its subject
- utilizes multiple discourses, multiple voices (including, of course, the writer's own distinctive voice)
- attempts to develop the significance of its subject in at least three directions: toward the personal/autobiographical, the objective/factual, and the abstract/universal

These explicit criteria help us frame our responses to all their drafts. As is the case with practically any writing assignment we give them, our students first need considerable assistance in narrowing and focusing their topics to the point where these topics can be developed in depth in a short text. While students typically prefer the safety of writing texts that are a mile wide and an inch deep, so to speak, we encourage them to write ones that are an inch wide and a mile deep. For example, we point out which aspects of their first drafts would seem most profitable for them to restrict their attention to as they move on. This brings us to the second major area of response we make to their first drafts, which is to suggest domains of knowledge, databases, and even particular sources they might want to investigate as they work to develop multiple perspectives on their narrowed and focused topic. As their drafts develop, we begin directing their attention to the other desiderata for their final products.

Let us conclude here by noting that while using the personal essay as research paper does not promise to make research writing easy, fun, or foolproof, it does result in research writing that we don't dread to teach and students don't fear to compose. And that, we submit, is no mean feat.

Works Cited

Ballenger, Bruce P. 2001. *The Curious Researcher: A Guide to Writing Research Papers.* 3rd edition. Boston: Allyn & Bacon.

Chapman, David W. 1991. "Forming and Meaning: Writing the Counterpoint Essay." *Journal of Advanced Composition* 11 (1): 73–81.

D'Angelo, Frank J. 1975. *A Conceptual Theory of Rhetoric.* Cambridge, MA: Winthrop.

Elbow, Peter. 1981. *Writing with Power.* New York: Oxford University Press.

Fulwiler, Toby. 1998. "Writing Snapshots." In *Teaching Writing Creatively,* edited by David Starkey, 102–10. Portsmouth, NH: Boynton/Cook.

Huxley, Aldous. 1959. "Preface." In *Collected Essays,* v–ix. New York: Harper.

Montaigne, Michel de Eyquemde. 1958. "Of Friendship." In *The Complete Essays of Montaigne*, translated by Donald M. Frame, 135–44. Stanford, CA: Stanford University Press.

Root, Robert L., Jr. 2002. "Beyond Linearity: Writing the Segmented Essay." In *The Fourth Genre: Contemporary Writers of/on Creative Nonfiction,* 2nd edition, edited by Robert L. Root Jr., and Michael Steinberg, 321–28. New York: Longman.

Spellmeyer, Kurt. 1989. "A Common Ground: The Essay and the Academy." *College English* 51 (3): 262–76.

Tate, Gary. 1989. "Theory of Composition." Lecture, Texas Christian University, Fort Worth. Fall.

Weathers, Winston. 1980. *An Alternate Style: Options in Composition.* Rochelle Park, NJ: Hayden.

PART III

Research Across Genres, Disciplines, and Settings

6

More Than Just Writing About Me?
Linking Self and Other in the Ethnographic Essay

Bonnie Sunstein and Elizabeth Chiseri-Strater

> The personal essay has this single quality of difference from fiction:
> it is bounded—some might say grounded—by reality. There are no
> unreliable narrators in personal essays; in a personal essay an
> unreliable narrator is just another name for a bad writer.
> —Joseph Epstein (1997, 14)

After the first hour of the first nonfiction essay class Bonnie taught the first time, two students dropped the course. "Yo," one mumbled, looking at his sandals, not at her. He handed her a green drop slip and sniffed, "Naaaah. No way. I didn't want to write about THE OTHER, I wanted to write about MYSELF. What kind of nonfiction is this?" She noted a grimace through the dreadlocks that curtained much of his face. In her creative nonfiction class, Elizabeth had a student, female, older, who tossed her head, swept her pencils into her book bag, tucked a silk scarf under her jacket, and pressed her cell phone to her cheek. "I was TRICKED," she whined to her husband. "I don't want to do any *research or reading*; I just want to write about MY LIFE. I'm going to drop this course. Come and take me home."

We hate it when that happens. We feel awful, and it continues to happen to each of us a few times a year when we distribute syllabi, reading, and research requirements during the first class meeting of our nonfiction writing courses infused with ethnographic research methods. "This looks like too much work," some of them mutter as they file out of the classroom, dumping the syllabus back on the desk. Students sometimes believe that taking a nonfiction writing course is a chance to write exclusively about the "self," to have a professor's permission to use the personal pronoun for a change, to "make meaning" in an institution in which the meaning is usually made for them. Nonfiction, despite what its name implies, is counterintuitive to them and to us. Few people are comfortable with what we're now calling "creative nonfiction." Maybe that's why we keep changing its course name. Some English faculty toss it off as "personal writing," "protean meanderings," or "this self-indulgent memoir phase we're currently in." Some people with composition or rhetoric backgrounds sneer at it lately under the categories of "expressivism," or "the personal essay," "confessional writing," and "whiny wanderings." Journalists' terms have covered recent years with the "old new journalism," "literary journalism," and the most recent and newer "narrative journalism." Yet even the "non" in *nonfiction* suggests confusion, as Robert Root likes to remind us; even dictionaries emphasize "the non-ness of the form," but that it is "not just not-fiction anymore—it's something positive and self-defining in its own right, an entity rather than a non-entity" (2003, 243).

We kind of relish our marginal status. And like any other literature, the nonfiction essay is both art and craft, a creation made up of words carefully drafted and rendered into a shifting variety of content and form. And despite this complicated nomenclature and confusion of academic sorting, smooth writing, wrought well, remains one of our contemporary culture's great reading pleasures. Do we try to classify the writing we read in *The New Yorker, Harper's,* and *The Atlantic*? Hear on National Public Radio? Consume at our Sunday leisure in the magazine supplements of our cities' newspapers? Traditionally and consistently, on the best-seller lists of *The New York Times*, Amazon.com, and Barnes and Noble, nonfiction sells twice the numbers as fiction. Our bookselling and book buying habits enhance all the critiquing, not to mention the categorizing, as we discuss and define our reading habits with other readers.

And so as coauthors (the "nonauthor"?) and in a voice that is both of ours and each of ours (a "nonvoice"), we'd like to complicate this classification even further by suggesting that we add yet another adjective—*ethnographic*—to the long line of descriptive adjectives that attach themselves to the term *essay*: creative, narrative, personal, literary, lyric, segmented, and even "nonfiction."

The ethnographic essay, as we see it and teach it, demands that the writer include documented attention to "the other," a way of guarding against the solipsism that misguides many student papers and many faculty attitudes, like the ones we've illustrated from our own students above. Is a course in the nonfiction essay a chance, as some of our students want, to purge the self but not learn the rigors of writing and research? Is it a chance, as some teachers want, to ignore the difficult part—teaching research—of teaching composition? We like to think about ways we can teach students to include the other without ignoring the self, to engage in thick description based on documented observation, to learn to conduct interviews and research in archives, to develop the critical and analytic strategies any writer needs in order to understand and write about the many cultures and many "others" that surround the self.

Linking Self and Other: Writing for a Reader

Is there really such a giant gap between "self" and "other" that a student should drop a course over it? Compositionists and nonfiction writers have long understood the centrality of the self in the traditional essay form. But even the most personal of personal essays has to be about some kind of idea shaped for a reader who hasn't, or doesn't want, the same life as the writer. Nancy Mairs (1994) meditates on the relationship between the writer, the reader, and the details the writer promises in any essay:

> I cannot write myself without writing you, my other. I don't believe literally that in writing my "life" I am writing yours as well. On the contrary, I feel certain I am not . . . you didn't get bitten on the foot by red ants when you were four, did you? . . . You don't eat the same thing for breakfast every morning of your life? . . . These are my details. And heaven knows I have enough trouble getting them straight without keeping track of yours. (119)

With our students, our course descriptions, our disciplinary polarities in mind, and borrowing a phrase from the contemporary frenzy about standards, what do essay writers "need to know and be able to do" (Sunstein and Lovell 2000)? Just as a writer must remember herself as she writes her "other," a teacher of writing must remember her teaching. We think we can help our students by reminding ourselves about some pedagogical strategies we've learned but not used very consistently over the last thirty-five years in the field of composition studies. We've learned from scholars, philosophers, and practitioners that essay writing means a self writing to an "other," about his or her relationship with some kind of information.

Sondra Perl's work, as she drew upon philosopher Eugene Gendlin, reminded us that writers need to recognize a "felt sense . . . the soft underbelly of thought," as they explore an idea, patiently looking ahead ("projective structuring") and behind ("retrospective structuring") as they blend the information (1980). Linda Flower, through the lens of cognitive psychology, helped us recognize that any writer must work a text, draft after draft, from "writer-based prose" toward "reader-based prose"; that any self writing must imagine another self reading (1979). James Britton's research showed us that all writing, whether it's the transactional, businesslike kind, or the poetic (to fit or break an artistic form), relies on beginning with self-exploration—that no writing for a reader simply ends with a writer simply engaging in "expressive writing" (1975).

There are a few conversations about representation in studies of literacy (Mortensen and Kirsch 1996), but we are not alone. The academic disciplines of folklore, sociology, and anthropology have sensed a similar paradigm shift (Hymes). They have long considered issues of the reflexivity that a writer must establish as a participant/observer both in research and in writing (Ruby 1982), as well as issues of self and other in writing (Van Maanen, Clifford and Marcus, Peacock, Rosaldo, Stoller, Behar). Qualitative researchers in education, too, discuss effectiveness in ethnographic writing involving self and other (Woolcott, Eisner, Lightfoot and Davis).

We'd like to look more closely at the teaching and learning involved in writing the ethnographic essay, which we feel provides a bridge between purely personal writing and purely research writing. We think attention to these skills can help balance the continuum between self and other. Good non-fiction, in addition to being creative writing, *is* about writing about the other, even when it is writing about the self. In an essay-writing class, too, we need a pedagogical plan, a scaffold of ways for our students to link themselves and their intuitions consciously to the information and details they're wanting to write about.

In the first week of Bonnie's undergraduate nonfiction class, Tyler, a senior, wrote this*:

ME, ME, ME, ME, ME. LATELY I HAVE BEEN WONDERING WHY I LIKE WHAT I LIKE, DO WHAT I DO, THINK HOW I THINK, READ WHAT I READ, AND QUIT WHAT I QUIT. I CAN'T FIGURE MYSELF OUT . . . FOR AS LONG AS I CAN REMEMBER, I HAVE BEEN VAIN. I JUST DIDN'T KNOW I POSSESSED THIS CHARACTERISTIC UNTIL RECENTLY SIMPLY BECAUSE I HAD NO IDEA WHAT "VANITY" MEANT.

I'LL TELL YOU WHAT CONTRIBUTES TO VANITY. COMPLI-MENTS. PLAIN AND SIMPLE COMPLIMENTS. . . . "EXCELLENT ANALYSIS," "LOOKIN GOOD, BUDDY," "GOOD QUESTION" . . . SCHOLARSHIPS, AWARDS, PAPERS THAT MEET CRITERIA. THE COMPLIMENTS BUILD AND BUILD AND THEN, WALLA [*sic*], A BONA FIDE EGOTIST. I WANT THESE COMPLIMENTS. I STRIVE FOR THESE COMPLIMENTS . . .

BUT, YOU SEE, I LIKE READING ABOUT CHARACTERS WHO ARE SCUM. GUYS THAT ARE REALLY STUCK ON THEMSELVES: HOLDEN CAULFIELD, THOMAS CHIPPERING, PIP, HARRY ANG-STROM, AND TED COLE. I LAUGH AT THESE GUYS FOR BEING IG-NORANT, EGOTISTICAL, CHASING THEIR IDEAS OF BLISS, USUALLY INVOLVING A FEMALE. . . . AND THEN I STOP. "SHIT," I THINK, "I'M NO DIFFERENT THAN THIS GUY."

Tyler goes on for two pages, all in capital letters, including other expletives, exploring what vanity would be like in Hollywood, and imagines himself with audiences of readers and movie viewers. The all-caps, he tells Bonnie when he hands the paper in, is because of two sprained fingers on his left hand. She sees the plastic brace, but she thinks how appropriate the capital letters are to his writing. The problem is certainly not his voice; he's as comfortable as he can be. The problem is that he's not going anywhere with his idea of compliments caus-

---

*Ellipses show text breaks and substitute for extra text, deleted for the purpose of this article.

ing vanity. He might cite his scum guys, offer a few quotes, discuss who has offered him those compliments that have made him vain, what he means by "ideas of bliss, usually involving a female." Those writing choices would be in the category of "data" about the other in order to elucidate his thoughts about himself. But Tyler takes no position; he inventories and narrates his intuitions—he "tells," as we like to say, without "showing" anything.

Along with his capital letters, Tyler SCREAMS his essay to anyone who will look, at least once before he graduates. But he's neither complicating his own thoughts with specifics nor thinking about what his reader might need from them. In his conclusion, he can only ask for more compliments— acknowledging his vanity in the company of his literary scum guys, and asking for more of what got him into the situation in the first place:

> THE VAIN MUST APPEAR TO BE HUMBLE . . . THAT THEY HAVE DONE BETTER THAN ALL THE OTHERS, AND THEY COMPLETELY SHUT DOWN WHEN THEY ARE EXPECTED TO RECIPROCATE OR RESPOND. WE'LL USE THE ANALOGY OF DRUGS HERE. COMPLIMENTS ARE THE DRUG THE VAIN CAN'T GET ENOUGH OF. SO, PLEASE, SHOWER ME WITH COMPLIMENTS.

By the end of Tyler's piece, we're not sure who his reader is and we don't think he's sure either. His drug analogy smacks the reader with a pun at the end—drugs and compliments in the vain (the vein?). In the last words of his conclusion, he raises yet another "other" (drugs) that he might want to further research, another line of investigation.

And so we wonder, *what is* that injection of compliments into our vanity and our writing veins, as Ty suggests, if not a shot of the "other"? We could go on citing other compositionists, but instead, we prefer to return to Tyler, five weeks and six assignments later:

> "Snow" to me does not mean recreation. It doesn't mean snow skiing, hunting, ice fishing, snowboarding, or sledding. "Snow" means hard blistering work, frostbitten fingers and toes, yearning for hot chocolate and a fireplace, nose running, snot sticking to my upper lip, sweating under seven layers of clothing, arms twitching as I toss shovelfuls of the stuff that don't form a mound when I want them to. "Snow" means scraping a windshield. . . .
>
> But for my roommate Jimmy, "snow" has another meaning.
>
> "Hey Jimmy," I call.
>
> "What's up?"
>
> "I've got this assignment . . . First I have to take notes on it. Then I'll ask you about it. Something you could talk to me about? Something that has a story behind it?
>
> "Hell yeah," he says as he makes for his room. "Write about this." He brings a bag into the hallway that stands on end. It is about five feet tall and reaches to my neck. Jimmy unzips the bag and removes his prize.

"Awesome," I say.

I knew Jimmy had a snowboard, but I had never seen it up close, felt it, read the inscriptions and stickers covering it. I grabbed a tape measure and a scale. . . .

Tyler continues for fifteen manuscript pages packed with details, dialogue, description, and analysis. He ends with an homage to Jimmy's language and his bedroom. Jimmy has become the "other" in his writing about the snowboard, but Tyler never loses himself in his piece:

Music, name brands of snowboarding gear, and records cover the walls and ceiling. Above his bed there are two posters of men with snowboards strapped to their feet, flying through the air in trees and snow, unfamiliar. . . . My thoughts of snot dripping from my nostrils, throwing shovelfuls of snow on a slowly ascending mound, and longing for cocoa diminish. I find myself wanting to believe that Jimmy found peace out there in the snow while scratching the bottom of his flying piece of plastic.

Tyler considers himself in relationship to Jimmy, his roommate, his "other," and he teaches himself and his reader a lot about snowboards: the details, language, and behaviors of snowboarders; he even contemplates the human differences when people confront the weather. What *happened* in the six assignments and five weeks between these papers? Tyler did a lot of reading and thinking about writing, as well as writing. And, as his teacher, Bonnie did a lot of planning. She "scaffolded" with specific assignments: write about a subculture you belong to—list its rituals, beliefs, language, behaviors. Record your observations in a double-entry journal in which the left side is for data only and the right side is for personal thoughts. Analyze what you wrote, try to think about what's missing, and share it with someone else before you draft it again. Read other nonfiction writing *as a writer*—what did the writer do to create images? What kinds of sources did she use? Notes might she have taken? Places and people she documented?

This is not new stuff, nor was it new when any one of us teaching now first encountered it. If we want students to write nonfiction with art and craft, we must give them ways to do it. Four centuries before Ken Macrorie offered the "I-Search Paper," Montaigne wrote, "We are all patchwork, and so shapeless and diverse in composition that each bit, each moment, plays its own game. And there is as much difference between us and ourselves as between us and others" (1973, 48). We must offer structure, strategies, and habits of mind to allow our students to explore combinations between their own thinking and the information they collect. The collected information— the research, that data—becomes part of the "other" with each topic our students write about, each time they write. In the remainder of this chapter, we'll offer four specific strategies we've developed to assist students as they craft ethnographic essays, strategies that help student writers pay

close attention to details of the "other" without losing the sense of self:
1) Linking the Self with Information: Positioning; 2) Linking the Self, the
Other, and the Information: Asking Reflective Questions for Analysis;
3) Linking the Writing and Reading "Selves"; and 4) Linking the Links: A
Research Portfolio in Two Parts.

1. Linking the Self with the Information: Positioning

Nonfiction writers need to "read" themselves and write that perspective into
their work. Instead of leaving out personal, subjective information, we should
write it in. These days, most contemporary scientists and postmodernists
would agree that objectivity (or measured, certain "truth") is not possible—
that the observer is always part of the observed.

But do students know that about their own writing? Despite their contemporary postmodern and politicized studies, do they feel they have univer-
sity-sanctioned permission to link themselves with the information they've
researched to write about? We don't think so. In fact, do they realize that a
meander around a set of ideas might involve research at all? They should.
Students need to recognize and practice a constant shuttle between self and
other, intuition and information, subjectivity and objectivity, the felt and the
observed, the meander and the argument, the whine and the critique. Not until a first draft is complete can a writer determine where on this continuum the
two features will fall. And each time, probably with each draft—certainly with
each separate essay—it will fall on a different place in the continuum.

We need to work with our students on the idea of "positioning": all
those subjective responses that affect how a writer collects and arranges
her information, how a researcher sees herself in relationship to her data.
Being the writer/guide through an ethnographic essay so influences your
work that it would be deceptive *not* to include relevant background information. We think that there are at least three ways a writer positions or situ-
ates herself in relationship to her information: fixed, subjective, and textual.
And, we believe, this is a skill we need to teach. When we first created
these categories writing our book *FieldWorking: Reading and Writing Research* (2002), we worried that they might become "orthodoxies," skills that
teachers would announce as three ways to position the self, somewhat like
a yoga book or a sex manual. But since then in our teaching, we have found
the following to be useful categories for ways of discussing how the essay
writer integrates or infuses herself into her text (2002, 118-24)

1. *Fixed positions* are the personal facts that might influence how the writer
   sees information—her age at the time, gender, class, nationality, race—factors that will not change during the course of a piece of writing but that are
   often taken for granted and unexamined.

2. *Subjective positions,* such as life history and personal experiences, may
   also affect field research.

3. Textual positions, the language choices you make to represent what you see, affect the research as well as the writing. The way that you position yourself with respect to those you write about determines the kind of information you'll gather, the voice you'll create in your finished text, and to some extent your credibility.

Marji, an undergraduate in a nonfiction writing class, positions herself this way as she answers the preceding questions in a week's writing assignment. She calls it "Mozart and Free Food":

> We are a string quartet. Before a gig, at least one of the four of us is in a bad mood. It's usually Liz, the cellist, or Carrie, the second violinist, because they are more thin-skinned than Bjorg, the violist, and me, the first violinist. Of course, Carrie and Liz are the ones to set up these wedding gigs, and are carrying on their shoulders bigger portions of responsibility for a strange couple's happiest day. Anyway, we all meet at the loading docks of the school of music, where we load our instruments into the trunk of Liz's senior-citizen car, then we get into our appropriate seats. Liz at the wheel, Bjorg sitting shotgun but not exercising her privilege as radio jockey or air controller, and Carrie and me, roommate violinists, in the back. Bjorg and Liz, like Carrie and me, are a natural pair. They're the low strings—we're the high. They're tidy people who study the sciences and do music for fun— we're performance majors who procrastinate and make messes. They are front seat people—we are back seat people.
>
> Whether the gig is hard to find or not (which small town are we looking for? Will the couple tie pink balloons on their mailbox to note the backyard tent?), we stay pretty quiet and grouchy on our way to the gig. Grouchy mostly because we feel ugly. Each of us performs in an average of three concerts each month, and each owns one and a half concert-black outfits. . . .

Marji works her way through this draft as she thinks about her positions in relationship to her music and her quartet, remarking on the "wedding gigs" they perform and on the bond they have as college friends. Her positions are clear from the beginning: she's skeptical but hungry, artistic but practical, a serious musician among others, needing money from a less musically sophisticated public. She shows the folding chairs, the sheet music ("the dorkified arrangements of Bach pieces"), the "twittery crowd," her own task as first violinist of cueing the processional, and how the music gets them out of their collective funk. Soon, writes Marji, like many college roommates, "we the quartet sit back and judge," hypothesizing questions about the couple's pasts, futures, relatives, critiquing their choices of music, readings, outfits, floral arrangements and fake tans. The mood lifts further, she writes:

> . . . until you've nailed a passage of a Spanish dance by Sarasate, or pulled a rich, teeth-rattling open C from a cello, I'm convinced you don't know the

full definition of "sexy"—we play our instruments for the reward of free roasted chicken, fresh green beans, baked potatoes, wedding cake, champagne, and a table reserved for us in the back of the reception hall. At that table, if it's isolated enough from the rest of the crowd, we share our opinions of the wedding and rate the dinner. Our ratings are based partly on the quality and temperature of the chicken, beans, and potatoes, but most importantly on the buns. A wedding bun can go many ways: it can be too soft, like Wonder Bread, or it can be tough and dry. Those kinds of flaws register a one-bun rating. It might have a perfect, crisp crust and an airy, warm center. Rating: four buns. There might not be any buns served, in which case the wedding reception dinner gets a rating of negative seven buns. Serve buns at your wedding, in a basket lined with a cloth napkin. Do it.

Marji positions herself with the help of the week's writing exercise on positioning as she asks herself about her fixed, textual, and subjective positions. Her response to the three categories reveals herself to herself to be a hardworking college student, a competent musician, a wedding and food critic. As readers, we learn about her positions in these short excerpts as she writes about her experience playing wedding music several times a month. To clarify her voice (and further position herself), she even includes us, the "reader," in her use of the intimate and chatty but ever difficult second person ("Serve buns at your wedding. Do it."). We see both her engagement and disengagement in relationship to the information she presents.

By the end of this exercise on positioning, she concludes with the tender meditations of one independent romantic young college woman—and those of her friends—about weddings, "I want there to be a tent far off where that someone (WHO ARE YOU?) and I can escape when nobody is watching. My quartet friends will be there, sharing a basket of buns." Marji doesn't give up her self in order to include the information she wants to explore in this draft, nor to offer us the perspectives of the others. She develops a way of offering information and description, turning back reflectively to herself, considering her friends along the way, and then turning again (reflexively) toward her experience. Her careful and strategic positioning is an act of both reflection and reflexivity, a "turn of thought," as compositionist Donna Qualley (1997) observes, "when the process of composition includes the habit of reflexive inquiry, then we begin to see more clearly how writing and reading the word, the world, and the self are always in continual dialectical interplay" (5). This positioning exercise urges essay writers to include the links between the self and information that are often assumed but not explicit.

2. Linking the Self, the Other, and the Information: Asking Reflective Questions for Analysis

As Marji discovered by continually considering her positions in relationship to her subject, both reflective and reflexive inquiry require conscious and constant questioning, sometimes asking the same question—to examine different answers—many times during the process of writing one piece. Writer Donald Murray has mentored two professionsful of writers—journalists and compositionists—how to ask the question "what surprised you," each time we write a draft or confer with a student. For the writing coach or teacher, asking this question helps a writer draw the details that turn telling into showing.

Murray's strategies helped us know that phrase for phrase, draft for draft, it's important to ask questions of your writing as you write. And so, in our book and in our courses, we suggest to students that they ask questions periodically and regularly in order to determine how their positions are changing during the research and development of an essay. Under Don's influence, we came up with three questions to determine a researcher's assumptions, positions, and personal biases in order to allow writing from both perspectives, the "self" and the "other."

The questions are deceptively simple. But the complexity of our assumptions, positions, and biases is critical to keep in mind when we set out to understand anything and then write about it for a reader. Keeping track of these shifts enables students to write honestly, reflectively, and reflexively as they continue to research and write about others without losing voice or perspective. Here's how we introduce the idea to our readers in *FieldWorking*.

> In ethnographic research, fieldnotes are the storehouse for data and, hence, the home of a project. They enhance your ability to step in and step out of the culture you've chosen. From the earliest "freewriting" as you think about a topic, through the notes you take as you enter your fieldsite, to the reflections you write as you look back, question, and add to what you wrote—draft to draft— fieldnotes offer you the details, language, perspectives, and perceptions that will eventually become a final written product. Take fieldnotes with care and patience. Although you may not realize it, your fieldnotes create an original source, a primary source that no one has recorded in the same way you have, at the site you've chosen, and with the people you've studied. (425–28)

1. *What surprised you? (to track assumptions)* helps you monitor your assumptions throughout the research and writing process. Asking yourself this question regularly throughout the research process helps you articulate your preconceived notions and record how they change.

2. *What intrigued you? (to see positions)* makes you aware of your personal stances in relationship to your topic. You as the writer *are one important instrument* (recorder and presenter) of the research process. What interests and attracts you about your topic will always influence what details you record and how you write about them. This question helps you understand the complex ideas and dilemmas of positioning.

3. *What disturbed you? (to understand tensions)* Expose yourself to yourself. In nonfiction writing, you need to be honest about your blind spots,

stereotypes, prejudices, and the things you find upsetting, no matter how small. Focusing on what bothers you about a topic or project is not always comfortable, but it often leads to important insights.

To illustrate with a student-researcher/writer as her essay evolves, we'd like to introduce you to Holly Richardson, a high school teacher in Alaska who grew up in western New York and worked with us in a summer writing course for teachers in Massachusetts. To prepare to teach her Alaskan students how to do fieldwork, she practiced by doing a field study of her own. Holly studied a bingo game at a local American Legion hall. "Ever since I was a young girl," she summarizes in a statement that positions herself,

> I have accompanied my mother and a slew of her friends to bingo games at various Veterans of Foreign War posts, Indian reservations, Catholic churches, and volunteer fire stations in Western New York. In my adult life, I have attended bingo games in central Alaska, sometimes just for fun, and sometimes games to raffle off items or do 50/50 drawings for my student government group. I've always been intrigued by the superstitions and rituals that surface at these games. Although I am not particularly superstitious, I find myself rubbing my neighbor's winnings, or coding a particular game by marking an edge with the dabber, hoping that the game will bring me luck. There are mostly women at the games and usually there is a mix of ages, although the majority are probably over 50. The men seem to accompany the women, not vice-versa. Until now, I never actually took notes on what people around me were doing at these games.

Holly continues to look at her "other" (the bingo players in the unfamiliar hall in Massachusetts) through her own lenses, meditating on her past as a bingo participant in both New York as a child and Alaska as an adult. She notes themes like gender and age, superstition and rituals, but in this research project she became interested in another quite different cultural ritual which eventually furnished her with an interesting angle from which to write her essay:

> *What surprised me?* I went outside before the game started and during the ten-minute break to smoke a cigarette and talk to some of my fellow addicts. As usual, the chitchat was of gas prices, cigarette prices, and our terrible habits. But there was an underlying feeling of camaraderie in this group that didn't seem directly related to bingo, but maybe it was. I realized I was being accepted into their bingo circle merely because we were smoking together. This surprised me; I just haven't thought about it before.

> *What intrigued me?* As I began to think about the ten years I have spent on front porches or in smoking sections, I realized that these strangers whom I meet have shared their life stories with me. I remember and am intrigued by the hundreds of people whose wisdom about life, strengths, and failures have been in my life. I wanted the smoking area to become my central area of focus.

What disturbed me? I went to the bingo game to observe the players, not to focus on the smokers! I was disturbed by my feeling when I was with them. They took me into their lives and shared with me. This has been happening for ten years and I am only now realizing it. I wonder if the kindness and closeness I feel with my fellow smokers is part of the addiction I can't seem to kick. I understand why AA meetings can be so important to people. But I'm here to study bingo!

As she reread her fieldnotes and wrote in her journal, Holly realized that she needed to either write more about the bingo games, or to focus only on the cluster of interesting and talkative people with whom she'd developed a relationship during their smoking breaks. Asking these three questions helped Holly understand that her "other," at least for that moment and that essay, was focused not on bingo players, but on the smokers at the bingo game. She was honest with her reader about her surprise change of focus, the discomfort she felt as she was shifting her interest as well as her understanding of bingo from other times in her life. She was documenting the influences to her work and acknowledging them, as she explained the shifts to her reader.

3. Linking the Writing and Reading "Selves"

Using a variety of readings in a nonfiction writing course provides yet another "other" for student writers, especially when you're asking them to write ethnographically; it's not always apparent to students why there are lists of readings in a writing course. While we should never focus exclusively on reading, the many voices, models, styles, and shapes that essays provide can offer inspiration, instruction, and even affirmation to student writers. Donald Murray often refers to "the ghost text" that forms between a writer reading and a writer writing—a ghost text providing a transparent trace that often goes unrecognized, even by the writer. In Elizabeth's literary nonfiction course, student writer Joe had read Philip Lopate's essay "Portrait of My Body" in his nonfiction textbook, *The Fourth Genre* (Root and Steinberg 2002), as well as a photocopied handout of Montaigne's essay "Of the Inconsistency of Our Actions." Both essays offer liberal descriptions as the authors meditate on their male body parts, the most intimate other. In "Portrait of My Body," Lopate considers his toes, his back, his stance, and then:

> About my penis there is nothing I think unusual. It has a brown stem, and a pink mushroom head where the foreskin is pulled back. Like most heterosexual males, I have little comparative knowledge to go by, so that I always feel like an outsider when I am around women or gay men who talk zestfully about differences in penises. I am afraid they might judge me harshly, ridicule me like the boys who stripped me of my bathing suit in summer camp when I was ten. But perhaps they would simply declare it an ordinary penis which changes size with the stimulus or weather or time of day. (110)

In another essay written four centuries before Lopate's, Montaigne's observations offer similar kinds of details:

> Those who know their members to be obedient by nature need only take care to out-manoeuvre the imagination. We have reason to remark the untractable liberties taken by this member, which intrudes so tiresomely when we do not require it and fails us so annoyingly when we need it most, imperiously pitting its authority against that of the will, and most proudly and obstinately refusing our solicitations both mental and manual. Yet if on being rebuked for rebellion and condemned on that score he were to engage me to plead his cause, I might perhaps cast some suspicion on our other members, his fellows, of having framed this fictitious case against him out of pure envy of the importance and pleasure attached to his functions. I might arraign them for plotting to make the world his enemy by maliciously blaming him alone for their common fault. For I ask you to consider whether there is a single part of our bodies that does not often refuse to work at our will, and does not often operate in defiance of it. Each one of them has its own passions that rouse it and put it to sleep without our leave. (1973, 42)

We believe that reading both essays provided Joe with a theme, some confidence and at least two "ghost texts" as he crafted his ethnographic essay, "A Night in My Grave (With My Shovel in Hand)." In it, Joe writes about the frightening threat of a sexually transmitted disease, which begins with a phone call from a girlfriend: "So I get a call from a girl. She has something awful, she says. It hurts to sit. It hurts to piss. It hurts to breathe. She wasn't sure yet what it was, but did she give it to me? Did she get it from me? One time's all it takes, you know. . . . and all I could hear, that one awful phrase, over and over, like some sort of perverse Gregorian chant."

Although Joe doesn't seem to mind sharing this intimate problem with his reader, he might have skirted around a descriptive paragraph about examining his male body part had he not been given license to do so from having read the sixteenth-century writing of Montaigne and the twentieth-century writing of Lopate.

> There is no water hot enough or no soap with hearty enough white lather to make you feel safe when you find yourself standing alone in your shower, trying in vain to contort yourself into some sort of solo kama sutra pretzel position that will allow you to see your own cock from every conceivable angle, down under your scrotum and on to the backs of your thighs.
>
> Once you've figured out you probably need a mirror and a flashlight, you're presented with another problem altogether. What's your cock supposed to look like? You know the answer in a general sense—size, shape, and approximate color, maybe. But if there was some change more subtle than a matching set of festering boils, or a sentient eyeball sprouting from nowhere, would you really have any clue? Who spends that kind of time

examining himself? The one certainty I had was that it didn't hurt to sit, piss, or breathe. I tallied these up under positive signs.

Joe claimed no direct link between what he had read and what he'd written, but it is difficult for a teacher not to see that what students read often influences what they write. In this direct example, it is the subject he's mirrored. But for many students, reading provides simply an "other" in either style or form. Readings should not be part of our essay writing courses for merely inspiration or auxiliary work. For any student writer, readings ought to be sources of data in all ways: as possible topics or larger themes, as forms, as stylistic models—so that they can become those ghost texts for the writer's mind. And they should learn to acknowledge and cite the influences these texts have on their writing. To teach writers' habits of mind to our students, it's important to make the ghost texts a little less valuable.

4. Linking the Links: A Research Portfolio in Two Parts

We're not sure Joe would have recognized these influences without stopping to examine and analyze what he'd done while writing his essay had he not kept a portfolio. Developing a research portfolio during the course of a project helps students sort through important data and see the array of materials they've read, collected, and used, and it helps them organize the chaotic process in which they've been immersed. Such a task assists a writer with the deeper task of analysis. By capturing the process, essentially creating a discursive snapshot several times during the writing of a paper, the portfolio offers insights as students put things in, take things out, and sort through it. This kind of self-research allows their ever-changing reading and writing processes. Students sometimes question the difference between a scrapbook and a portfolio. A scrapbook, as some of us like to say, is a "pasted down" moment in time. But a portfolio is its opposite: it is a shifting document of the multiple processes of learning, writing, and understanding, constantly changing as the researcher continues to learn about the research site, its people, and its contexts. In short, a research portfolio can be a student's very own silent research assistant. The most useful strategy we've developed for portfolios for students engaged in their nonfiction ethnographic writing is a double strategy, which offers a simple shortcut for including a research portfolio as a part of a finished work (see *FieldWorking* for a more detailed explanation):

- *An annotated table of contents* made from a list of the artifacts in the portfolio, along with explanations in short sentences or phrases to accompany each item
- *A one-page analysis* of your portfolio's current contents, which offers you an opportunity to explore current ideas about the overall themes in your research: connections between items, between sites and informants, between past and present, between yourself and the people

you've met, between your current materials and the writing or organizational goals you still want to meet. Checking the history of these (three or four during the course of the development of one project, for example), you will have a documentation of your thinking as it has changed throughout the project. Set beside one another, these will assist you to see how your own process of thinking about your topic has changed as you've gathered, sorted, and thought about your research materials. (2002, xx)

With these two documents summarizing what's in the portfolio, students offer themselves a clearer picture of their research and its progress. And they offer us two pages of very important synthesized, summarized, categorized documentation each time we collect these pages and respond or evaluate what our students have written along the way. Of course, like much in our own lives, there's no substitute for the real thing; the portfolio is merely a snapshot of the rich and textured living they've experienced in their research—and want to write about effectively. But we don't need or want to haul portfolios around. In fact, the student needs to keep the actual portfolio; we merely need to see the student's progress in keeping it. We've found this to be a manageable and successful way to guide students in both the process and the product of their research and writing.

Elyse is a first-year graduate student in a course called "Varieties of the Essay: The Ethnographic Essay." During the summer between college and graduate school, she had worked in South Dakota as an interpretive ranger at Wind Cave National Park, taking tourists through the cave. As Elyse writes, "I knew a lot about caves, but virtually nothing about the people who explored, mapped, and managed them. As I found, cavers have an intriguing internal culture. My position as an 'interpretive ranger' (ever connected to the public), a 'surface dweller' (I'd take the prairie over the cave any day), and a woman (sensitive to 'who's left out' issues) without a lot of extra money (who can afford to be a caver?) may have affected the way I perceived them." She organized her first portfolio according to her data sources:

1. Literature (websites, journals, newsletters, guidebooks, fiction and non-fiction books)
2. Other people (observations and notes from a reunion/celebration and surrounding activities, interviews with resource management, interpretive staffs, U.S. and British cavers, and tourists)
3. Telephone and email exchanges (from people at the celebration and fellow rangers)
4. Myself (journal entries, formal class workshops, others' responses to drafts)

The portfolio serves not only as an organizational tool, but as the project continues, it becomes an analytic tool as well. In the process of annotating her table of contents, Elyse saw themes emerge and tested out connections between sources of data. Gradually, she became more confident with the materials, and organized them into these broad categories:

1. In preparation for my research . . .
2. *Show and Tell:* This section reveals what I learned about caver culture from studying the way cavers represented themselves (or allow themselves to be represented) to the public.
3. *Labor of Love:* This section reveals the tension I witnessed in the caving community between loving the cave and laboring on its behalf—a tension just under the surface of what the public is able to perceive.
4. *Playing for Keeps:* This section reveals a bit about resource managers, the "keepers" of cave health; these people seem to be driving the development of the "work" culture revealed in the previous section.
5. *Mapping the Middle Ground:* This section reveals how tensions between work and recreational culture are manifested in the caving community at large, and explores ways in which cavers transcend them.
6. In reflection of my research . . .

Each of these sections held sample representative artifacts and data Elyse had collected as part of her study, along with a short explanation. The "Mapping the Middle Ground" section includes, for example, six items, each with a short explanation: a guest list for the celebration of the one-hundredth mile discovery at Wind Cave (the event she attended and wrote about); a diagram of the public center in which the celebration took place; a verbal collage in which she discusses her own position in relationship to the subject; a transcript of a conversation with two fellow cavers and a few follow-up emails she wrote when the themes were becoming apparent; a class exercise on finding a focal point in which she explored the importance of maps in cavers' sense of space and time; and, finally, the cover of Simon Winchester's book *The Map That Changed the World*, which she'd read during the course of her project, and which had been an important influence on her thinking.

After she'd spent time drafting her essay, reorganizing her portfolio, studying its themes, and combining her data, her interpretations began to make sense of the data and offered her an effective controlling metaphor and colorful, specific, real-life details for a compelling piece of writing. Her final portfolio's newest categories also served as the subheadings for her essay. Here are three short excerpts from Elyse's final ethnographic essay called "Mapping the Middle Ground: Work, Play, and Unity in the Caving World."

- *From her prologue:*

  Minnesota was yellow on my new map, and South Dakota brown. Wyoming was tan. Dry, mixed-grass prairie, this said to me, an admitted surface-lover. Though the public tours I had given at Wind Cave never lasted more than two hours and rarely veered from a paved, lighted path, I was always ecstatic to get my feet back on the prairie.

- *From the first section, called "Labor of Love":*

   Jewell Cave's visitors' center has—hands down—the biggest map I've ever seen. Standing before this map, I could see how the caver narratives I'd read likened caving to being on a treasure map hunt: passageways had such kid-fantasy names as Penny Arcade, Humdinger, and Hobgoblin's Ballroom . . . "jewels" a treasure hunter might find at such depths—bulbous pearls of calcite that I recognized from my interpreter days as "cave popcorn," hair-like needles of aragonite known as "frostwork," and bluish, pyramidal crystals the size of nail heads. . . .

- *From the last section, "Mapping the Middle Ground":*

   . . . maps seemed to bring the community together. People pored over them during the social part of the celebration, using them as centerpieces for caving memories and shared stories. During the official part of the celebration, the presenters used a PowerPoint map to illustrate milestones in the cave's shared history. . . . I left the celebration that night believing that the negotiations between work and play I had seen—in the community and within individuals—were just that, negotiations. Not fights, not all-out wars, but obligations to compromise. I've done several heavy months of research and writing since that night, but I have yet to find a caver—or a map—that's proved me wrong.

In her reflective commentary, Elyse mentions the value of working with the portfolio; in categorizing her research materials and juxtaposing them with her observations, her journal, and interviews—as well as with the comments of the very important others she'd met, she found the "middle ground" metaphor that undergirded her final essay. As anthropologists have long known, in writing about the other, Elyse learned something about herself. And most important to us, she had learned to write eloquently about both:

   I had thought I was an insider as an interpretive ranger and had found I hadn't been. But compared to the people in the cars driving next to me—returning from their horizontal trips to Rapid City or Minneapolis—I certainly wasn't an outsider. I seemed to be somewhere in the middle, an odd and potentially incriminating place to be writing an ethnographic essay.

   But perhaps it was an important place for the story I thought I might want to tell. The cavers I had met were trying to create a middle ground, for themselves and their communities, between work and play. Who to better recognize and express that position than someone standing in the middle of things herself? Someone who is curious about the underground yet in love with the surface; someone who has to compromise doing the things she loves in order to pay the bills. . . . [Elyse includes here a quote from a caver about the "real weird contrast between the surface and the cave."] Cavers are constantly positioning and repositioning themselves, it occurred to me. . . . The world could learn a lot—I could learn a lot—by witnessing this act of negotiating for the middle, this act of physically, intellectually, individually, and collectively cultivating a culture of compromise. I think this study has just begun.

Cultivating a "Culture of Compromise" on the Page

Elyse achieved sophisticated writing as she worked her way through her project, knowing her job was to represent more than just her own perspective. And she learned it using specific strategies. We think there's a place for what we know about teaching composition in the teaching of nonfiction. We must not reserve what we've learned over the past thirty years in composition studies for the beginning student. We must not reserve what we've learned over several centuries about the value of finding universal ideas inside the specifics of personal thought. We must not reserve what we've learned from our colleagues in the other social sciences about the value of participant-observation, research, and fieldwork in the artful practice of writing interesting essays about the other without losing sight of the self.

Tyler, Marji, Holly, Joe, and Elyse did not want to drop our nonfiction/ethnographic essay courses. In the process of using these ethnographic strategies—linking self with other—they each learned how to make their own narrator more reliable. For, as Joseph Epstein writes in the quote that opens this chapter, "there are no unreliable narrators in personal essays." But rather than allowing ourselves to produce unreliable or "bad" writers, we, as teachers of essay writing, can borrow from ethnographic techniques to show our students how positioning, questioning, close reading, and portfolio keeping can help nonfiction writers strengthen their narrating selves as they link with the information around them. Tyler, Marji, Holly, Joe, and Elyse found that their research essays were as much about themselves as they were about their subjects. As they wrote about the data they'd gathered, the language they heard and spoke, the surroundings they experienced, the cultural habits they learned, the people they met, and finally, how they made their artistic and rhetorical writing choices, they composed themselves more fully for us, their readers.

Works Cited

Behar, Ruth. 1993. *Translated Woman: Crossing the Border with Esperanza's Story.* Boston: Beacon Press.

———. 1997. *The Vulnerable Observer: Anthroplogy That Breaks Your Heart.* Boston: Beacon Press.

Britton, James, et al. 1975. *The Development of Writing Abilities 11–18.* London: Macmillan Education; Schools Council Research Studies.

Clifford, James, and George Marcus. 1986. *Writing Culture: The Poetics and Politiecs of Ethnography.* Berkeley: University of California Press.

Eisner, Elliott. 1991. *The Enlightened Eye: Qualitative Inquiry and the Enhancement of Educational Practice.* New York: Prentice Hall.

Elbow, Peter. 1981. *Writing with Power: Techniques for Mastering the Writing Process.* New York: Oxford University Press.

Epstein, Joseph. 1997. "The Personal Essay: A Form of Discovery," *The Norton Book of Personal Essays.* New York: Norton.

Flower, Linda. 1979. "Writer-Based Prose: A Cognitive Basis for Problems in Writing" *College English* 41 (1): 19–37.

Lightfoot, Sara Lawrence, and Jessica H. Davis 1997. *The Art and Science of Portraiture.* San Francisco: Jossey-Bass.

Mairs, Nancy. 1994. "Reading Houses, Writing Lives." *Voice Lessons: On Becoming a (Woman) Writer.* Boston: Beacon Press.

Macrorie, Ken. 1980. *Searching Writing.* Rochelle Park, NJ: Hayden.

Montaigne, Michel de. 1973. "Of the Inconsistency of Our Actions." *Selections from the Essays.* Ed. and trans. Donald M. Frame. Arlington Heights, IL: AHM Publishing Corp.

Mortensen, P., and G. E. Kirsch, eds. 1996. *Ethics and Representation in Qualitative Studies of Literacy.* Urbana, IL: National Council of Teachers of English.

Peacock, James. 1989. *The Anthropological Lens: Harsh Light, Soft Focus.* London: Cambridge University Press.

Perl, Sondra. 1980. "Understanding Composing." *College Composition and Communication* 31 (4): 363–69.

Qualley, Donna. 1997. *Turns of Thought: Teaching Composition as Reflexive Inquiry.* Portsmouth, NH: Boynton/Cook.

Root, Robert. 2002. "Variations on a Theme of Putting Nonfiction in Its Place." CCCC presentation, March 23.

———. 2003. "Naming Nonfiction (a Polyptych)." *College English* 65 (3): January.

Root, Robert, and Michael Steinberg. 2002. *The Fourth Genre: Contemporary Writers of/on Creative Nonfiction.* 2nd edition. New York: Longman.

Rosaldo, Renato. 1989. *Culture and Truth: The Remaking of Social Analysis.* Boston: Beacon.

Ruby, Jay. 1982. *A Crack in the Mirror: Reflextive Perspectives in Anthropolgy.* Philadelphia: University of Pennsylvania Press.

Stoller, Paul. 1989. *The Taste of Ethnographic Things: The Senses in Anthropology.* Philadelphia: Univeristy of Pennsylvania Press.

Sunstein, Bonnie Stone, and Elizabeth Chiseri-Strater. 2002. *FieldWorking: Reading and Writing Research.* 2nd edition. New York: Bedford/ St. Martin's.

Sunstein, Bonnie S., and Jonathan H. Lovell. 2000. *The Portfolio Standard: How Students Can Show Us What They Know and Are Able to Do.* Portsmouth, NH: Heinemann.

Van Maanen, John. 1988. *Tales of the Field: On Writing Ethnography.* Chicago: University of Chicago Press.

Winchester, Simon. 2002. *The Map That Changed the World.* New York: Perennial.

Woolcott, Harry. 1995. *The Art of Fieldwork.* Walnut Creek, CA: Sage/Altamira.

7

A Piñata of Theory and Autobiography
Research Writing Breaks Open Academe

Mark Shadle and Robert Davis

Art is . . . the reinforcement of the capacity to endure disorientation
so that a real and significant problem may emerge.
—Morse Peckham, *Man's Rage for Chaos*

. . . I listened and realized there are some things you simply cannot
prepare for.
—David Antin in "durations" in *what it means to be avant-garde*

People think the blues is sad. They hear people moaning and such.
That's not the blues. That's just somebody singing slow. . . . The
blues is about truth-telling.
—Alberta Hunter, in Nikki Giovanni's *Blues: For All the Changes*

A penguin has no eyelids. A traditional college research essay writer may be
interested in merely explaining or noting that this creature cannot prevent crying. But the human being in us is also interested in moving toward writing research with this question in mind: "Do we care if a penguin cries, maybe even
constantly?" Don't curiosity and inquiry flow from what we see expressed in
the world, and our attempts to understand how it moves us? Whether we agree
with James Elkins that knowing and seeing always carry our intentions and
personal histories, or with those scientists trying so hard to correct for bias
and remain as "objective" and "truthful" as possible, research is the glass of
cold water in the desert of not-knowing.

This chapter will argue that research can be especially rewarding when it engages both personal and academic passions and theories to discover, shape, and express a topic with "multiwriting" in multiple genres, disciplines, media, and cultures. Such work weaves together the epigraphs by Peckham, Antin, and Hunter, reminding us that the art and craft of writing demands that the researcher-writer live inside tensions and mysteries as she looks for the truths that emerge from not-knowing. We will offer a minihistory of how research writing needs to be reconnected with theory across the disciplines through autobiographical knowing. Then we'll contrast the steps in traditional research writing with multiwriting, to reveal the pedagogies of each. Next we'll offer a look at how to grow the consciousness of multiwriting by looking at lists of student projects, excerpts of syllabi, reading suggestions, lists of literary and rhetorical tropes, and a closer examination of one student project.

We argue that traditional research writing was often answer-driven, while multiwriting is designed to return student research to inquiry that ends with better questions. Multiwriting also attempts to be seriously playful, incorporating humor and making use of self-consciousness as cosmology.

Along the way there will be discussion of invention strategies for multiwriting—including writing on autobiography, bodylore, and the senses—and how these expressive writings can be matched with analysis and theory to shape a project. A discussion of student reflections upon the multiwriting process will follow. Supplementary materials for this chapter are on the website for this book.

Multiwriting developed out of listening to students talk about what did and did not motivate them in research writing. After years of interviewing students doing research writing at "research universities," small liberal arts colleges, community colleges, and even adult schools, we have heard the same complaints about both research writing and theory courses. Students consistently see them as difficult, abstract, unnecessarily complex, and inapplicable. Yet faculty continue to value the importance of research (a necessity for attaining tenure and promotion, as well as "advancing" humankind) and theory (seen as proof of higher-order thinking and tastefully French).

Here we will show how theory and research can be linked in ways that also begin to transform these views of research as sterile and useless or (deadly) serious. We see, and want to teach, research as a passionate attempt to understand those parts of the world that move us not only to ask questions, but often also to act (even when we lack answers). Further, we believe that research may open the world and the self for the reflective, question-centered stance that we know as theory.

We begin with the way we have arrived in the present predicament of a research writing that is often seen as boring or top-heavy with theory. Although it is disappearing, the tradition at many universities in the last thirty years was a three-course sequence of freshman composition that ended with either an argument-persuasion course or a research-writing course. In addition, programs in writing across the curriculum grew out of English/writing departments as a plea for making all disciplines responsible for teaching writing. The research-writing course was often transferred into the disciplines, where it became the responsibility of each department to train its students in the traditional style and documentation system.

Wherever and however it is taught, the actual research process is always more complex than any textbook can present it, ranging through dozens of steps that begin with mulling over possible topics, through investigation of a rich variety of sources, into the invention and drafting through which sources are integrated, and on to revision, editing, documentation, and presentation or publication.

Embedded or implied within this process are various theories of learning, knowledge, or conceptualization that are rarely made conscious to students trying to learn the process. Ironically, students learn theories as both the topic and process of research only in upper-division courses. Most applied theory courses are below "pure" theory courses, but both are above the research writing that is expected of first-year students. Even more paradoxical is the way we allow so many theory courses to seem "inapplicable" for undergraduates nearing graduation. There is an assumption that theory is either unnecessary or too difficult for first-year research writers, or that theory is studied for its own sake, without any need to apply it beyond a traditional "term paper" that is rarely found in the world beyond academe.

Even a quick search of syllabi on the Internet confirms that many theory classes are taught with anthologies of theoretical essays that represent an unofficially approved canon of theories of composition and rhetoric, often also featuring some of the greatest hits of continental philosophy, including structuralism, post-structuralism, and deconstruction. Reading the primary texts of these postmodern philosophies can be a daunting task for graduate students, and an overwhelming one for undergraduates. Often the reading strategies are limited to a close formalist interpretation of the text, followed by either a literary-critical or rhetorical analysis of the theory or research concept.

Our alternative viewpoint is to emphasize theory as something written as much as read, which involves the creative work of theorizing about the world, one's place in it, and the subject of one's research. One of the keys to enacting this idea of helping student writers discover their inner theoretician is to remove the burden of knowing from their shoulders. It is strange that it has been placed there at all, as much of what interests most experienced researchers, in the academy and elsewhere, about their own work is that they do *not* know, but are trying to find out. Pointing out the known gets us nowhere in the research world, so why do we ask students to do it?

If, however, our stance and expectation is that we want students to find and engage in questions of interest to them—which may not be answered, but can be explored in a committed manner—then theorizing is a natural act. A quick template for such a method would involve asking key questions and then presenting the various theories that try to answer them, or connecting (or rejecting) these theories as one builds one's own. As the discourse that follows suggests, we bring theory into the research world most self-consciously in a 300-level course called "Writing Theory," which has gone from being an overview of various theories of writing, rhetoric, and the teaching of writing, to a course about the writing of theory, always in relation to inquiry and research. However, this practice of helping students toward theory has carried over, even into our first-year courses, which require inquiry and theorizing.

Theory is not a luxury; in fact, it is hard to live without almost constantly theorizing. We believe that students need to learn how to see the challenges of research and theory as an invitation to an academic life that is satisfying and enlightening in a world that calls for both contemplation and action. Students need to start using whatever theory they know across the disciplines to begin researching a project that mixes their academic and personal passions. Beyond any fashionable topics generated by our times (e.g., gene-splicing), students must search for those that speak to them where they actually reside, intellectually and emotionally.

Over the past ten years we have worked to help students at Eastern Oregon University, as well as kindergarten through college students throughout other parts of the country, to construct research-writing projects of personal interest to them in multiple genres, disciplines, cultures, and media—what we call "multiwriting." We have used this method to break open the form of research writing and reveal how the template of the term paper may have been hiding the goodies of multiple viewpoints and hybrid discourses all along.

Multiwriting does not so much seek to displace traditional research as to expand, supplement, complement, and transform it. Before we tour the multiwriting approach, it may be useful for students and teachers interested in changing their approach to contrast the parallel steps in traditional research writing with multiwriting in this two-column table.

Steps in Traditional Research	*Steps in Multiwriting Research*
Be assigned or find topics	Multiautobiographical writing to discover connections between personal and academic passions
	Bodylore writing to anchor topic in the senses and to mix emotion and intellect in detail
Study research writing model and singular audience of teacher and classmates	Select genres, forms and media relevant to topic and multiple audiences (including multicultural ones) in and beyond classroom
Begin library research	Begin research using libraries, bookstores, Internet, ethnography, and other fieldwork

Steps in Traditional Research (cont.)	*Steps in Multiwriting Research (cont.)*
Discover thesis, if not already decided	Remain open to various themes, memes, theses, messages and purposes on topic
Draft research paper	Draft various genres that move project along
Share draft with peers in class or in writing center, mostly focusing upon editing grammar and mechanics	Share sample genres and discuss forms and media with teacher, peers in class and writing center, and with friends and family, focusing upon form, organization, style, and mechanics
Check revised draft against style and documentation guides	Connect relevant styles and documentation devices of various genres, disciplines, media, and cultures by choosing the most suitable form/container for project
Print and turn in final draft of paper to teacher for grade	Create deadline portfolio, including the multiwriting research project, including self-evaluation of course and project, with ideas for future revision or application (e.g., as conference or research symposium presentation or publication)
Pick up paper for grade and comments	Retrieve multiwriting project and discuss further use of it with teacher and classmates and perform project for future students

The traditional research-writing process has burst like a piñata to reveal, through multiwriting, the previously hidden candies of autobiography and theory. In multiwriting the personal becomes the theoretical as students begin with subjects that matter to them, and develop these by learning to step into the open spaces of inquiry, where the known gives way to wonder.

The sweet heresy of the autobiographic allows us to turn our teaching on its head, so that nurturing curiosity and mentoring inquiry become our chief purposes and methods. Such teaching looks beyond the confines of any one project or course, so that even the most complete student text is a stage on the way. Of course, following this heresy requires reeducation of ourselves, the academy, and our students (who often feel that academic discourse should lock them out of their own lives, as it frequently has).

For instance, students are used to creating multiple drafts of papers. However, the first-year writing students' belief that anything written but not evaluated is wasted usually disappears when topics are chosen that reflect a personal interest. It also helps to let students know that most professional writers publish only about a fifth of what they write—a consequence or process we might, for the students' sake, call "overwriting"! There is the belief that all writing expertise is somehow front-loaded and then over; it's like comedian Steven Wright saying he bought a puppy and walked it two thousand miles so that he would never have to walk it again. Students learn that they have to keep walking the dog of their research and writing; their ambitions grow with their skills. Turning research into not only vocation, but also avocation, allows for more research and writing.

The first step for students is to choose a topic that matters to them for their multiwriting project. These may turn out to be nouns (such as people or places) or the verbs of process (such as events). Students often find their topic rather quickly just by looking at a list of the titles of previous projects that jog their memories. A list can be found on the companion website. It demonstrates that some students do choose the kind of topics (such as capital punishment) labeled "serious" in many reader-based textbooks generated for writers. Topics reveal a wide range of choices, from highbrow culture (academic poet Adrienne Rich) and pop culture (*The Dukes of Hazzard*) to folk culture (sheep herding). Some topics form around hobbies (windowbox gardening) or work on campus (the writing center) or off campus (construction crew literacy).

Often the projects are loosely directed, according to the class. For example, students in a first-year exploratory writing class research a dream trip they would like to take, which helps them move sooner toward a cornerstone requirement of study abroad or with a different ethnic group. Our Writing 206: Applied Discourse Theory and our Writing 328: Writing Theory classes insist that students incorporate not theories per se, but theorizing in their multiwriting project; they move to inhabit the nouns of theories as the verbs of applying them.

Sometimes this theorizing stems from seeing autobiography more as stance than form. That is, students often do some autobiographical writing in various forms that are either summative (the older, wiser narrator summing up her life near its end) or generative (creating a new incarnation of self that the writer is moving herself toward). This results in projects like *The Urge to Destroy What We Cannot Be*, where the author looks at images and processes of perfectionism or idealism that can become competitive and hateful. Projects like *Theories of Good and Evil* or *Theories of the Afterlife* are often generated by autobiographical writing about personal fears. Some autobiographical assignments, including writing about the body and through the senses, and a three-column list that links unusual experiences with hobbies/habits and personality traits, can be found on the website. That is where students will also find such research strategies as field trips to libraries, bookstores, and museums.

Projects like *The Literary Canon Debate* begin with and explore an academic world. But often the ones that most inhabit primary theories begin by expanding or filling in a basic annotation of a theory. For example, a fascinating one on digital surveillance grew out of Nietsche's notions of the superman, as well as a post-structuralist notion of autobiography. A partial list of such projects and their theories is on the website.

To understand how this kind of multiwriting unfolds, it may be helpful to examine the syllabus for Writing 328: Writing Theory, which can be found, along with a class schedule for the term, on the website. It begins by transforming parts of the syllabus often seen merely as attachments for accreditation into meaningful goals. For example, *student outcomes* is a place to replace fear of the abstract with an excitement about uncovering truths about how the world seems to work. The *objectives* center upon the need to redefine both "writing" and "theory" as verbs that help students discover theorizing in their lives, and apply it across disciplines and cultures.

In turn, these objectives are met with *methods* that are purposefully unusual in remaining analogies as different as mapping, medical trauma, and a thunder and lightning storm. Rather than any step-by-step delivery systems, methods are processes students create to match the objectives of their projects.

This multiwriting is nontraditional, and can therefore sometimes be frightening. To warn students about what is coming we often include humor, as when we offer interruptions to the boilerplate in the syllabus that include the illusion of being hypnotized, or an allergy alert that warns that constant linear and traditional thinking can be unhealthy. In the same spirit, we often have assignments that let students enjoy doing parodies of traditional forms of literature or rhetoric. This is important because it allows students to see that form is a flexible thing. More on how multiwriters learn to mix genres, discover form within content, and revise and edit can be found in the further materials on the website, especially the Multiwriting Book Review.

The syllabus often includes voyeuristic invitations toward multiwork; for example, a passage by multigenre practitioner Tom Romano (1995) shows that multigenre writing results from seeing the world in different, simultaneous ways. We also like to have an excerpt that eggs students on toward practicing multiwork without any further hesitation. So there's a quotation from scholar Winston Weathers (1980) that urges students to think literally outside the box of the traditional research paper. As this kind of research-based theory course unfolds, we often introduce some of Weathers' alternate "Grammar B" forms, sometimes as practiced by Romano; these can be found on the website.

Often a good way to encourage students to complicate their thought as they move into theorizing is to incorporate some oxymorons in their writing. A list of these—including our favorite, "tight slacks"—is attached to the sample syllabus on the website.

Some students discover the topic of their research and begin to understand multiwriting by simply reading some published multiwriting books, so we include a very brief bibliography with the syllabus, which can be viewed on the website. A typical one usually includes theoretical works, such as

Richard Wilbur's *A Brief History of Everything*, which groups theories into categories. Ishmael Reed's novel, *Mumbo Jumbo*, enacts multiple genres, including lyrics, ads, quotations, and more. Belinda Recio's nonfiction work, *Blue*, embodies multiple disciplines as it studies this color in art, architecture, psychology, fashion, mythology, healing, gardening, and music. Barton Lidice Benes' *Curiosa,* a collection of peculiar celebrity relics, shows how multiple media can be used effectively. Dan Eldon mixes a variety of genres across multiple cultures in his trip through Africa in *The Journey Is the Destination*. Once students read and view these books, they are able to quickly discover many more on their own, as well as with the help of their teachers.

Literary tropes can also be helpful, as a way of opening up ways of writing and thinking. Annotating a brief list, like the one attached to the syllabus on the website, may help move students toward using glossaries of literary or rhetorical criticism or dictionaries, where etymology can lead to theory or form or even topic. For example, *hyperbole* might lead to a project on urban legends or tall tales, just as *puns* could be a path to a project on cartoons.

As students add to their projects and try various invention methods, we begin to introduce words/tropes with "syn" prefixes—attached to the website syllabus—that help students make connections across the disciplines. For instance, the idea of *symbiosis* might help a student working on a project on sharks consider the way pilot fish that follow sharks are like a parasite that lives from, but does not kill, its host. *Synecdoche* might become the microcosm of a project, and a perfect way to perform it, just as *syncope* might provide a part of a project that escapes. *Syncretic* sources are those that absorb others and are more inclusive.

With many choices of subjects and patterns of connection open to them, students can become overwhelmed or paralyzed by their own sudden freedom (especially after years of academic bondage). The key to helping them appreciate and use their freedom and make wise choices comes not from any particular classroom exercise, or assignment, although we try many to see what will work for individuals. Rather, the more important strategy is the holistic one, practiced by teachers ranging from Socrates to Donald Graves, of referring students back to their lives, interests, and questions. When students find a subject that is autobiographic in the best sense—engaging the self and world as mysteries, rather than known quantities—then the project can begin to appear in the space of an open inquiry, to which theory becomes essential, rather than abstract.

Below we will model the process of discovering a multiwriting for one student in a writing theory course. Having student multiwriters from previous terms perform their project for new students is a key part of the pedagogy, but we have to emphasize that the former projects are samples more than models. It also helps to ground students in some solid practices—including field trips to libraries, museums, and bookstores—which we offer as research strategies on the website.

In the writing theory course discussed earlier, a project by Aby illustrates this process of theorizing with writing that emerges from an autobiographical stance that discovers connections between personal and academic passions. She began her project at the center of her life, thinking about how she might do research from or about her kitchen, alcove, and garden. She thought more about what she wanted to show people about her world than about the ideas she would research.

All she knew was that she would write autobiographically with some self-reflection/reflexion. So she thumbed through collections of theory books across the disciplines, looking for an approach that would involve such a stance. This included a comic documentary read by the class entitled *Introducing Postmodernism* by Richard Appignanesi and Chris Garratt. A brief annotation on deconstruction caught her eye, and she decided to look further into this critical theory. She found a passage from Derrida in *Psyche: Invention of the Other* (1984) that led her to understand how deconstruction was not just disassembling, but also inventive—an act of *re*construction:

> Deconstruction is inventive or it is nothing at all; it does not settle for methodological procedures, it opens up a passageway, it marches ahead and marks a trail; its writing is not only performative, it produces rules—other convention—for new performativities and never installs itself in the theoretical assurances of a simple opposition between performative and the constative. Its process involves an affirmation, this latter being linked to the coming in event, advent, invention.

Next she returned to the world of her home, and thought about images of de-/reconstruction that occurred there. Her young daughter's birthday reminded her of piñatas—a subject she began to look into. She was surprised to find that the piñata existed across cultures. In Christianity, it symbolized the seven deadly sins, and she found an example of how these had been translated across religious and cultural boundaries in Mahatma Ghandi's revision of them in India. It surprised her that the piñata in ancient China carried seeds and decorative papers, which were burned for good luck and a bountiful harvest. This burning was a second destruction and deconstruction. Marco Polo brought this artifact and process back from China to Italy, which spread to Spain and on to the New World with the Conquistadors. The Aztecs either had their own parallel or borrowed from the Spaniards when they broke a colorful pot full of treasures as an offering to their god of war on his birthday.

As Aby researched the piñata through time, ideas came to her about how to expand and shape her multiwriting project. At first the piñata became a poem about a father, broken by divorce. Then the narrator reconsidered in another excerpt, understanding that, unlike people, the piñata cannot be reconstructed. Similarly, she equated the piñata with a tomb—using the Mausoleum of Halicanarsus—that can be raided, deconstructed, and used to fortify a crusader castle.

Eventually Aby decided that her project had to be housed in a piñata. The first aspect of deconstruction for her was to "disappear" some texts she didn't want to read anymore, including Edgar Allan Poe's "The Tell-Tale Heart" and Jonathan Edwards' sermon, "Sinners in the Hands of an Angry God." She dipped these texts into wallpaper paste to make the shell of the piñata. Then she painted over them with mysterious symbols that represented the traceries of lost meaning in, and beyond, language.

Next she found and created texts about and toward both de-/reconstruction to embody Derrida's words about affirmation and invention. These went inside the piñata as surprises and treasures. They included critiques of structuralism and deconstruction, including those that attempt to undo any easy look at deconstruction. For example, Aby used Derek Attridge's "Singularities, Responsibilities: Derrida, Deconstruction and Literary Criticism" (1995) to complicate Derrida's work:

> We now know—or have no excuse for not knowing—that deconstruction is not a technique or a method, and hence that there is no question of "applying" it. We know that it is not a moment of carnival or liberation, but a moment of the deepest concern with limits. We know that it is not a hymn to indeterminacy, or a life-imprisonment within language, or a denial of history: reference, mimesis, context, historicity, are among the most repeatedly emphasized and carefully scrutinized topics in Derrida's writing. And we know—though this myth perhaps dies hardest of all—that the ethical and the political are not avoided by deconstruction, but are implicated at every step. (109–10)

These many assumptions about deconstruction made Aby able to loosely wrap herself up in the piñata as fragments about both the processes of creating self and her own life. The piece was performed as the class broke open the piñata, swinging from a ponderosa pine outside the classroom, to the Incan sounds of the Batista Family Players. Various writings and candies fell out as the piñata was whacked with a stick. These texts were then read aloud by class members standing in a circle. The de(con)struction circled back to reconstruction, even as the self outran anything that could be written or imagined by or about it. Secrets were exposed, though the texts used to make the piñata were not.

While Aby's was a purposeful, self-conscious use of theory in an upper-division course, even first-year students can follow a similar dynamic of deconstruction and reconstruction into inquiries that lead to theorizing. For instance, students in a course in a later term—an interdisciplinary study of the relationship between animals and people that is part of our general education program—worked to create multiwriting research projects that began to show some of the differences between people and animals, as well as the connections. They had been prompted, in part, by a reading of Barry Lopez's *Of Wolves and Men*, which not only deconstructs Western ways of "relating to" wolves (which generally involved killing them), but also reconstructs Native American understandings of wolves (which make room for mystery, and for open theorizing about why wolves do what they do). Beyond even the carefully considered positions of people who are closest to wolves, however, is the understanding that humans will not understand or fully know wolves—that wolves are wolves and people are people, and that wolves do as they do because they are themselves and not us, or what we would have them be.

Lopez recounts an episode in which the piñata of Western knowledge is inadvertently broken up by the conversational theorizing of Native Americans. A group of Nunamiut are watching wolves from a high pass in the Brooks Range of Alaska, using spotting scopes to survey a broad field of vision. They watch a wolf follow a grizzly bear for hours, a behavior they have not seen before. A member of the party recounts a recent episode in which a family of wolves howled every day for two weeks during the denning season, another apparently new behavior. An elder wonders aloud if wolves change their behaviors over time, if they do things now they never would have considered years before. Lopez's inner scientist goes quietly nuts:

> If he is correct, then the implications for wildlife biology are staggering. It means that social animals evolve, that what you learn today may not apply tomorrow, that in striving to create a generalized static animal you have lost the real, dynamic animal. (81)

The Natives, conversely, are observing the "real, dynamic animal," and negating dichotomies of Western thought with a simple, but fertile, "maybe" in response to all questions.

Writing theories of animals that entail research and leave room for not knowing are now part of the course's challenge. It is also part of our opportunity as teachers: how do we teach writing in the open space where research and theory meet? How do we help people write what they do not know, and what no one does? How do we think beyond "knowing," and into a deeper understanding that includes inquiry, ignorance, and mystery? What, really, are these things—thinking, researching and writing—about? These are the questions that occupy us this spring in Oregon, as the days grow longer, and we enter into the work that we are still just defining. We are still thawing the definition of "teacher" Upik-speaking students from so far north of us have loaned us: "one who creates the conditions under which learning is possible."

As we join our students in trying to cosmologically order and understand the world around us, our research and writing simultaneously resist this necessary impulse and pull us into the fascinating chaos that is inquiry and research. Somehow, while presenting and performing what we have discovered as new questions, we must find room in our research writing—as poems with multiple meanings do—to honor the mystery of what we don't yet understand, as we move toward better questions. Believing in the creativity of our students, we take these words from Morse Peckham, in *Man's Rage for Chaos*, with us into our next classes:

> There must, it seems to me, be some human activity which serves to break up orientations, to weaken and frustrate the tyrannous drive to order, to prepare the individual to observe what the orientation tells him is irrelevant, but what very well may be highly relevant. (xi)

Works Cited

Antin, David. 1984–1993. *what it means to be avant-garde.* New York: New Directions.

Attridge, Derek. 1995. "Singularities, Responsibilities: Derrida, Deconstruction and Literary Criticism." In *Critical Encounters: Reference and Responsibility in Deconstructive Writing,* edited by Cathy Caruth and Deborah Esch. Piscataway, NJ: Rutgers University Press.

Elkins, James. 1996. *The Object Stares Back: On the Nature of Seeing.* New York: Simon & Schuster.

Giovanni, Nikki. 1999. *Blues for All the Changes.* New York: William Morrow and Company.

Lopez, Barry Holstun. 1978. *Of Wolves and Men.* New York: Touchstone.

Peckham, Morse. 1965. *Man's Rage for Chaos: Biology, Behavior & the Arts.* New York: Schocken Books.

Romaro, Tom. 1995. *Writing with Passion.* Portsmouth, NH. Heinemann.

Weathers, Winston. 1980. *An Alternate Style: Options in Composition.* New York: Boynton/Cook.

8

Working Together
Teaching Collaborative Research to Professional Writing Students

Joyce Magnotto Neff

Teaching workplace research in an academic setting is challenging. Academic and workplace practices can differ dramatically, causing students in professional writing courses to struggle with the conflicting conventions that surround collaboration, genre, sources, audience, assessment, culture, and power. These conflicts require creative teaching that can help students develop effective practices applicable to both current and future assignments. In this chapter I describe a collaborative research project in a senior-level management writing course that is delivered face-to-face as well as over a televised, interactive, distance-learning system. Students who register for the course are majoring in English, interdisciplinary studies, or business. Some are employed full-time and have managerial experience in corporate or government settings. A few have participated in on-the-job research, and most have completed research assignments in their college courses. Ideally, students should bring their varied experiences to the classroom, enrich the work we do there, and transfer what they learn to other research opportunities. In reality, the path from nascent idea to project to transfer of knowledge is like a mountain road with switchbacks, steep hills, pull-offs to reread the map, and some downhill thrills. Actually, it's the unpredictability of the journey that makes teaching workplace research in an academic setting so exciting to me, and one of my goals is to convey the excitement and value of research to students.

Academic and Workplace Contexts

Scholars have done some important work on differences between academic and workplace writing (Matalene 1989; Schreiber 1993; Dias et al. 1999;

Mirel and Spilka 2002; Russell 2001). As Matalene notes in the introduction to *Worlds of Writing: Teaching and Learning in Discourse Communities of Work*, the student who is preparing for writing in a profession has multiple negotiations to manage—audience, beliefs, cultures, intent, and language, to name a few, and these negotiations differ across discourse communities. Zimmerman and Marsh's (1989) study of a proposal team shows that workplace writers must also be able to face complex rhetorical tasks, produce effective documents quickly, make rapid improvement in writing, work collaboratively, and stifle the pride of authorship.

Dias, Freedman, Medway, and Paré (1999), in their book-length study, describe how wide the gap between academic and workplace contexts can be. In the workplace, professional documents serve as legal records and are part of a paper trail that confirms when, by whom, and how well work was completed. In contrast to the notes from sources that a student might make during a school assignment, the notes of a workplace writer "represent individuals, agencies, and involvements with whom he or she has some interactive relationship. The professional is required to take action that will affect the people and states of affairs that the bits of paper represent" (227). Furthermore, while students write in the library, at home, or in the student union, most professionals write in spaces that their employer owns. This centralized space facilitates circulation of drafts and the building of networks among cowriters, but it also allows a kind of surveillance that students do not experience when they sit down to write. Dias et al. emphasize the distinction between writing as an *activity* and writing as an *action* contributing to a larger *activity system* (230). Thus, when students move from academic writing to professional writing, "they may not realize how much of workplace knowledge is tacit rather than explicit, how much the written text is implicated in a complex, multisymbolic communicative web, and that their moving into full participation may be much more a process of enculturation and much less a matter of transferring school learning or receiving deliberate instruction" (231). Writing is not something discrete that professionals *do* because, in the workplace, "writing is not separate from the actions and activities it serves" (Paré 2002, 59). For academics, an analogy to email might help. Most of us open, read, and respond to email every day. However, we do not think of ourselves as "emailers." We are teachers who use email as a means of achieving our academic goals, just as architects are experts who use writing to achieve their design goals.

As for the best way to connect academic instruction in technical and management writing courses to workplace performance, Dias et al. suggest teaching writing as a means of thinking; that is, taking advantage of the epistemic function of writing, what is known as "writing to learn" in the WAC community. Examples include informal, exploratory, low-stakes responses such as those posted to online discussion boards, captured in journals, or recorded in process logs. Dias et al. also encourage the teaching of current theory and critical analysis of texts and rhetorical contexts. While the workplace does not pro-

vide time or space for employees to learn those skills, they are noticed and often appreciated by teammates and supervisors. Other ways to bridge the gap
include realizing that writing is "embedded in workplace practices and cultures" (235). When students write in classrooms, they are writing in a culture
that emphasizes solo authorship and ownership; workplace cultures are more
likely to expect collaboration in both research and authorship so that the documents produced address multiple audiences and complex rhetorical situations.
Professionals write as experts who can effect change rather than as novices
who must prove their know-how to someone who is more expert than they are.
"If there is one major, obvious-seeming way in which educational courses
might prepare people better for the demands of writing at work, it is through
constituting the class as a working group with some degree of complexity, con-
tinuity, and interdependency of joint activity. Such arrangements will go some
way toward realizing the far richer communicative relations that contextualize
writing in the workplace" (Dias et al. 1999, 235; see also Paré 2002).

In other words, because people in the workplace *do* things with their research, the question in professional writing courses is whether we can make
research and writing *actions with consequences*. David Russell (2001), in his
succinct review of qualitative research on writing in the disciplines, concludes
that the best assignments for teaching disciplinary and workplace writing take
into account student motivation, student identity with the discipline, and tools
of the profession (e.g., specialized genres). Furthermore, the best assignments
model processes that reflect those of disciplinary professionals (284–89). Faculty must keep in mind not only what they want students to know at the end of
the course. They must also ask themselves, "What do we want students to be
able to do with the material of the course?" (290).

This short review shows that differences between academic and workplace cultures raise questions about whether workplace research and writing
can or should be taught in an academic setting. What's a teacher to do if
"school-based simulations of workplace writing fail to prepare students for
professional writing because they cannot adequately replicate the local rhetorical complexity of workplace contexts," as Dias et al. claim (1999, 201)?
How might we teach the disciplinary content we want students to know while
we make their writing an "action" as well as an "activity"? The rest of this
chapter describes a semester-long assignment that addresses these questions.

An Extended Example of an Academic/Workplace Research Assignment

Management Writing is a 400/500-level course offered in the English curriculum as part of the undergraduate and graduate (MA) emphases in professional
writing at Old Dominion University, a doctoral-granting, comprehensive state
university with a Carnegie Research I designation. The population for the
course depends on the delivery method in a given semester. When the course

is taught on campus, those who register are usually full-time students majoring in English, communications, or management. When the course is taught
through interactive television (synchronous two-way audio, one-way video
known as ITV), those enrolled are part-time students who are also working
adults. They have completed an AA degree at their local community college
and are progressing toward a BS in interdisciplinary studies with an emphasis
in strategic communications or professional writing.

Class time is divided among lecture, discussion, and group work. In the
ITV sections, synchronous group work and presentations are difficult, although the university's recent adoption of Blackboard has provided excellent
virtual alternatives (see Neff 1998; Whithaus and Neff, forthcoming). The core
assignment of the semester is a team project that asks students to research
and write about a current and significant workplace issue (see "Collaborative
Project and Presentation Assignment Sheet" on the companion website). The
stated goals are:

- to enable students to research topics of importance in their professional lives
- to provide experience in business research methods
- to provide experience in collaborative research and writing
- to enhance skills in rhetorical analysis of business documents
- to practice meta-analysis of collaborative research and writing
- to prepare students to contribute to and eventually manage a workplace research/writing team

Students begin their work individually by listing problems, needs, or opportunities that interest them and that can be addressed in the available time
frame. After some initial research to determine the staying power of their topics, students negotiate their membership on a team. In Phase 2, teams do more
research and write preliminary proposals explaining their research plans for
accruing relevant data from primary and secondary sources. In Phase 3, teams
carry out their surveys, interviews, and library and electronic searches, and
they describe their progress in short reports and minutes. In Phase 4, students
give oral briefings on their projects, and in Phase 5 they finalize the projects.
The documents they produce mirror workplace genres: emails, memos of intent, memos of record, proposals, agendas and minutes of team meetings, job
descriptions for team members, performance evaluations, drafts and final copies of project documents, and graphic aids.

Teaching Strategies for Workplace Research Assignments

Earlier I mentioned the challenges of teaching workplace research in an academic setting. The following sections gives some suggestions with attendant
strategies for addressing those challenges. The strategies were developed

over time and work well for the team project, which I hasten to add is an assignment embedded in a course embedded in a curriculum embedded in a degree program. The strategies take into account who the students are in a given semester and how the assignment might better meet their individual and professional needs. They support my goal of making research a more familiar practice for students and one with a payoff that is greater than the grade. With that in mind, please read the strategies and imagine how you might tailor them to your students and local context. Note that each suggestion entails overt and explicit teaching of concrete steps or techniques that help students progress even when the project as a whole might seem daunting to them. Yet I believe the strategies are more than mere devices because they are taught in the context of the larger project with its long-term action agenda.

Suggestion 1: Don't avoid theory.

Teaching current critical and rhetorical theory is important in improving the transferability of academic writing and research practices to workplace contexts. When I begin the semester with a review of communication, management, and rhetorical theories, students have a framework for later discussions and actions. Once students learn these theories, they are eager to tell stories about particular supervisors who were Total Quality Management (TQM) driven or ACE Theory proponents. They especially like Douglas McGregor's (1960) Theories X and Y, which paint employees as lazy and needing direction or as liking to take responsibility, and William Ouchi's (1981) Theory Z, in which the company is a "family" and managers encourage teamwork. The discussion then moves to how writing and research are practiced within certain management frameworks. Throughout the rest of the semester, whether we're talking about document cycling or performance appraisals, students can see how the theories under which a manager operates influence the way writing is done in a specific workplace.

Suggestion 2: See research writing as a practice rather than as a process or product.

Writing teachers have long focused on process versus product, and some of us now consider ourselves post-process practitioners (Kent 1999). I prefer to use the term *practice,* which I see as more than the process, procedure, or product alone, and which I draw from my study of yoga. A thoughtful, mindful practice becomes a way of being, knowing, and doing (Schon 1991; Yancey 1998). Barbara Couture (1999) talks about the design and ethical components that make writing a form of personal agency. She reminds us of Moffett's later work in which he suggests a "'project' approach, which encourages students to work together to address contemporary problems. Projects simulate 'what practitioners do in real life' in making connections between people and sites to solve our common problems" (36). Couture also argues that we should move beyond the idea that teaching writing is a matter of providing devices and tools. She proposes "that we treat writing as design and that writing skills are developed through emulation" (43). Emulation allows for social engagement and thus personal development (40). By constructing workplace research in an academic setting as a *practice*, teachers can work across the borders. For example, a progress report pushes students to analyze what they have done, what has changed in their practice, and how they intend to shape their practice for the next round. Periodic freewrites encourage meta-analysis of what the student knows and needs to know. Sample prompts include: "What do I need to know to incorporate survey results into the proposal?" "Where will my reader benefit from data converted into graphics?" "What happens to proprietary research if my document is sent to the media?"

Suggestion 3: Emphasize rhetorical analysis for planning and reviewing research.

At the end of each semester, students in my technical and management writing courses tell me that the most important strategy they have mastered is rhetorical analysis. One method I teach is GRACE, which is an acronym for goals, readers, arguments, conventions, and expression (Inkster and Kilborn 1999). Students complete a GRACE analysis of their research plan at the beginning of the project and reconsider their answers to the GRACE questions several times: when they draft the proposal, when they prepare briefings, when they review their own and others' projects, and when they present their final reports. Repeated analysis of goals, readers (especially multiple audiences with varying levels of technical expertise and managerial authority), arguments (claims, evidence, warrants), conventions (genre, formatting, design, mechanics, usage), and expression (style and tone) teaches students the language of analysis and leaves them with written evidence of how rhetoric informs the success of their practice.

Suggestion 4: Teach students how to choose topics that will hold their value for a full semester and beyond.

After I share a list of projects completed by teams in previous semesters (websites for English majors; communication audits of the company where a student is employed; proposals for a child-care cooperative at the university; workshops on diversity), then each student submits three potential topics drawn from problems, needs, or opportunities that are current and important in the student's academic or professional life. In the next class session students select one topic from the collated list and answer three questions about it. We read some answers aloud. Then students spend fifteen minutes answering a second set of questions that address the topic's complexity, its capacity to sustain interest over a semester, and the level of expertise the student has in the topic area. In the third round, students keep the same topic or select one that better matches their needs, and then they answer two questions about rhetorical exigencies and compelling reasons for continuing with the topic. Using their answers, I compile a list of viable topics for the next class session. At that point, we hold a wide-ranging debate and negotiation session that ends when the teams are formed and a preliminary topic for each team is agreed upon. During the negotiations, students must convince others to join their team (until they have three to six members). Sometimes the topic is massaged to recruit members; sometimes the expertise of certain individuals convinces others to join them. This messy, but exhilarating, process produces self-selected groups that have agreed to study an issue critical to their members and to produce a report or proposal that contributes new knowledge on the topic. (See the companion website, Collaborative Project and Presentation Assignment Sheet, "Teaching Notes for Choosing Research Topics.")

Suggestion 5: Fully explore with students the concept of genre.

By reviewing the surface features of research reports in the academy and in industry, I invite students to share their experiences with genre. We move beyond surface features to how genres and discourse communities shape one another. (See Blakeslee [2002] for a discussion of the overlap between workplace and academic genres.) Eventually, students learn to take genre into consideration when they plan their research projects, and they see that practitioners adapt multiple genres to their purposes as a project progresses. An early memo of intent for an internal review board may morph into a proposal for a funding agency and then into a progress report for a supervisor, a periodic report for stockholders, a briefing for a regulatory agency, or a brochure for medical technicians. In shaping each genre, students revisit their research sources to select information that supports a different rhetorical purpose.

Suggestion 6: Address collaboration and teamwork directly.

Too often we tell students they will do a group project, but we do not teach them how to research and write collaboratively. Fortunately, technical writing textbooks and handbooks now include sections on successful team strategies, such as how to negotiate differences, how to deal with difficult people, and how to fire nonproductive team members. On the first day of the semester, students freewrite about their recent academic, personal, or workplace research projects. Next, they freewrite about collaboration. Some of their classroom memories are negative and involve the typical stumbling blocks—group grades and one member not doing anything while another takes on too much. However, I'm always pleased by how many students can recall successful team experiences, especially at work. I explain that team projects allow contributions from more than one expert, an important consideration in business where the stakes may be too high to leave the responsibility to one person, or the task may be too large for one person to complete by the deadline. As for some of the pitfalls of collaboration, we discuss solutions such as assigning each team member a particular role—document manager, leader, editor, chief researcher, data analyst, graphic artist, budget expert, to name a few. Each member then writes a job description of the tasks she or he will complete in that role, and teammates use the job descriptions to write performance evaluations of their colleagues at the end of the project. Teams take minutes at all meetings and submit them along with the transcripts of their virtual chats in a research notebook that accompanies the final project. The notebook provides a record and paper trail of the team's practices.

Suggestion 7: Implement document cycling in research projects.

Document cycling is an industry term for response and revision. In Chapter 8 of the companion website for this volume, I've included a document-cycling workshop adapted from review practices used at the U.S. General Accounting Office (see Collaborative Project and Presentation Assignment Sheet, "Document-Cycling Workshop"). The constructive critique that results from self and outside review points researchers to gaps in evidence and argumentation. It helps students learn the difference between a data dump and data analysis (as does class time spent on analytic methods). (See the companion website, Collaborative Project and Presentation Assignment Sheet, "Data Analysis: Fire in the Lumber Mill" for a sample exercise that introduces data analysis.)

Suggestion 8: Make use of technology.

Course software such as Blackboard supports both virtual teams and face-to-face teams in the same course through group discussion boards, drop boxes for files, and tools for inserting and tracking revisions. Document cycling is most effective when revision is practical. Technology makes revision easier, especially when revision is defined as strengthening the support for a report by inserting additional research findings.

Suggestion 9: Stress the recursive nature of workplace research.

By interviewing a practicing professional the first week of class, students begin the journey of collecting and evaluating information. Research practices become more demanding as the project progresses. One text used in the course sets up a "continuum of complexity" for research: mnemonic, minimal, consultative, and creative/collaborative (Inkster and Kilborn 1999, 472). The progression moves from capturing what one knows (mnemonic) to searching company files and interviewing colleagues (minimal) to seeking out experts and reviewing professional literature (consultative) to developing and processing surveys and other research instruments (creative). Students, who are or soon will be practicing professionals, must understand the costs of research, in dollars and hours. By following the continuum, they can balance costs with results and deadlines.

Suggestion 10: Include a cross-cultural component in the research project.

The modern workforce is diverse. Employees need to understand other cultures so that they can be contributing team members and can better meet the needs of their audiences in terms of data and argument. Yet industry may not be as up to date on managing diversity as teachers are. Schreiber (1996) reminds faculty that current pedagogies tackle diversity through analysis of difference and "active engagement with the perspective of others" (n.p.). Inclusiveness and cooperation are watchwords in these pedagogies, and faculty can point out the transfer value of these approaches to the workplace. For example, when students present their research orally, we can teach them how to adjust their content and delivery for an audience from either a high-context or a low-context culture.

Assessing Workplace Research in an Academic Setting

The recent literature on service learning is one place to look for feedback on whether the ways we teach research in technical and management writing courses are effective. Students engaged in service learning have one foot in each world as they take academic courses that require them to write for community institutions and nonprofits. When Teresa Redd (2003) compared client, student, and instructor assessments of the service-learning documents produced in her technical writing course, she found that the instructor assessed primarily for readability and the writer's proficiency while clients assessed primarily for meaning and usability. Drawing on work by Nora Bacon, Redd reiterates the "limits of our expertise" when we as faculty find ourselves assessing documents written in contexts that we know little about (29). In Management Writing, the semester project is assessed several times as it progresses. Response comes from the instructor, classmates, teammates, and the individual writer. Students often seek responses from those outside the course as well. Self-assessments, peer responses, and cold-reader responses are integrated into the project. (See Collaborative Project and Presentation Assignment Sheet, "Self-Assessment of Project Draft" and "Document-Cycling Workshop" on the website.)

It is fun to teach collaborative, workplace-based, research projects because student enthusiasm builds during the semester and becomes contagious. Students who might be skeptical from earlier experiences with group projects come to see collaborative research as a means of producing a product that is richer for the multiple expertise that shapes it. They find themselves collaborating with teammates who may not be physically present but who are eager to research solutions to problems that matter to all members of the team, and they dedicate time and energy beyond what they intended. By the end of the semester they have to adjust their goals, as writers almost always do, and they accept the limits of their projects, realizing they are part of ongoing actions. It's okay if the project is not final or perfect. For example, the team that proposed a day-care cooperative for part-time students was unable to overcome legal constraints that prohibited an on-campus center. They now use a phone list as an informal child-care co-op and have asked me to seek a team from next semester's class to carry on their work. One group of distance students, who were finishing their bachelor's degrees, prepared a proposal for a distance master's degree in English so they could continue their studies. Their proposal has not been approved, but they are pleased to share their project with readers of this book so their research on distance education can reach a wider audience (see "Students Seeking Knowledge: A Proposal" on the website).

The effort that went into these projects has enriched students' understanding of *research as action* in a larger context. As for those of us who teach workplace research in an academic setting, Faber and Johnson-Eilola (2002) suggest that we restructure the relationship between industry and academia by increasing our "migrations" between these worlds and by valuing knowledge flow and the knowledge-based work that goes on in industry. The benefits are many: "improved, value-added experiences and practices in both academia and the workplace" (146). Teaching collaborative workplace research in an academic setting is an unfinished journey. When one mountain road is successfully negotiated, another exciting one lies ahead.

Works Cited

Bacon, Nora. 1997. "Community Service Writing: Problems, Challenges, Questions." In *Writing the Community: Concepts and Models for Service Learning in Composition,* edited by Linda Adler-Kasner, Robert Cooks, and Ann Watters, 39–55. Washington, DC: AAHE and NCTE.

Blakeslee, Ann M. 2002. "Researching a Common Ground: Exploring the Space Where Academic and Workplace Cultures Meet." In Mirel and Spilka, 41–55.

Couture, Barbara. 1999. "Modeling and Emulating: Rethinking Agency in the Writing Process." In *Post-Process Theory: Beyond the Writing-Process Paradigm,* edited by Thomas Kent, 30–48. Carbondale: Southern Illinois University Press.

Dias, Patrick, Aviva Freedman, Peter Medway, and Anthony Paré. 1999. *Worlds Apart: Acting and Writing in Academic and Workplace Contexts.* Mahwah, NJ: Erlbaum.

Faber, Brenton, and Johndan Johnson-Eilola. 2002. "Migrations: Strategic Thinking About the Future(s) of Technical Communication." In Mirel and Spilka, 135–48.

Hager, Peter J., and H. J. Scheiber. 1992. *Report Writing for Management Decisions*. New York: Macmillan.

Inkster, Robert P., and Judith M. Kilborn. 1999. *The Writing of Business*. Boston: Allyn & Bacon.

Kent, Thomas, ed. 1999. *Post-Process Theory: Beyond the Writing-Process Paradigm*. Carbondale: Southern Illinois University Press.

Matalene, Carolyn B., ed. 1989. *Worlds of Writing: Teaching and Learning in Discourse Communities of Work*. New York: Random House.

McGregor, Douglas. 1960. *The Human Side of Enterprise*. New York: McGraw-Hill.

Mirel, Barbara, and Rachel Spilka, eds. 2002. *Reshaping Technical Communication: New Directions and Challenges for the 21st Century*. Mahway, NJ: Erlbaum.

Moffett, James. 1994. "Coming Out Right." In *Taking Stock: The Writing Process Movement in the '90s,* edited by Lad Tobin and Thomas Newkirk, 18–30. Portsmouth, NH: Boynton/Cook.

Neff, Joyce Magnotto. 1998. "From a Distance: Teaching Writing on Interactive Television." *Research in the Teaching of English* 33 (November): 136–57.

Ouchi, William G. 1981. *Theory Z: How American Management Can Meet the Japanese Challenge*. Reading, MA: Addison-Wesley.

Paré, Anthony. 2002. "Keeping Writing in Its Place: A Participatory Action Approach to Workplace Communication." In Mirel and Spilka, 57–73.

Redd, Teresa M. 2003. "In the Eye of the Beholder: Contrasting Views of Community Service Writing." *Reflections* III, 1 (Winter): 14–35.

Russell, David R. 2001. "Where Do the Naturalistic Studies of WAC/WID Point?" In *WAC for the New Millennium: Strategies for Continuing Writing-Across-the-Curriculum Programs*, edited by Susan McLeod, Eric Miraglia, Margot Soven, and Christopher Thaiss, 259–98. Urbana, IL: NCTE.

Schon, Donald, ed. 1991. *The Reflective Turn: Case Studies in and on Educational Practice*. New York: Teachers College Press.

Schreiber, Evelyn Jaffe. 1993. "From Academic Writing to Job-Related Writing: Achieving a Smooth Transition." *IEEE Transactions on Professional Communication* 36 (December): 178–84.

———. 1996. "Muddles and Huddles: Facilitating a Multicultural Workforce through Team Management Theory." *Journal of Business Communication* 33 (October): start page 459. Electronic version.

Whithaus, Carl, and Joyce Magnotto Neff. (forthcoming). "You Can't Just Circle the Chairs: Interactive Television, Video Streaming, and Writing Pedagogy."

Yancey, Kathleen Blake. 1998. *Reflection in the Writing Classroom*. Logan, UT: Utah State University Press.

Zimmerman, Muriel, and Hugh Marsh. 1989. "Storyboarding an Industrial Proposal: A Case Study of Teaching and Producing Writing." In Matalene, 203–21.

9

Developing a New Generation of Scholars
"Search and Re-Search" Reader Response and Writing in the Literature Classroom

Georgia A. Newman

For some students, the word *scholar* conjures up an image of a bespectacled, severely myopic reader, hunched over books and journals and puzzling over esoteric texts in dusty, distant archives, until, at length, he (the image is usually male) makes a discovery that, once set forth in print, provides *the* authoritative word on a subject. A corollary to this figure in today's college classroom is seen as one-dimensional, a "nerd" who is content to sit all day in the library and never engage in Instant Messaging with friends. Perhaps it is this stereotype of the scholar that drives so many students to become bewildered by, even disdainful of scholarship and to seek "creative," if not desperate, ways to circumvent the research process. Meanwhile, college teachers watch woefully as students abandon critical thinking, borrow heavily from the work of perceived *real* scholars, and, with navigational (but often not evaluative) skills in the familiar environment of computers, tap into easily accessed but often unexamined and frequently inappropriate websites in a futile effort to conduct "research."

Could it be that we classroom teachers have unwittingly created an environment that works counter to sound research? Have we prompted students to distrust their own voices and seek authority instead in other, more clearly "established" sources? If so, what can we do to recapture students' imaginations and coax hitherto reluctant scholars to find value in a new identity? And how can we promote in our own classrooms the particular patterns and habits of thinking, writing, and speaking that authenticate true scholars?

The questions I posit suggest, I hope, an enlarged vision of scholarship in the college classroom, a vision that goes far beyond assignments of end-of-semester term papers and that sees documentation as an issue much larger than adherence to the mechanics of a particular manual of style.

It is my contention that the assign-and-run paper—in particular, the conventional research paper—does little to promote the type of scholarship that language and literature teachers desire; that, more often than not, this type of assignment assumes but actually inhibits critical thinking. It is my further contention that when we teachers fail to ground our teaching of documentation in the need to build credibility for an argument, when we focus documentation primarily on our students' mastery of citation forms, we ultimately thwart the academic goal of preparing students to be scholars.

In what I call a "search and re-search" process of inquiry, I have found an inviting alternative to more traditional research assignments in the literature classroom. This alternative, equally compelling for general education courses and seminars in the major, has four key components: 1) evoking creative reader-response to a literary text; 2) developing student habits of critical thinking and documentation in daily, focused-question journal entries (or weekly, short writing assignments) that center initially on primary texts; 3) incorporating the repeated testing of ideas into carefully structured class discussions and cooperative learning groups; and, ultimately, 4) integrating more traditional research of secondary sources into student scholarship.

Developing Creative Reader-Response

Vigorous intellectual inquiry begins with active reading and creative response to questions a reading provokes. Reader-response theory, with its emphasis on alternative ways of viewing a text, provides a particularly useful frame for structuring and evaluating assignments that engage students in their own text-search process long before they commit themselves to more traditional investigation of secondary sources. While reader-response theory is hardly new to academe, few students have learned how to respond to primary texts in ways other than the superficial "I can relate to that" or "I just don't connect with that writer" response. Accustomed to equating "opinion" and "judgment" with a gut response in which anything goes, yet equally accustomed to being told what and how to think (whether by advertising moguls, TV commentators, parents or spouses, or teachers themselves), many students are reluctant to believe that they can approach a subject new to them with both reasoned and reasonable authority, or that they themselves have imagination, knowledge, and logic to bring to literary analysis. Thus in an early lesson, I want to engage classes in a provocative reader-response activity, one that will illustrate the validity of multiple readings of literary texts while also demonstrating the scholar's need to provide evidence informed by critical thinking.

Although subject matter for an effective reader-response activity—one that will generate a variety of creative readings—varies considerably from course to course, Robert Frost's poem "Stopping by Woods on a Snowy Evening" serves as a useful illustration. If I ask, for example, who the "I" in this poem might be, freshman students in a writing about literature course will often assume, without interrogation, that poet and persona must be one and the same. "Robert Frost," one student may reply. Yet when pressed to state what she or he knows about Frost that could explain why the poet stops by woods on a snowy evening this "darkest evening of the year," the student will typically shrug, "I have no idea." To stimulate creative thinking and resist coming to premature closure on the question, a small-group discussion or "think-pair-share" process in which each student has a speaking and listening role will allow students to begin to examine more thoughtfully such questions as "What do we know for sure about the speaker of this poem? What can we imagine? Where is this person? Why or how do you suppose the persona has come to this place? What attitude do you sense? What details hint at this attitude? Whom do you picture here?"

Most students are astonished when they discover that some classmates have readings quite different from their own, presumably "obvious" reading. For example, one student in a group may declare, "I think the persona of this poem is a tired St. Nicholas on Christmas Eve." Another may query, "Could this be a young man in a dark depression, maybe someone trying to break his drug addiction to 'snow'?" The more startling or seemingly outrageous suggestions are those that invariably evoke the most engaged discussions; stimulated to defend or challenge a reading, students are eager to return to the text for more studied investigation. They become fascinated now by such questions as "What details within the text itself support this reading? Are there any details that seem to contradict? Are there multiple ways of viewing evidence? If contradictions are present, can these be explained or accounted for in some other logical way, or do they compel us to dismiss this particular reading?" Through this search process, students can see how creative and critical thinking work together to generate an interpretation of a text. And as they discover how a single work can evoke more than one response, they also begin to understand why literary critics sometimes disagree in their analyses and evaluations of texts. In fact, students taking on the role of investigative scholar, perhaps for the very first time, typically begin to feel less concerned about being *right* than being *engaged*, and they become much more willing to search and re-search a primary text before hastening to outside sources for opinion.

A search activity of the type just described does not preempt more traditional research but rather prepares students for it. Indeed, as students formulate their own readings, and later as they listen to and reflect upon the ideas of others, they are learning to anticipate and welcome multiple viewpoints, to examine assumptions, to weigh the logic in a particular argument, and to spot logical fallacies.

Eliciting Short, Focused-Question Writing
About Primary Texts

Weary from reading traditional, end-of-semester term papers and writing "unity needed" and "document this" on page after page of lengthy but patch-work and undocumented text, discouraged teachers (myself included, once upon a time) collide with equally discouraged students. "Haven't they learned how to do this by now?" is the all too familiar complaint. Thus with sighs heavy and joyous exclamations few, these same teachers are happy to reward with an "A" a paper that simply synthesizes well and documents accurately the thinking of others; creative and original insights fall into the category of "wishful thinking" rather than "requirement and realistic expectation."

From repeated poor results, one might assume that students have not had enough exposure to term papers. Yet a closer look will show that even those students who have written myriad term papers in multiple subjects over many years can still fall far short of excellence, their work revealing serious gaps in an understanding of focused topic, specific audience, controlled viewpoint, and appropriate evidence. Repeatedly expected to take giant leaps without first practicing in small steps, uneasy young scholars become frustrated, pro-duce poorly written papers, and emerge from the experience tired of, certainly not valuing, the research process.

To help students gain the practice they need in reading, thinking, and writing, I am partial to nontraditional, short assignments focused exclusively at first on primary texts; these in turn, become catalysts for in-class, reader-response discussions. For freshman-level classes, a focused-question, literary journal helps students acquire a daily habit of scholarly reading, thinking (both creatively and critically), and writing. Students prepare for each class session by reading the literary selection(s) assigned with a particular question in mind, then writing a full page of single-spaced, properly documented text in response to the question. The questions themselves are carefully designed to stir interest, provoke reflection, and encourage original response. Consider the following example:

> Reflecting on Poe's "A Cask of Amontillado," why do you believe Montressor plotted revenge against Fortunato in the manner described? Although Montressor never identifies the "thousand injuries" nor the "insult" that he mentions at the beginning of the story, what type of in-sult do you believe is most in character for Fortunato and most likely to offend Montressor? Cite specific details and/or quotations from the story to reinforce your argument.

In early writing assignments, I want to keep students focused on primary texts, on developing their own ideas before they turn to the ideas of others. For this reason, in freshman classes, I delay more formal essay writing until stu-dents have had weeks of experience with the literary journal—a discipline repeated over time in a process that helps to ensure a scholarly product not only for the present assignment, but for later, more traditional, research as well. For sophomore survey and upper-division courses in the major, I replace the daily journal with short, weekly or biweekly essay assignments (these too prompted by focused questions) that continue to stimulate creative, original readings of primary texts. More advanced than the literary journal entries (which, although documented, are essentially informal and focused on a single text), assignments for upper-level courses more often call for synthesis of ideas in two or three primary texts and require students to employ more deliberately the standardized conventions of academic diction and style that characterize scholars at their best. Following is an example of a writing assignment from a sophomore survey course that is designed to prompt the imagination, stimulate student engagement with a text, and encourage original response:

> Imagine that you are the genial host who accompanies Chaucer's pilgrims on their way to Canterbury and who has been asked to judge the tales. What three to four literary criteria will you employ to evaluate each tale? Briefly explain your rationale for selecting these criteria. Applying the criteria named to the four tales studied in class this week, select the pilgrim you will honor with first prize and a free dinner at the Tabard Inn. Justify your choice through careful presentation of your criteria and supporting analysis of the literary texts.

Understanding that students, even at upper levels, too often equate documentation with the need merely to follow a particular convention of style and, as a result, miss the more fundamental need to provide material support for their arguments, I often repeat the phrase "cite specific evidence" in instructions for the assigned questions. Furthermore, before I teach the mechanics of documentation, I want students to understand their need to *show* and *demonstrate*, not just *tell* the reader that a particular point is valid. I find it helpful to remind students that there is not a specific *correct* or *incorrect* response, but that there are *valid* and *invalid* readings, a valid reading defended by specific details of the text and not contradicted by any detail for which the student cannot make a reasonable account.

The benefits of focused-question assignments are many. When these assignments are given *in advance* of reading, as is the case with the literary journal, students obviously read with more attention and care, and are much better prepared in follow-up class discussions to respond actively to what they have read. When the short assignments are written as a *follow-up* to class discussion, the focused questions continue to help stimulate original (and, as the course progresses, more complex) thinking in ways that student-selected topics seldom do.

In their search and re-search of *primary* texts, students acquire a heightened awareness of evidence, an awareness that enables them to become not only better scholars themselves, but also better readers and evaluators of the work of their peers and, ultimately, of all secondary sources. In the process, they also develop ease with the conventions of the documentation process as their repetitive need to cite evidence in support of different readings develops into a scholarly habit.

Focused questions also allow me, in my teaching role, to reinforce particular concepts that may need more attention. For example, in a literature-based composition class, if I want to reinforce awareness of setting in a short story while simultaneously helping students learn the concept of literary viewpoint, I may design a question such as the following:

> What appears to be the setting of Jamaica Kincaid's "Girl"? Cite specific contextual clues that form your impression of place, time, and atmosphere. Within this setting, who appears to be the narrator? Speaking to whom? What evidence supports your reading? To what extent do you think setting affects or does not affect the narrator's attitudes? Cite supporting evidence to make your case.

Although a question such as this requires close reading of the text, it does not presume just one valid response. My objective is to get students to search the primary text, to activate their imaginations while also sharpening their eyes for facts and details that provide the evidence they need to support creative readings. Through questions focused specifically on a primary text, students quickly discover that their own analytical reading and reasoning skills are their best search tools.

A final benefit of the focused-question writing assignment is that it engages all students in the same project, preparing them to read and reflect on one another's work more thoughtfully, in much the same way as scholarly articles are peer-reviewed by other scholars with expertise in the subject.

Developing, Not Just Generating Critical Thinking

Like any skill, good critical thinking requires development. Levels of cognition originally theorized by Benjamin Bloom in his *Taxonomy of Educational Objectives* (1956) and, with minor adaptations, still given strong credence by educators today, point to the need for educators to move students from recall, comprehension, and application of terminology to "higher order" skills of analysis, synthesis, and critical evaluation—essential components in scholarly inquiry and debate.

If carefully constructed, focused-question writing assignments will allow students to sharpen their skills in critical analysis as a course progresses. The following examples from a freshman-level writing-about-literature class illustrate the principle:

> *Application:* Review the literary viewpoints defined in class before and after you read Faulkner's story "A Rose for Emily." Which of these points of

view does Faulkner employ, and with what effect(s)? Cite and document specific quotations as evidence.

Analysis: Choose one of the following lenses through which Milcha Sanchez Scott's one-act play, "The Cuban Swimmer," could be read: allegory of life; religious allegory; feminist allegory; allegory of the [Olympic] athlete; political allegory of immigrants in America; cultural allegory of Hispanic (alternatively, Latino/Cuban) culture within the United States. Within the frame/lens you choose, discuss the allegorical role and import of each of the following: Margarita; family members; the competition; the ocean; reporters Mel and Mary Beth; the biting fish; the dolphins; the oil slick; the "miracle." Document your evidence, citing supporting quotations as appropriate.

Comparison-Contrast: Examine two versions of May Swenson's poem "Women": one in traditional, block style, the other in shaped verse. What poetic techniques are found in both versions? Which, if any, in one version only? Cite evidence. To what extent does shape affect your reading of and response to the poem? Illustrate and document your analysis.

Synthesis: Examine "Young Goodman Brown" (Hawthorne), "A Good Man Is Hard to Find" (O'Connor), and "Big, Black Good Man" (Wright). Does the definition of "good" remain constant in these three stories? shift from one story to another? have different meanings even to different characters within a single story? Cite specific evidence, including direct quotations, to support each point.

Critical thinking develops over years, not just weeks, of course. Therefore, just as it is appropriate for writing assignments to become progressively more sophisticated from freshman to senior to graduate levels, so too should focus questions for a sophomore survey course offer more challenge than those for an introductory, general education course, and questions for an upper-level course in the major require more analysis than those for a survey course. (See companion website for examples.) Even so, it is important to continue to develop, not just generate, critical thinking in all of these courses; indeed, the gradual progression from one level of critical thinking to another *within* a course always needs attention.

Using Cooperative Learning Groups to Promote Scholarly Discussion and Debate

Traditional research usually presumes thinking and writing, but rarely is speaking a component. Regardless of how well structured a research assignment may be, however, writing alone will seldom develop a student as a full-fledged scholar. Just as professionals test their theories through informal discussion with peers, through publication in peer-reviewed journals and the like, and through engagement with others in professional conference presentations, so students benefit from opportunities to test their own ideas before a public audience of their peers. Small, well-designed, carefully monitored, cooperative learning groups can afford students an ongoing opportunity to hone critical thinking and to engage in the process of evaluation that characterizes scholars at their best.

I am particularly indebted to the work of Johnson and Johnson (1989) for group modes and strategies that ensure good results. Varying the size and composition of groups from one class session to another (sometimes even within a class session) adds vitality to a class, and students' anticipation of a class in which they know they will contribute actively encourages them to read assigned texts carefully. Students do not know in advance with whom they are likely to be paired or grouped, but they do know that class discussion will always follow up on the reading and thinking they have done in advance. They can thus have confidence that their work will be acknowledged, that their ideas will be taken seriously, and that their own participation matters.

Sometimes I structure an activity that allows students to push a particular reading even further through discussion with others of like mind. Sometimes I group students with others taking quite different approaches. Occasionally I require students to formulate for class debate a position opposite the one they have taken in their journal writing assignment. In such instances, students are compelled to search a literary text in even more depth and to see subtleties they might otherwise overlook.

I also use cooperative learning groups for peer evaluation, and find that students are generally much more careful and deliberate with their work when they know it must pass the scrutiny of their peers.

When all students are engaged in oral discussion—whether in vigorous debate or reflective evaluation, whether as a member of a team, a pair, a triad, or other group configuration—every student in the class gains practice, and multiple viewpoints are always explored. Even those who claim no interest in literary scholarship find themselves stimulated to play the role of literary detective—either to defend their own readings or to challenge or support the readings of others.

Students actively engaged in such groups over time enjoy developing relationships with others within a learning community. With exposure to myriad voices and viewpoints, they become not only more critical in their analytical reading and reasoning, but also more open to difference and more appreciative of alternative ways of seeing. They are sometimes surprised to discover how intellectually stimulated they are and how quickly class time passes when vigorous debate ensues.

Interestingly, while my personal observation, as well as students' anonymous course evaluations and end-of-term critiques, confirm students' perception of personal and intellectual growth throughout the semester, most at this early stage of the process do not realize they are becoming scholars. Only later do they come to discover that the term *scholar* is not restricted (rarely even relegated) to a one-dimensional, stuffy person. When they eventually come to see themselves and their peers as participants in a public literary debate, these heretofore-reluctant scholars now seem to wear the label with pride.

Integrating Secondary Sources into the Research Process

Because I want students first to acquire a scholarly habit of engaging actively with a text, reflecting upon what they read, and using both creative and critical thinking to formulate interpretations, the early assignments in my courses compel the reader to focus on a primary text alone and to write in response to a question for which an outside source (especially a direct Internet site) is likely to be of little value. The process of searching a primary text first moves students well away from the traditional research assignment before it conceives of moving them *toward* that end. As a course progresses, however, and as students gain confidence in their creative and critical thinking abilities, I begin to integrate lessons and assignments that encourage the use of appropriate outside sources.

One way in which I prepare students in a literature class for this transition into more traditional research is to introduce them to major literary theories and critical approaches—from biographical, historical, and formalist to postmodern sociological, psychoanalytic, deconstructionist, and the like. Students who have seen already how their peers can read a text differently from them quickly perceive how various theoretical lenses, like the varying colored lenses of sunglasses, filter the readings of professional scholars too, allowing certain details or evidence to surface while other details recede. With this preparation, students read with greater awareness and understanding the work of professional scholars, and they come to regard secondary sources as ancillary to, not a substitute for, their own thinking.

Extra-credit-research "teasers" are also useful for *encouraging* exploration of secondary sources long before students are *required* to do so. I may well give a dozen or so such optional assignments during the semester, each one slightly different from the one before, all short, and all encouraging students to search and re-search. These short assignments, offering as they do the opportunity for "free" mistakes, become learning tools; they are especially effective in helping students develop research skills in small steps over time. Subtly, the association of research with extra credit places research in a positive light; students freely choose to go on a "search and re-search" mission.

Always short, and seldom generating more than two or three extra credit points, research teasers, when carefully constructed send students to scholarly sources. As the students analyze the ideas they discover from these sources, they exercise even further their critical reading and thinking skills. Students who undertake extra-credit "search and re-search" projects always report back to the class on their findings; their classmates thus share in the discovery process, with the result that all see once again how two or more sources may define terms differently, how scholars may disagree with one another even on supposed "facts," how two literary critics can read the same text in very different ways.

When the process of searching primary texts has become habitual and when students have had ample extra-credit opportunities to engage in limited research of secondary sources, I consider my students to be ready for a more in-depth, more traditional research assignment, one that will require them to seek out and evaluate a variety of secondary sources, then to synthesize and integrate their findings into their own thinking and writing. At this point, usually after mid-term, I introduce in all my classes a *collaborative research* project that fosters teamwork skills (an extension of the cooperative learning groups in class) while simultaneously encouraging an investigative and reporting process foundational to most academic disciplines and careers. Assignment specifics for a collaborative research project vary from course to course and from one academic level to another, but in each case, the *development* of critical thinking is ever at the fore.

Just as in-class discussions are improved when students have had the reading and writing preparation of focused-question journaling, so too I find that the quality of research at each academic level is enhanced when students work together and when they have specific questions they want to answer. In most courses I provide a set of questions that student groups will use as a springboard to research; however, I also facilitate students in generating additional questions of their own. In a collaborative research project on a novel, for example, I may ask freshmen students to seek out information about a particular author, locate several critical reviews, investigate elements of literary style and genre, read several different interpretations of the literary work under study, and explore broader questions of context for a particular setting or theme. Unfamiliar terms and settings in a novel may also generate questions that further establish research parameters. For example, students who elect to read Eli Wiesel's *The Fifth Son* may choose to investigate Hasidic Judaism, learn about Jewish mysticism and the Cabala; do historical research into WWII Nazi concentration camps and Polish ghettos; discover when, where, and why Wiesel elected to write the novel; and determine what, if any, autobiographical elements are present in the text. Students reading Flannery O'Connor's *The Violent Bear It Away* may investigate "the Grotesque" as a literary style; find out what O'Connor stated in her essays and letters about technology, religion, and the South; and see what critics have written about sun imagery and other symbolism in the novel.

How I teach students to develop and refine their methods of searching secondary sources and primary texts other than those used in class varies considerably from course to course and from one academic level to another. In a beginning freshman composition class in which the writing process itself is the chief content, I devote nearly a month to teaching the research process step by step with assignments that systematically take students to different types of resources—from college-level print encyclopedias to Internet sites; from specialized references to books in circulation; from popular magazines and newspapers to peer-reviewed, scholarly journals; from government documents to vertical files ephemera; from nonprint sources such as films, recordings, and TV documentaries to live, personal interviews. Yet, even with specific questions to focus the investigation, even with concrete guidelines to establish number of sources and types of sources to be consulted, even with collaborations encouraged to ease the burden on individuals while making more extensive research possible over all, and even with evaluation throughout the process to help build student confidence and ensure a good final product, I find that most of my students benefit also from formal instruction time in class and opportunity for individualized help outside of class. Simply assigning a research project is insufficient.

Individual writing is an important part of the research process; however, nearly every goal of a traditional term paper (ten to twenty pages) can be achieved—and with better results—in a short (usually five-page), documented writing assignment. When students collaborate on research, each individual within the group can focus on a specific, limited aspect of the research topic; as resources are pooled, every student in the group learns a great deal more about the subject than would be possible otherwise. Furthermore, students daunted by a twenty-page term paper assignment seldom fear the five-page essay, even if the same number and types of sources are specified in each case. Shorter assignments encourage students to be more careful in their selection of facts, details, and quotations, and to synthesize more smoothly what they learn from their research.

Requiring an annotated bibliography in advance of (or even along with) a formal essay is a particularly effective strategy for encouraging students to read more carefully, to summarize and paraphrase more ably, and to assess sources more critically. Specifications for an annotated bibliography, as for the formal essay, should be level appropriate. While the bibliography can be any length the instructor specifies, less can mean more. I have found, for example, that if I require annotations of only five sources, I can ensure broadened research and quality reading by specifying that the bibliography reflect at least three different types of sources (such as scholarly articles, personal interview with expert in the field, film documentary, specialized reference, and the like). I can also specify minimum lengths of the sources consulted (such as a half-hour interview, a twenty-page article, an hour-long documentary, and so on). In each case, the goal is to stretch students to discover and work with resources they may not find if told simply to "write a paper and make a presentation about your discoveries."

When students are required to submit print copies of all sources consulted along with their annotated bibliographies and to highlight central points of interest on the printouts or photocopies attached, they are far less likely to plagiarize text (either intentionally or unintentionally) or to "borrow" the work of someone else. Once again, the emphasis is on building research skills step by step.

I prefer to evaluate the annotated bibliography (together with the highlighted sources attached) before students submit the penultimate draft of a documented essay. This step in the process allows me an opportunity to intervene where help is needed—perhaps to flag a questionable source before the research has gone too far, perhaps to point out where and how a student can paraphrase, quote from, and document text more effectively. This intervention goes a long way toward ensuring a well-researched, well-written, and clearly documented essay.

This step-by-step development of the collaborative research project allows my students to develop new skills at the same time they are exercising and reinforcing skills acquired earlier. It should come as no surprise that virtually all students, guided in this way, produce quality work with lasting effects. I may still bemoan students' problems with language, syntax, mechanics, and the like (as I have from my first days in academe), but I seldom have cause to weep over lack of substantive content, insufficient development, problematic organization, missing documentation, excessive or purposeless quotation, or factual inaccuracies. I actually enjoy reading the essays, and I look forward to the group presentations that will synthesize the research of these student scholars.

Theory into Practice

The learning process I have described for a literature class involves specific steps from reading and writing about primary texts to testing ideas both in real-time discussion and in consultation with professional scholars through their articles and books. Nevertheless, this learning process, like the act of writing itself, is neither linear nor entirely sequential; it is, rather, recursive—or perhaps more accurately, a spiraling upward or drilling downward, a process through which students develop new skills even as they repeatedly practice skills learned earlier. At the same time, it is also a *seeing* and *re-viewing* process, or as I prefer to label it, a search and re-search approach to scholarship.

In my attempt to create an in-class environment (and even a climate outside of class) conducive to the development of the student-scholar, I find that I have borrowed, with purposeful eclecticism, from different philosophical schools—perennialist, essentialist, behaviorist, progressivist, existentialist, and reconstructionist. Nonetheless, while the search and re-search assignments and activities that form the core of all my courses are adaptable to a variety of instructional modes, including distance learning, I find that they work most effectively in real time and within the framework of a less lecture-oriented, more student-centered classroom, where reader response is encouraged in every aspect of the class and where cooperative learning groups provide emerging scholars with the live feedback of a public audience.

I have also found useful many of the theories of cognitive development, right brain/left brain functioning, multiple intelligences, study skills strategies, and personality type and academic process that are in wide circulation today. All of these suggest the need for a synthesis of creative and critical thinking activities coupled with provision for both independent and collaborative assignments.

In order to accommodate a variety of student learning preferences, I design my curriculum to draw on the strengths of introverted writers and extraverted speakers, analytical thinkers and creative performers, independent learners and learners with social needs, those who require structure and those who prefer more freedom (Myers and Briggs 1975). While I realize the impossibility of creating a classroom in which "one size fits all equally well," I do take care to provide some class time for quiet reflection and time for active sharing; to elicit both the imaginative "what if . . ." and the factual "this is . . ."; to give students a chance to experience the emotive and personalized "I can relate to . . ." and the logical, impersonal "see how these words undercut the idea that. . . ." My goal is to ensure that all my students have some opportunity to exercise their learning preferences even as they develop their less practiced skills.

To create variety and balance in my classes as well as to accommodate different learning preferences, I try to provide students with ample opportunities for "writing to think" and "writing to speak" as well as for "thinking to write" and "thinking to speak." In the process, I want them to have repeated practice in search and re-search methodologies that develop their skills in active reading, critical thinking, cooperative and collaborative learning, and independent research and writing.

Students in my classes know that they are working hard and writing a lot, but they seldom feel intimidated. With ample opportunity to collaborate with others, to have regular feedback, to test their ideas and theories in an atmosphere that encourages originality, and to write on topics that address specific questions of immediate relevance to their mastery of course content, students experience success and feel rewarded by their efforts. In the process, they experience too the intellectual stimulation that professionals enjoy in their own discussions and debates with one another. I, of course, take satisfaction and pleasure in watching my students become more creative and critical thinkers, more polished writers, and most self-assured and articulate presenters—in short, a new generation of real scholars.

Works Cited

Bloom, Benjamin S. 1956. *Taxonomy of Educational Objectives: The Classification of Educational Goals: Handbook I—Cognitive Domain.* New York: Longman.

Johnson, David W., and Roger T. Johnson. 1989. *Cooperation and Competition. Theory and Research.* Edina, MN: Interaction Book Co.

Myers, Isabelle Briggs, and Katharine C. Briggs. 1975. *Myers-Briggs Type Indicator.* Palo Alto, CA: CPP, Inc.

10

The Collage Connection
Using Hypertext to Teach Research Writing

Shelley Aley

The world is a warehouse of forms which the writer raids.
—Annie Dillard (1982, 20)

Writing needs the drama of thinking and the performance of voices.
—Peter Elbow (1999, 13)

From this Derridian emphasis upon discontinuity comes the conception of hypertext as a vast assemblage. . . . To carry Derrida's instinctive theorizing of hypertext further, one may also point to his recognition that such a montagelike textuality marks or foregrounds the writing process and therefore rejects a deceptive transparency.
—George P. Landow (2001, 151)

Chelsea opens her paper with a quote from one of her sources: "A computer simulation exercise designed to provide virtual utopia has demonstrated that human beings cannot get on with one another without rules and regulations to restrict anti-social behavior." She goes on to explain that in this quote, her source, someone named Andrew Smith, is "talking about how an online community can go awry."

I check Chelsea's list of works cited and see that the title of the piece Andrew Smith has written is "Lucifer Is Part of the Program in Paradise," and it appeared in *The Sunday Times* on the 27th of December in 1998. Chelsea got the article in its full-text form from Infotrac, via our university's library website. As a reader, my interest may have been raised by Chelsea's use of this particular source, but I cannot follow her trail and find the source with any ease. A search of the Infotrac database pulls up nothing. Evidently, the article was removed from the system sometime after Chelsea accessed it. As a reader, if I were to find her essay in print, I would have to go find the source article she cited by conducting a search. It is a task that few casual readers pursue, unless their interest in a source is very high. This is nothing new. Readers of scholarly works look sources up all the time. But how many would pursue more sources if they could do it more quickly and easily?

Chelsea fulfilled the traditional research writing assignment I gave my freshman composition students by enriching her writing and her credibility with outside sources. She has a pretty good idea of why she is using outside sources, too. She is on her way to becoming a member of the academic community. Maybe I have done my job and reinforced the lessons about research writing that Chelsea has already absorbed over the years through her education. Maybe.

Or maybe I should have provided Chelsea with another way of thinking about research writing, using sources, and addressing a reader's curiosity. Chelsea's "raid," as Annie Dillard (1982, 20) calls it, her use of an outside source to open her paper and pique a reader's interest, pays off, but only to a degree. I have to wonder if there isn't more I could be doing for my students, besides reinforcing what they already know about research writing.

Isn't it interesting to see the ways that our students choose sources and employ them in their own writing? Sometimes they get it just right. On the other hand, sometimes it seems like the students are just tossing in quotes because they know the assignment is supposed to contain "outside sources." At times I've seen papers that effectively use outside sources in one place and yet are dismal in another. Sometimes student writers are in command of their writing; other times their sources take over. One of our jobs is to teach novice writers to conduct effective source "raids" and then make good use of what they have found. It is quite possible to get them involved in bringing the outsider in to enrich their own thinking and writing and to create a piece of writing that involves some of the multitude of voices caught up in the conversations about topics that have been going on long before we became involved in the din. But we try to get our students to be tidy about it all, reserving any indication that they have spent days or maybe weeks wading through a muck of sources in order to write a paper, by merely leaving a documentation track through the writing for their readers to follow. We teach our students to rope in those pushy sources that shove their thinking against or beyond their masterfully stated thesis statement. But how do we help our students stand aside sometimes and let the sources challenge them? And how do we get our students to allow their readers to become involved in the messy research process, beyond allowing them a curious glance at the works cited, references, or bibliography section at the end of a piece? Getting our students to think about research writing as creating a sort of collage can help, and giving them effective assignments involving hypertext can get them to encourage the active reader's involvement in a piece of writing. (For more information about the definition of hypertext, consult the companion website for this book.)

Students' Erroneous Conceptions of Research Writing

Probably the first, biggest problem I see with my students' understanding of research writing is ownership. They do not see research writing as something that they own. They have written too many of what I call "regurgitation reports"—ugh! This is the paper that brings in a multitude of voices to summarize what every expert (including *Webster's*) has said on a topic, yet the paper itself says nothing—not even intimating that an actual writer had a hand in putting it together. Inputting the entire collection of anything and everything on a topic into Microsoft Word and then hitting the AutoSummarize button could have created it. Ever try this? I think that some of my students have.

While this kind of writing assignment can be useful in teaching students to write summaries of their sources or use writing to assimilate and learn information, the regurgitation report should not be their only exposure to research writing, no matter how useful it may seem. Because of their experience with this kind of writing, students think that research writing is anything but creative, interactive, and challenging. They do not see it as a form of personal expression. Many have been told by teachers that they cannot use "I" in this type of writing, and instead of connecting this directive to audience and register, they think that the restriction limits the formation of any ideas of their own. Many of my students are shocked when they get my assignments and ask, "Do you mean that I can write my opinion in this paper?"

In contrast to the regurgitation report, the kind of research writing I am interested in getting my students involved in moves well beyond summarizing and reporting. After some unlearning, my students begin to understand that the essay's focus or thesis—whatever one calls it—is their own (formulated not in a vacuum, but in a conversation with many voices). And the word *research* does not mean that creativity and the writer's voice are unnecessary. Quite the contrary!

This being said, the next biggest problem I have with research writing is getting the students to understand that using sources has a purpose for both them and their readers. Many students resist this instruction, however. Frankly, I've found that they would like to avoid using research, if possible, because college students are scared of plagiarism. Teachers, they find, are using "cheat-detection" websites to determine if their students are plagiarizing. This response to student writing is unfortunate, I believe, because plagiarism can be dealt with so much more effectively than by resorting to scare tactics. With the blurring of boundaries between writers and readers and writers who are readers, it is no wonder that students think that they are cheating when they do research writing. Teachers should note that their students hold this belief in common with other writers. Peter Elbow (2000), for example, notes this truth about research writing in his discussions of collage writing, which he calls a "cheatin' art" (26). And as Annie Dillard points out, we writers are raiders of the world's warehouses; "this is a stickup," she proclaims (qtd. in Elbow 2000, 301). Both Elbow and Dillard see the writer's pilfering as both positive and necessary—and it has little to do with plagiarism or a teacher's concern that sources aren't getting proper credit and that students are not doing their own work and may be stealing someone else's ideas. But the difference between what Elbow and Dillard are saying and the teacher's (not unimportant) concern over plagiarism is sometimes not always getting translated to students. Research writing poses students with a field of plagiarism land mines to maneuver. After all, there are all kinds of boundaries between what parts of the paper are theirs and what parts are their sources'. Unless care is taken to involve students in finding their own point of view within the context of their sources, they will simply avoid using a rich tapestry of sources to stay out of trouble.

Here's the good news: ownership and fear of plagiarism can both be addressed by developing research-writing assignments involving collage and hypertext. Such assignments strive to reveal the pasted-together nature of research writing, which is characteristic of hypertext itself. At the same time, while these assignments can help students more clearly see boundaries between their own work and their sources', they also generally challenge students' conception of boundaries, which can be good.

Such assignments redefine the roles of both writers and readers, as well as the activities of writing and reading. These assignments get students involved with their sources and carry them beyond their fears of plagiarism. Students feel confident when they can link to an actual document they used in their research. While it is not always possible to link to the actual document, when students do create a link for the reader, it can literally lead to the citation of the source, if not the actual document.

In the past, I often used my students' knowledge of and experience with hypertext to reinforce the use of citations. I got them to imagine that their in-text citations or references to sources were actual hypertext links (blended into the writing the way artists create a collage) that would take them directly to the citation. As a result of this thinking, they began to see how active readers could read their writing and actually link to their citations—if not the sources themselves. The collage connection, using hypertext, was a way to help students think more creatively and effectively about their own research writing.

Now that I teach in a computer lab, I can actually show my students how to create hypertext links in Word documents and on webpages. I've found that the assignments can be fairly easily developed for composition courses, especially for those taught in computer labs—but they can even be developed when a computer lab is not available. Using the technologies available today and our students' own experience with these technologies, we can assign collage hypertext writing assignments, which engage students in activities requiring them to think critically about their sources of information, the boundaries separating readers from writers and writers from their sources of information, and the role of both writers and readers in the process of knowledge making.

The Collage: Background for Hypertext Research Writing Assignments

To develop effective assignments, I've found it is helpful to draw on what others have been doing. We don't have to recreate the wheel. This chapter is primarily grounded on George P. Landow's "Hypertext as Collage-Writing" (2001, 150–70), an analysis of hypertext as collage, but it also draws from Elbow's body of work, which is familiar and easily at hand.

Both Landow and Elbow use the term *collage*, a word that describes an artistic composition made of various materials glued on a surface, and relate it to writing. The term itself comes from the French word for gluing. For more background on collage, Landow (2001) provides an in-depth definition in his essay. Other composition theorists have used the term in relation to writing as well. Elbow points out that Winston Weathers published the first description of collage writing in *Freshman English News* (now *Composition Studies*) in a 1976 article titled "The Grammars of Style: New Options in Composition." In 1992, Gregory Ulmer linked collage to hypertext by defining the act of hypertext writing as "relying on the remotivation of preexisting fragments in a new context for the production of its own significance" (142). This is exactly what a collage seeks to accomplish. It is also a pretty good description of what we call research writing.

Elbow (1981, 1999) is best known for his use of the term as it relates to "mastering the writing process," a phrase he uses in the title of one of his books (*Writing with Power: Techniques for Mastering the Writing Process*). Elbow encourages writing instructors to employ collage-writing assignments to aid invention (specifically in "looping," a type of prewriting exercise) and before assigning collaborative writing projects to prepare students to build bridges for the interactive demands of working in groups. He sees collage writing as a way for students to quickly take the very best of their writing and revise it through cutting, ordering, and presenting it intuitively. His use of collage is one technique among many that he draws on to teach writing process. He sees it as a form his students are already exposed to every day, through television and newsmedia documentaries, for example. The advertisement-spliced programming students watch on TV is another example. Magazines themselves are a form of collage, not to mention the Internet. Elbow's (1999) instructions for collage writing are as follows:

- Produce or gather as much of your writing on your topic as you can. Go fast, don't worry. Freewriting is a good method. Take thoughts in any order (Option: add fragments of writing by others.)
- Go through what you have and choose the best or potentially best bits— freely cutting to create long and short sections.
- Revise what you have, mostly by cutting, not rewriting. Cut paragraphs and sentences; cut phrases and words. It's amazing what is possible with just cutting.
- Figure out a pleasing order for the bits: perhaps logical, more likely intuitive and associative—maybe even random. (8)

Elbow's collage-writing assignment, whether used by a solo writer or collaboratively, separates the wheat from the chaff, so to speak, and reveals connections, contradictions, and possible patterns. This kind of writing can help student writers who, according to Elbow (1999), "feel pressure always to have a clear 'thesis,'" to avoid "settling for the lowest common denominator point that the various parts of the self can agree on" (13). It can also help student writers who are "tempted to stop writing when they feel perplexed or come across conflicting feelings and ideas, nervously sweeping complications under the rug" (13). When done well, collage writing can present the "drama of thinking" and the "performance of voices" Elbow feels are so vital (13). It isn't a stretch at all to see how collage writing, especially as hypertext, can lead to dynamic research writing.

Writing and Publishing a Research-Writing Assignment Online

When a colleague of mine told me about an assignment he has his students do at the beginning of the semester, I was excited to try it. The first time I developed a project based, in part, on his assignment, it was not designed with collage or hypertext in mind; however, I was teaching in a computer lab and eventually found it more effective to connect the assignment to concepts of collage and hypertext.

The overall project I developed involves three parts: a narrative, an analysis, and an argument. The narrative portion of the project, which was based on my colleague's assignment, involved having the students imagine they were having dinner (or involved in some sort of social engagement) with three key sources (editorialists, for example) who were writing about a controversial, current issue.

The instructions I developed for the narrative asked the students to imagine what the editorialists would say about the issue, based reasonably on what each person wrote in his or her editorial. The objective of this portion of the project was to get students to see their sources as people involved in real issues and to think critically about what they were saying.

To write the narrative, the students had to think critically about the editorialists in order to characterize them, and they had to think about the give-and-take of an oral exchange. To characterize their "characters," the students had to think about what motivated them. Were the sources truly informed? Did they reveal their biases and prejudices? Ultimately, were their points of view important to take into consideration? Why or why not?

Writing the narrative itself was an act of collage writing. The students read their sources and noted key phrasing that they could use to develop the "conversation." I instructed them to make each source clear to the reader through narrative technique and not try to formally document the source material they used. It would be clear from reading the narrative that the narrator was talking to such-and-such editorialist from such-and-such newspaper without having parenthetical citations. Instead of formally documenting this portion of the project, I had the students create hypertexts to the editorials and to the editorialists' personal websites (if available). If a website was not available, I had them hypertext to background information about the editorialist that they characterized, based on research on the author or his or her publication. I encouraged the students to link to anything that they felt would inform and interest their readers about the "characters" in the narrative.

In the analysis, the students were supposed to consider the points the editorialists "raised" in the narrative and write reflectively about them. Here is where they were supposed to articulate what the sources had to say and why. In this section, I had the students document their sources formally, although I encouraged them to think of the citations as hypertext links to the list of documents they were citing.

Again, they were to examine the sources critically during this phase of the project and take into consideration what they learned from their "interaction" with the sources in the narrative assignment. They could bring in information they learned from their background reading to provide more information for the reader about the issue and how the editorialists either did or did not take that information into consideration.

In the argument, the students were supposed to articulate their own (now more fully) informed point of view. They were to sow the seeds for a full-length piece of research writing, which could now be developed from this project. I required formal documentation in this phase of the project, much in the same way as I did in the second phase. At this point, I encouraged the students to seek ways to use sources to educate their readers and to illustrate or support their own point of view.

In all three phases of the project, I encouraged the students to use print and nontraditional resources. I wanted them to get information from a variety of places. Because the issues they were supposed to research were so current, they found Internet news sites helpful. Often, the editorials they read were available online and easy to link to, although they were only available for a limited time.

The project was extremely well received by my students, and it led to some good writing. Toward the end of the semester, I had my students "publish" writing to a website they created using Yahoo! GeoCities' PageBuilder online software. Yahoo! GeoCities is a commercial site that enables students to publish independently, so I didn't have to deal with their files or take up server space of my own. Some students already had their own websites and could publish their work in a variety of other ways. Some students could use such software as Netscape Composer; however, increasingly I'm seeing students publish on their own using Microsoft FrontPage and Macromedia Dreamweaver. Many schools provide students with server space for publishing class-related work online. Students register for the space and maintain their own files. However, the space is limited and sometimes the servers do not support the type of software the students may know how to use. At this time, because most students have not published to the Web and have limited experience with hypertext, the commercial sites, such as Yahoo! GeoCities, can be an effective way to display their work. Whatever the choice, it isn't difficult to get students "published" online.

Because I encouraged my students to use Yahoo! GeoCities, I used it myself to create a "portal" website that linked to my students' pages once they were published. My guidelines for the website assignment included the following:

- It had to have multiple pages.
- It needed a main page serving as a starting point where the student could introduce himself or herself and the purpose for the website.
- It needed to publish a piece of writing arranged on multiple pages with hyperlinks leading to and from each page.
- The sources cited in the paper had to be hyperlinked to the works cited or the references page (depending on the type of documentation used), to quickly carry the reader to the source documentation. If Web-based support was used, hyperlinks had to lead to these sites from the paper. Relevant hyperlinks were also to be used to lead readers to additional credible information created by the student or by others.

Essentially, I've found through these assignments that hypertext *is* collage. Hypertexts are linked, or glued, texts (and other media)—but mostly they are stuck together like sticky notes, because the order the links are opened is up to the reader. It is a pasted-together, open-ended, dynamic composition process that essentially never ends, as long as it is read.

Both Landow and Elbow can be helpful in getting students to recognize the pasted-together, open-ended nature of composition itself. Hypertext writing only makes this nature more explicit. Landow especially recognizes the connection between research and the messy, disconnected process of relating various sources during the writing process, as well as how hypertext writing reveals and embraces this connection. He finds that, along with challenging traditional concepts of reading and writing, hypertext writing helps writers become more aware of their readers. Hypertext, according to Landow (2001), must be made easy for the reader to follow (154). Its works must also be large, made up of multiple pages of material with many links to multiple places, providing the reader with a variety of choices. Finally, hypertext works must enable the reader to become involved—to be able to interact with the hypertext work itself, drawing the reader into the work and involving him or her in the discourse (Landow 2001, 154).

Hypertext research writing enables student writers to expose more explicitly the research behind their own writing—including the research behind traditional texts they use as sources. It also exposes the way discourse distributes authority and power. The hypertext allows the writer to explore and then expose what Landow (2001) calls the "multivocality" of a research project, while "decentering" authority and "inviting a bit of anarchy" (154). Through hypertext, the research-writing project can be viewed as a controlled collaboration between the author and the reader, where the author actually encourages the reader to make his or her own connections. Aesthetically, this process involves the pleasure of linking, juxtaposition, and surprise (Landow 2001, 54–58).

Thus, hypertext produces a new kind of reading, as well as writing. Writing becomes visual as well as alphanumeric, and links our literate tradition back to its oral heritage (Landow 2001, 159). Finally, through the experience of hypertext research writing, student writers can begin to understand how the "changeable jumble of voices" they have been interacting with during their research project can be sequenced into a connective whole that involves readers in the process (Landow 2001, 159).

Reflections for the Future

The conclusion of this chapter brings me back to my student, Chelsea. She effectively addressed my traditional research-writing assignment to use sources in her paper to support her own point of view. However, like many of my students, she was able to do this before taking my class and beginning my assignment. She already understood why we require the use of sources in research writing. But after doing my traditional research-writing assignment, did she learn anything about the nature of discourse and the process of knowledge making? Did she fully realize the multivocality of the sources she raided, from which she pilfered the material she cited in her own writing? And did she learn from my assignment the importance of stepping aside and allowing her reader some autonomy, some power over how he or she will, in turn, make and make use of this knowledge?

I've only begun to use the technologies at hand in the computer lab to teach research writing. As I reflect on what I've been learning about collage and hypertext, I want to continue rethinking my traditional research-writing assignments for freshman composition and take my students beyond their current conceptions of research writing—both negative and positive.

Works Cited

Bolter, Jay D. 1991. *Writing Space: The Computer, Hypertext, and the History of Writing*. Hillsdale, NJ: Lawrence Erlbaum.

Dillard, Annie. 1982. *Living by Fiction*. New York: Harper and Row.

Douglas, Jane Yellowlees. 1998. "Will the Most Reflexive Relativist Please Stand Up: Hypertext, Argument and Relativism." In *Page to Screen: Taking Literacy into the Electronic Era*, edited by Ilana Snyder. London: Routledge.

Elbow, Peter. 2000. "Your Cheatin' Art: A Collage." *Everyone Can Write: Essays Toward a Hopeful Theory of Writing and Teaching Writing*. New York: Oxford University Press. (First published in 1997/98 as "Collage: Your Cheatin' Art," in *Writing on the Edge* 9: 26–40.)

———. 1999. "Using the Collage for Collaborative Writing." *Composition Studies* 27 (1): 7–14.

———. 1981. *Writing with Power: Techniques for Mastering the Writing Process.* Oxford: Oxford University Press.

Haraway, Donna. 1991. "A Cyborg Manifesto: Science, Technology, and Socialist-Feminism in the Late Twentieth Century." *Simians, Cyborgs and Women.* New York: Routledge.

Johnson-Eilola, Johndan. 1994. "Reading and Writing in Hypertext: Vertigo and Euphoria." In *Literacy and Computers: The Complications of Teaching and Learning with Technology*, edited by C. L. Selfe and S. Hilligoss. New York: MLA.

———. 1998. "Negative Spaces: From Production to Connections in Composition." In *Literacy Theory in the Age of the Internet*, edited by Todd Taylor and Irene Ward. New York: Columbia University Press.

Joyce, M. 1990. *afternoon, a story.* Unpublished electronic document, Cambridge, MA: Eastgate Systems.

———. 1998. "New Stories for New Readers: Contour, Coherence and Constructive Hypertext." In *Page to Screen: Taking Literacy into the Electronic Era*, edited by Ilana Snyder. London: Routledge.

Landow, George P. 1994. "What's a Critic to Do? Critical Theory in the Age of Hypertext." In *Hyper/text/theory*, edited by G. P. Landow. Baltimore: Johns Hopkins University Press.

———. 2001. "Hypertext as Collage-Writing." *The Digital Dialectic: New Essays on New Media.* Cambridge: MIT Press.

Lanham, R. A. 1993. *The Electronic Word: Democracy, Technology and the Arts.* Chicago: University of Chicago Press.

Selfe, C. L., and R. J. Selfe. 1994. "The Politics of the Interface: Power and Its Exercise in Electronic Contact Zones." *College Composition and Communication* 45 (4): 480–504.

Snyder, Ilana. 1998. "Beyond the Hype: Reassessing Hypertext." In *Page to Screen: Taking Literacy into the Electronic Era*, edited by Ilana Snyder. London: Routledge.

Ulmer, Gregory. 1992. "Grammatology (in the Stacks) of Hypermedia: A Simulation." In *Literacy Online: The Promise (and Peril) of Reading and Writing with Computers*, edited by Myron C. Tuman. Pittsburgh: University of Pittsburgh Press.

Weathers, Winston. 1976. "The Grammars of Style: New Options in Composition." In *Freshman English News* (Now *Composition Studies*) 4.3: 1–4, 12–18.

PART IV

Research as Collaboration and Service to the Community

11

Agents of Change

Catherine Gabor and Carrie Leverenz

The real learning and teaching with this kind of project cannot be duplicated in the classroom—I can tell students over and over again that employees who work full time and earn minimum wage barely scrape by, and I can point out the various class, race, and gender dynamics, which complicate students' notions that people who work for minimum wage should "go back to school" or work harder to qualify for a better, higher paying job; but my descriptions cannot compare to a face-to-face conversation with a 62-year-old black male, who served in the armed forces, has a wife and two grown sons, has held at least one and often two jobs from the day he was old enough to work, has been sweeping the floor of the student center in a prestigious, private university for over 20 years, and is worth nine dollars/hour to our university's "ethical leaders."
—Teacher of primary-research assignment

Why Conduct Primary Research?

We begin with this comment from a graduate instructor in our composition program (Carrie is director of composition; Cathy is assistant director) because it reflects one of the principal reasons we advocate the inclusion of primary-research assignments in writing classes. When students are asked to plan a research project that requires the systematic gathering and interpretation of data that has not previously been interpreted, they learn in a powerful way that research is rhetorical and that it has the capacity to effect change. Primary research that involves human participants (the kind of primary research we will be focusing on here) teaches other important lessons about both the potential and limits of human agency and the degree to which writing enacts that agency.

Whether teachers view composition courses as the place to prepare students for future academic writing, as a preprofessional training ground, or as a liberal art, primary research can contribute to those aims. For example, honing the ability to collect and analyze data can support future assignments for biology, chemistry, and anthropology as well as other social sciences. In addition, many students will be asked to collect and analyze sources as part of their job—professional consultants survey and interview their client's employees, gather corporate documents, and inductively reason about better business practices. It is not just the hard and social sciences that emphasize primary research skills; with the popularity of service-learning courses, many students conduct community-based primary research in liberal arts courses as well. Regardless of which of these aims composition courses pursue, what is important is that students experience research as a means of knowledge-making.

If the publication of textbooks such as Elizabeth Chiseri-Strater and Bonnie Sunstein's *FieldWorking*, Thomas Deans' *Writing and Community Action*, and John Trimbur's *Call to Write* are any indication, primary-research assignments are becoming increasingly popular in composition courses. This should not be a surprise, since primary research methods have long been key to knowledge-making in the field of composition. From experimental research in the 1960s to protocol analysis in the 1980s to teacher research and community ethnographies in the 1990s, researchers in composition have relied not only on the analysis of secondary sources but also on the systematic collection and interpretation of primary data in order to come to new understandings of writers and writing. Perhaps because for too long composition courses have been seen as a service to other university courses that demand thesis-driven essays based on library sources, only recently have compositionists begun teaching research methods that more closely represent those they themselves use. For example, in *FieldWorking*, Chiseri-Strater and Sunstein, both authors of ethnographic studies, teach students to "step out" of the classroom and conduct field research by offering chapters on different kinds of data-gathering activities that fall under the *primary research* umbrella: archival research, observation, oral histories and interviews, and so on. Also interested in fostering a sense of how language shapes our world outside the classroom, Deans, the author of several important scholarly works on service learning, arranges his textbook around ways of interacting with communities—both local and academic. He helps students see how data can be gathered (and put to use) whether one is writing about a community, writing for a community, or writing with a community. Trimbur, who has long advocated expanding the purview of composition studies to include all kinds of public discourse, focuses his textbook, *The Call to Write,* on various rhetorical exigencies that might lead someone to take action through writing. His textbook features chapters on analyzing public documents with substantive attention to fieldwork practices. Informed by current research methods in composition studies, all three of these textbooks ask students to do research in the context of some larger knowledge-making enterprise rather than as an end in itself.

A number of recent scholarly articles have also argued that student research can have important material consequences. Linda Flower has published extensively about her work with Carnegie Mellon students and the Pittsburgh Community Literacy Center, where students from both groups work together to write documents and prepare presentations that elicit community discussion about contentious issues. In "Sustainable Service Learning Programs," Ellen Cushman insists that for service-learning research to benefit the community as well as students, teacher/scholars and their students should engage in primary research side by side, "studying similar kinds of problems and issues" (55). She persuasively points out that "when the service-learning researcher is on site with students, the teaching, methodology, and research *all* contribute to collaborative inquiry and problem solving with community members" (50). Seth Kahn, who prefers that students conduct ethnographic research that is not part of a service or volunteer arrangement, insists that such research can be a form of action. As Kahn describes it, his approach to student research is "drawn from radical anthropology, one that emphasizes the material implications of engaging in processes of producing and circulating texts, [and] offers students, teachers, and participants in ethnographic research some powerful options for collaborating in processes of grassroots democratic action" (63). Although it may be unrealistic to expect all primary research conducted by students in required composition classes to produce change, we believe that such research can lead students to a stronger sense of agency as researchers and writers and that such agency can lead students to take action.

Material Conditions

For primary-research assignments to be successful, the material conditions of teachers and students need to be considered. Unlike research based on library sources, where library holdings and access to academic databases are the main material concerns, primary research often requires different distributions of time and different kinds of research expertise, as well as access to an appropriate research site or participants. While Cushman's argument for teacher-student research is inspiring, Cushman acknowledges that the material conditions of many composition teachers—graduate students, adjuncts, two-year college instructors with 5-5 loads—prevent them from conducting primary research themselves. Even if the bulk of practitioners had the resources to engage in primary research projects, many do not have the training to do so. Similarly, students who enroll in composition courses while also juggling work and family responsibilities may find it more difficult to schedule interviews, do field research, or distribute surveys than to do Internet searches and write a traditional research paper. However, we contend that primary research is so beneficial to composition pedagogy that it is worth trying even if material conditions are less than ideal. Our goal in this chapter, then, is to give practitioners some ideas for how to teach primary research even if in measured doses, a sense of the benefits that accrue, and the confidence to give it a try.

Doing primary research in a composition class has to make sense in the context of your writing program objectives, your specific pedagogical commitments, and your students. We are aware that at our institution we benefit from several material conditions that help make possible our inclusion of primary research as part of our required sophomore-level course in argument. First, we are both researchers who have conducted primary research, and as such, our definitions of "research" have naturally expanded beyond traditional library and Internet texts to include observation, surveys, the gathering of primary materials, and interviews. Because we have this experience, we can help guide other teachers who are asking their students to do primary research for the first time. For teachers who are themselves new to primary research methods, having sources of information and advice can be crucial to feeling confident about teaching these research methods to students. We offer more specific advice about tapping such resources here.

Although it seems obvious that the research method ought to be determined by the knowledge-making goals of a project, too often students are made to do certain kinds of research only so that they will learn a particular research skill (like how to use microfilm or academic journals). In our view, requiring students to do primary research just so they will learn to do primary research is not likely to lead to student engagement. Instead, the widespread use of primary research in our writing program is tied to a specific assignment, one that asks students to work in groups to research a local problem and propose a solution targeted to a specific audience. The proposal is then presented to the class in a collaboratively authored ten-page written document and also in an oral presentation. This assignment meets several course objectives: that students learn to research and write collaboratively, that they gain experience with oral and visual as well as print rhetorics, and that they engage with what we call "real" rhetoric—rhetoric that is situated in real-life circumstances where effective argument can have material consequences. (See the assignment and course objectives in Chapter 11 of the companion website.) As such, the assignment functions as the culmination of the course, following assignments where students write arguments using both personal experience and library research, analyze argumentative websites, and produce a rhetorical case study of a current controversy.

The use of primary research is especially appropriate to the proposal project, as students explore local problems about which there is little if any secondary material. Although students are encouraged to find library sources that inform them about their subjects (especially about alternate proposals), increase their ethos, and help them situate their local problem in a broader context, typically few authorities beyond the student newspaper have written on their specific subjects (such as lack of racial diversity on our campus, wheelchair access issues, food service monopoly, need for campus recycling, a problem with stray cats, or problems faced by local community partners with whom some students are collaborating). Secondary sources alone would not be enough to convince the local audiences for these proposals that there is a problem that should be addressed. The need for primary research is determined by real audience considerations. For example, one student group, who wrote a proposal addressed to the university chancellor arguing for improved wheelchair access on campus, found their most persuasive evidence came not from research on the Americans with Disabilities Act but from videotaping their own attempts to navigate campus in a wheelchair and interviewing others who use a wheelchair.

Another factor that makes primary research a good choice is that it is particularly amenable to collaboration, which we require of students in the sophomore class. We know from experience and from scholarship that for collaboration to be successful, students must see it as contributing to rather than inhibiting their personal success. If the research project is one that could (more) easily be completed by individuals, then students will resent the requirement to collaborate. In the proposal assignment, students clearly see the benefit of having four or five people distributing surveys, doing interviews, and observing, rather than having to do all of the research themselves. Because primary research is time-consuming and can be challenging for students who are new to this kind of work or are naturally shy, there have to be clear benefits that make it worth the initial discomfort and likely frustration of depending on people to participate in one's research. In the case of our assignment, students are typically invested in trying to solve problems that affect them, and they see that gathering information from other students, faculty, administrators, and community leaders is crucial to making a case for their proposed solution. The means of research is determined by the purpose of the project.

There are also some material conditions specific to our students and campus that make primary research a good option. Our campus is predominantly residential. Students live and socialize together and although many of them work at least part time, they are used to a high level of engagement with each other. Many of our students also own cars, so asking them to do community-based primary research is not a particular hardship. Students with very complicated lives (full-time jobs, families, commuting) may find that the challenges of primary research outweigh the benefits, unless you can help them find ways to do primary research where they live and work—interviewing family members, doing surveys at work (with their employer's permission), and so on. Even though our full-time students may not have the time-management issues described above, when we surveyed teachers about the challenges of teaching primary research, "time to adequately design and complete primary research projects" came up most often. Primary research is most successful when teachers design syllabi that take account of these time demands. Notably, time to (figure out how to) *teach* primary research also came up frequently in the surveys.

Learning—and Teaching—Primary Research Methods

Many writing teachers new to assigning primary research express anxiety about how to do so effectively. Most instructors surveyed worried that students would not collect adequate data and/or would not collect it properly. This worry is exacerbated by teachers' confusion about what to expect when students are asked to do primary research. For example, if teachers are predominantly literature scholars, their understanding of primary research is text-based rather than people-based. One instructor, who was concurrently do-ing archival research for her dissertation, expressed exasperation at needing to help her students "find the one original document that started it all"—a mis-read of the kind of primary research our sophomore composition class intends for students to do that was caused by this teacher's previous experience with primary research. Even those instructors who understood that the proposal as-signment involved researching people, not texts, expressed concerns that stu-dents' research might go astray despite their best efforts to teach ethical data collection or that they would not be able to teach primary research adequately. And teachers who have experience with human participant research may still be anxious about managing (and minimizing) the difficulties students will likely face.

Based on our experience as researchers and as administrators who have helped others teach primary research methods to their students, as well as on the surveys we conducted with teachers in our composition program, we want to recommend three ways that teachers can prepare themselves and their stu-dents to do primary research: 1) by understanding similarities and differences between primary research and library research, 2) by understanding key tenets of Institutional Review Board guidelines for human subjects research, and 3) by pooling knowledge through collaboration with other teachers and students.

Comparing Primary Research to Library Research

One obvious difference between primary research and secondary research is that teachers and students typically have experience doing library research and documenting the kinds of evidence found in libraries, whereas they may have little experience writing survey questions, planning interviews, taking field notes, and writing up their findings. Teachers must build in time to teach stu-dents the research skills they need to perform these tasks and also set aside time to intervene in the research process. Asking students to bring in their re-search experience from other classes can also help bridge the gap between stu-dents' expectations regarding research papers in English classes and the primary research we are recommending. Obviously, explicitly teaching students to do the research we ask them to do and then making sure they know how to do it are key to successful research assignments of any kind. But because some teachers expect students to know how to do library and Internet searches, they do not spend time on such matters in class. Taking a similar stance toward pri-mary research can be especially problematic since mishandling human sources has arguably greater consequences than mishandling texts.

Another important difference is that library research is often deductive (thesis-driven) while primary research is often inductive (question-driven). Though more traditional, library-based research can be inductive when a writer gathers sources to explore a topic without having a thesis or conclusion in mind, many assignments based on library research are still thesis-driven—they begin with a thesis (rather than a question) which the writer uses research to prove. With primary research, the writer cannot begin with a thesis or conclusion since the writer can't possibly know what kind of argument to make prior to doing the research. A writer might believe that there is a problem with inadequate parking or too few minority students on campus or that a local nonprofit agency needs better computer equipment, but the writer who relies on primary research cannot move from that belief to gather sources that support only that claim. Instead, the writer designs a survey to find out what other students, faculty, and staff think of the lack of racial diversity on campus, and if one finds (as some of our students did) that the majority of students at this predominantly white university are happy to go to college with others who are just like them, then the writer has an ethical responsibility to report those findings. (Of course, a good researcher would also interview students from underrepresented groups in order to get a different point of view.) Similarly, arguing for better computer equipment means researching what such equipment would cost and how it might be paid for; if students cannot come up with a feasible means of paying for the new equipment, they have to alter their proposal. Although researchers set out to answer a question rather than prove a point, they do draw conclusions from their data that they hope will be persuasive.

All research is time-intensive, but primary research demands a different kind of time management. Unlike traditional library research, where students are constrained only by the library's hours and the time frame required for interlibrary loan (and Internet searching has lessened both of those constraints), primary research requires that researchers plan surveys, interviews, and observations according to others' schedules, not just their own. There has to be time to have survey questions vetted, copied, and distributed, and time to conduct additional surveys if needed. Interviews have to be scheduled and sometimes rescheduled. The time needed for observation varies depending on what happens at each observation. Once students have gathered this kind of data, it takes time for them to assess what they have. A survey that took days to produce, distribute, and analyze might be boiled down into a single chart or list of percentages, not all of which are relevant. Students cannot wait to analyze data until right before a draft is due because then it will be too late to collect additional data. It is not unusual for students to find in the midst of their research that their ideas about the causes of a problem or their tentative plans for a solution are disproven by their data, necessitating either a change in their ideas about what kind of problem they're looking at or what kind of solution is feasible. As teachers, we see these moments when primary research leads students to change their minds about local problems as the point of doing research—to learn something new—but changing one's mind in the middle of a research project costs students time, and teachers need to plan the schedule with enough time to allow for such changes to occur.

Perhaps most obviously, the evidence students collect in primary research projects differs from library research. Although students may make use of some kinds of traditional print sources, most of the evidence that students marshal in support of their proposals has been gathered not from books or newspapers but from people. Both print sources and human sources must be handled ethically. But evidence from human subjects research can be more complicated to record, analyze, and present. For example, interviews and observations must be recorded reliably; unlike print sources, they cannot be looked up again later to see if the notes made were accurate. If students misuse print sources, we tend to hold them, not us, responsible, whereas if students misuse human sources, we as teachers must assume that responsibility.

Understanding IRB Guidelines

One way to help students understand the special responsibilities entailed when doing research that involves people is by discussing Institutional Review Boards and the National Institutes of Health Guidelines for Human Subjects Research. Although these NIH guidelines were created especially to protect participants in medical and psychological research, researchers who depend on human participants must show that their research complies with these guidelines. All organizations that receive research funding from the federal government (including colleges and universities) must have Institutional Review Boards that review research proposals to ensure that they meet these guidelines. Although students who do not plan to publish their research do not need to submit their research proposals to IRB committees, teachers who ask their students to conduct human participant research should be aware of these guidelines and should ask students to comply with them. Discussing these guidelines helps to educate students about ethical issues in research, and not having these discussions can lead to unpleasant consequences for both teachers and students. For example, one teacher new to primary research told her students that collecting the data was out-of-class homework and that she did not need to know the details. When students went to the student center to distribute a survey regarding campus diversity, they were stopped by a member of the student life staff, who demanded to know who had approved their survey and for what purpose. Although these students were not doing anything illegal, the teacher bore some responsibility for not having the survey approved, including telling students to identify their purpose on the survey form. Teaching students to follow IRB guidelines even when student research does not need to be formally approved by an IRB committee gives teachers and students solid ground to stand on when their research is questioned.

So what guidelines for human subjects research should teachers consider? Perhaps the most important principle is that of *informed consent*. Researchers are responsible for making sure that participants understand who is conducting the research and why. They must also be sure that participants choose to participate freely, having been made aware of both the risks and the benefits. (See the website for sample permission forms and survey introductions that make this principal clear.) Additionally, researchers should take measures to *protect the privacy and confidentiality of research participants.* Surveys should be anonymous; interview participants should be assigned pseudonyms or represented very generally (e.g., "one junior business major commented . . ."). Though arguably little harm is done when students fail to acknowledge that the survey is part of a class project or use the real names of students in their research reports, learning that there are specific conventions for conducting and presenting human participant research helps students see that all research is subject to disciplinary guidelines.

Pooling Resources

If thinking about implementing primary-research assignments in light of these unfamiliar guidelines is a bit daunting, our best advice is to pool your resources. Most obviously, contact your office for research and find out who chairs the IRB at your institution. Although students do not need to get formal permission from the IRB, knowing that such a committee exists helps sensitize students to the ethics of research involving people, especially if IRB members are willing to speak to your class about the importance of the NIH Guidelines for Human Subjects Research. IRB members can also point you to other helpful resources as well as identifying people on campus who conduct primary research. If you are interested in having your students conduct research off-campus, find out if your university has an office or person in charge of service learning who might be able to recommend groups to work with. (Doing research with people whom you are presumably serving has special ethical considerations, such as making sure the research benefits the community, not just the students who need to complete a research assignment.) A community of teachers is another invaluable resource to instructors teaching primary research–based assignments, especially for the first time. If no one in your composition program has asked students to do this kind of research, find someone adventurous who is willing to try primary research–based assignments along with you. Plan to meet regularly to develop handouts and activities and to discuss your students' work. You might even decide to study the experiences you and your students have had with primary research and to share your reflections with a larger group of teachers or a professional organization. (Keep in mind that if you want to be able to publish your research, you will need to submit your project to your campus IRB for approval.) Students, too, can be an important resource. We're happy to report that the teacher we described earlier who didn't want to know how her students were collecting their research data now invites students from previous classes to coteach with her when she introduces the proposal assignment. By asking students to reflect on their research processes, we teachers can learn a lot about the ins and outs of conducting primary research. Sharing those reflections with subsequent classes can help to familiarize wary students with what are often new research activities and gives them the chance to question students who have done what they are being asked to do.

Challenges and Benefits

In light of these special responsibilities of human participant research, students must be made to feel accountable for their research methods and teachers should expect to intervene regularly during the research process—vetting interview and survey questions, reviewing transcripts and field notes—as well as asking students to write reflections of their research experience and share reports of their research-in-process with the rest of the class. During such discussions, teachers may find out that students have naively planned to interview Ku Klux Klan members or that the questions they wish to ask at the local mosque about the position of women could be seen as inappropriate. These are extreme but real examples that illustrate how new such research procedures are for students but also how exciting it can be for them to see the world rather than just the library as a source of knowledge about important issues.

Students are not the only ones who come to see the power of research based on local knowledge and real-world evidence. Even if students abide by all the appropriate procedures for doing primary research, administrators or others in power may be critical of assignments that ask students to investigate the workings of the university or other local sites. For example, during Carrie's first year at her present institution, one group of students wrote a proposal calling for a boycott of the campus food service to protest what they felt were high prices and poor quality. Imagine her surprise when she showed up on campus to find signs everywhere asking students to boycott food services that day. The boycott made the front page of the student newspaper (whose reporters students had contacted), and Carrie had calls from the English department chair, the dean, and the vice provost for student affairs, asking for copies of the assignment and advising her to consider having students research solutions to international problems instead. She assured everyone that actually implementing the proposal was not a requirement and that students had gone forward with the boycott without her knowledge.

This kind of conflict with authority can be especially threatening for teachers who are not tenured or in tenure-track positions and thus more likely to have their authority and autonomy questioned. Just the fear of such a confrontation might be enough to dissuade teachers from initiating a primary research project. To be honest, there is no way to guarantee that teachers and students doing this kind of research can avoid such conflicts (though out of the fifty or sixty sections of this course offered each year, maybe one or two groups encounter conflicts). Clearly, what makes primary research intellectually stimulating—the immediacy of the process and the uncertainty of the outcome—can also make it feel threatening. But if teachers are willing to keep in close contact with students as they conduct their research and to advise students and to intervene if necessary (but only if necessary—students should feel responsible for their data-gathering), the learning that can result is worth the risk, at least in our experience.

For example, one of the most dedicated graduate instructors in our department (and winner of an annual teaching award given to graduate students) emphasized to her students the ethics of data collection, such as stipulating that all surveys and interviews are voluntary. Nevertheless, a group of her students still encountered a challenge from an authority figure. One collaborative group was gathering data to support the writing of a proposal that would argue for an increase in university staff wages. In the beginning of the data-collection process, the two female members of this group went into the university cafeteria and saw a group of cafeteria employees eating together. The students approached them, explained that they were researching staff wages and asked if they were on a break and would be willing to fill out anonymous surveys; all agreed. Five minutes later a man who the students described as "the cafeteria supervisor" walked up to the table, grabbed a survey out of an employee's hand, demanded the rest of the surveys, told the students to leave, and warned that the cafeteria employees could be punished for participating in the research.

Even though the students followed proper protocol, they faced a reality of primary research: external conditions impinge. Their methods were "right," but the *kairos* was wrong. Following the confrontation, the teacher commented that she "wanted to use the situation to impress upon them how important their topic was." So, I told the students that although this incident was perhaps embarrassing and uncomfortable, it was not useless. I asked them how this incident could be used as evidence in their proposal. They decided that they could use the incident as evidence that a problem existed. Some of the students in the class suggested that perhaps the group could still survey the staff after work and/or off-site.

In spite of the special challenges associated with assigning primary research involving human participants in composition classes, we believe that there are important benefits for students, teachers, programs, and institutions. By teaching students to do primary research, we help them see the power of writing as social action, not simply as academic exercise. A well-crafted primary-research assignment can help students see and *use* rhetoric for problem posing and problem solving. With primary research, students must engage with their sources, for they are the only ones with access to them: they are compiling the survey data or transcribing the interview or conducting the observation or writing the field journal. This relationship to the data often leads to strong evidence of engagement among students in both the gathering and presentation of the data. For example, two of Cathy's students working on a research project complained that they could not find any sources in the library about their topic. When Cathy told them that they would need to make phone calls and interview people, they responded by enthusiastically stating: "When we can't find the sources in the library, we can make them ourselves!" While we might quibble about students "making sources," this vignette exemplifies the student-as-agent role that primary-research assignments promote.

Instead of impeding the students' understanding of primary research and how to conduct it, the incident with the cafeteria workers pushed students' knowledge even further. Their instructor describes the most significant benefit to the students: "I think that the students who encountered problems in conducting interviews/surveys/observations due to 'permission' issues learned that research is important, and that knowledge is powerful and at times threatening." One student states that through "incorporat[ing] primary research" she learned that writing a proposal "was to be taken seriously and not just as a part of an English course." In primary research projects, which are so heavily dependent upon local conditions, the classroom environment needs to be flexible enough that students and teachers can learn from arising situations and from each other.

Perhaps not surprisingly, students in Carrie's class identified the food service boycott as one of the most important learning experiences in her class—students saw other students take action to solve a problem. We'll never know whether the boycott would have happened without the primary research students did—the surveys that showed widespread student discontent and willingness to participate in a boycott, the interviews with local restaurants that indicated a willingness to offer student discounts if students could use their meal plan cards there (as students learned happens at other universities). But another student in the group told Carrie how proud she felt when she interviewed the vice provost of student affairs who, expecting an annoying meeting with a disgruntled student, was instead impressed with how much research the student had done prior to the interview.

What do teachers gain from asking students to do primary research? Because for many students these proposals are the first project where they have to make use of primary data and also write collaboratively, students' negotiations of these complex demands don't always lead to the high-quality polished drafts that we would like to see at the end of the semester. However, because the proposals are also presented orally with a visual component, there is often more bang for the buck than a regular ten-page research paper would provide. Obviously, teachers benefit when students are engaged with their work and write papers that teachers actually learn something from.

We also believe that our writing program has benefited from having primary research on a local problem be a visible part of the second-year course curriculum, arguing that such work is closely tied to our institution's mission: "To educate individuals to think and act as ethical leaders and responsible citizens in the global community." In fact, we've been so impressed by the quality of thinking that grows out of students' use of primary research to argue for solutions to local problems that we're looking for ways to enable a more public distribution of the best proposals, perhaps through our composition program's website or even through a public forum where students do poster presentations; display videos; and distribute print copies of their proposals to students, faculty, administrators, and community leaders. Making the proposals even more public will raise new concerns about the reliability of survey and interview data, feasibility, and so on, but making the audience for this project more real and making the proposals even more consequential, we believe, will only improve engagement. And teachers will also learn as they negotiate the ethics of sharing their students' research more publicly. Ultimately, students will learn not just how to do primary research but how to use this research to persuade those in power to make changes. In doing so, they themselves will be acting as agents of change.

Works Cited

Cushman, Ellen. 2002. "Sustainable Service Learning Programs." *College Composition and Communicating* 54: 40–65.

Deans, Thomas. 2003. *Writing and Community Action: A Service-Learning Rhetoric with Readings.* New York: Addison Wesley Longman.

Flower, Linda, Elenore Long, and Lorraine Higgins, eds. 2000. *Learning to Rival: A Literate Practice for Intercultural Inquiry.* Mahwah, NJ: Lawrence Erlbaum.

Kahn, Seth. 2003. "Ethnographic Writing as Grassroots Democratic Action." *Composition Studies* 31(1): 63–81.

Peterson, Melanie. 2003. Personal interview. Texas Christian University, Fort Worth, TX. 15 April.

Sunstein, Bonnie Stone, and Elizabeth Chiseri-Starter. 2002. *FieldWorking: Reading and Writing Research.* Boston: Bedford/St. Martin's.

Trimbur, John. 2003. *The Call to Write, Concise Edition.* New York: Addison Wesley Longman.

12

Creating Successful Research Projects Through Collaboration

Cindy Moore and Peggy O'Neill

Composition scholarship has supported collaboration during the writing process, most often in the form of peer-response groups, since the early 1980s. Kenneth Bruffee (1984), one of its earliest proponents, points out that collaborative learning appeared in the list of suggested CCCC topics for the first time in 1982. By the end of that decade, collaboration was a standard feature in most process-based writing classes.[1] The rationale for collaborative learning, according to Bruffee, is located in theories of social construction, most notably in the ideas of thinkers such as Lev Vygotsky, Thomas Kuhn, and Richard Rorty, who link thought and knowledge to community, conversation, and social interaction (1984, 1999). Bruffee, in his landmark essay "Collaborative Learning and the 'Conversation of Mankind,'" summarizes the rationale for collaboration "for those of us who teach English" this way: If thought is internalized public and social talk, then writing of all kinds is internalized social talk made public and social again. "If thought is internalized conversation, then writing is internalized conversation re-externalized" (1984, 400).

According to Bruffee, writing teachers should engage students in collaborative learning to provide "a context in which students can experience and practice" the kinds of conversation valued by the academic community (400). Through this conversation, students contribute to the production of knowledge, becoming both active learners and active community members.

In addition to the benefits proposed by Bruffee, collaboration in writing classrooms can help students develop both a sense of themselves as writers and an appreciation for diverse viewpoints and experiences. Through collaborative activities such as group brainstorming and peer review, students learn about negotiating time for writing, how to "maintain ownership" for their writing, the necessity of feedback, and the importance of "exposure" to the ideas and experiences of others. In other words, collaboration "invites" students to identify as a writer, to practice the "essential elements" of a writer's life (Brooke 1994, 12–13). Also, because successful collaborations depend on conversation, challenge, and negotiation, they can promote the feelings of empathy and understanding that are so crucial for full participation in increasingly diverse academic (and nonacademic) contexts. Among their reasons for advocating collaborative writing, for example, Kami Day and Michele Eodice (2001) include the potential to promote an ethic of caring. As they suggest, students "don't *learn about* working through differences, finding common ground, and appreciating the strengths of others. They *find* common ground, *work through* differences, and *learn from each other's strengths* as they talk" (emphasis in original, 178).

Another rationale for encouraging collaboration in composition courses is that it has become a common activity in workplace settings, as demonstrated by scholars such as Lisa Ede and Andrea Lunsford (1990), Geoffrey Cross (1994), Ronald Schleifer (1997), Kitty Locker (1992), and others. For example, technical writers in a construction firm described by Ede and Lunsford (1990), use a "complex and highly collaborative process" in researching and writing a document, noting that the "job cannot be done alone" (31). The research typically includes gathering data from engineers, looking at drawings, reviewing material from similar projects, and even disassembling and reassembling a product. With respect to academic contexts, collaboration is also widely accepted. "Multiple authorship" (which involves collaborative research and analysis as well as writing) is now the norm in the natural and social sciences and is becoming more prevalent in the humanities.[2]

In short, there are many good reasons to include collaborative learning opportunities in composition courses. And, given the emphasis on collaborative research and writing in the workplace, there are special—and practical—reasons for encouraging students to work together during the research process. Unfortunately, although composition and rhetoric scholars have recognized the value of collaboration in many realms of professional life, undergraduate students are rarely encouraged to collaborate on research projects, especially in general education courses. Though teachers may acknowledge the many benefits of collaboration in theory, they often have trouble imagining how collaborative research projects might work in their classrooms—what such collaborations might actually look like and how they can be effectively encouraged and assessed. Further, teachers who try to encourage collaboration are often met with resistance from students who lack experience with real collaboration, which demands active participation, a willingness to express and negotiate differences, and shared responsibility for the final product, as Bruffee (1984, 1999), Day and Eodice (2001), and others explain. One potential source of student resistance is that collaboration "skates dangerously close to the supreme academic sin, plagiarism" (Bruffee 1999, 19). As Rebecca Moore Howard (2000) explains, in spite of contemporary theory and research that suggests that all writing is collaborative, the academy and English studies in particular "continue to require originality in student writing" (475). Within this individualistic scheme of writing and learning, working with others—especially during the research process—can be misconstrued as cheating: after all, if a student uses an idea generated by a classmate without "proper citation," the student might feel like she has plagiarized. While we believe that most composition instructors would not categorize collaborative activities as plagiarism, it is important to note that some teachers might. As we suggest later, articulating the difference between collaborating and cheating—what Howard (2000) calls fraud—can be important in helping students commit to collaborations.

In the following pages, we offer many examples of classroom activities for collaboration through all phases of the research-writing process. We also offer practical suggestions for addressing problems associated with collaboration, including inexperience on the part of student collaborators and uncertainty about how to fairly evaluate collaborative work. Please note that we are using the term *collaboration* to indicate an activity that requires students to engage in conversation, contribute ideas, negotiate differences, and take responsibility for the results of a task. Collaborative writing, then, can include one or more phases of composing, from generating ideas to drafting and revising—although, as Day and Eodice (2001) suggest, the benefits of collaboration are most fully realized when participants work together from beginning to end of the research process.

Setting the Stage for Collaboration

Again, although collaboration in college-level writing classrooms has been common for many years, we cannot always assume that our students collaborated much in their high school classes. In fact, students may have been discouraged from working together as a way of ensuring that they were capable of completing assignments on their own. Because of potential inexperience with collaboration and because "collaboration" can indicate many different types of interaction, as noted in the introduction to this chapter, first-year students may need you to define what you mean by collaboration and what you expect from collaborative efforts.

One way to begin defining collaboration for yourself and your students is to distinguish it from other terms or activities. For instance, given that many students have been taught to "do your own work" or "don't look on your neighbor's paper," it might be helpful to point out early on that collaboration is not cheating. For collaboration to be effective, one person doesn't take from another; instead both (or all) parties give to the project in a way that ensures mutual ownership of the final product. Additionally, collaboration should be distinguished from simply sharing ideas, which is a frequent activity in writing classrooms. In sharing, students divulge their ideas or texts and listen to others; they are not required to do much beyond this. Sharing, however, may be a good starting place for real collaboration (as we suggest later).

In addition to defining and distinguishing terms, it can be very helpful to discuss with students the benefits of collaboration. Students need to know not only what they are doing, but why they are doing it. One way of educating students about benefits would be to simply share with them what you have learned through reading about collaboration, encouraging it among students, and, if applicable, through collaborating yourself. Even if you haven't co-authored an essay with a colleague, chances are you have had to collaborate, in some fashion, as part of a university or professional committee. Another strategy would be to actually supply students with a scholarly text on collaboration. Sometimes students simply need to know that an activity or assignment is not just another class requirement, but actually a bona fide teaching method that has received serious attention by scholars, and is promoted by educators as well as business professionals. You could copy and distribute the introduction of this chapter, for example, or some of the articles on the works cited page. Knowing that they will need to collaborate in their writing after college might also help motivate those students resistant to collaboration, which often include high achievers who may have had negative experiences in the past or who may be reluctant to allow other students to do any work. Another strategy would be to plan a simple collaborative activity early in the semester that requires students to solve a problem or answer a question together, using everyone's expertise. A colleague of Cindy's who teaches ESL courses asks students to work in groups to define a familiar concept like "home," "family," or "education." Unless students are from amazingly similar backgrounds (Cindy's colleague's students are not), they will need to negotiate their own experiences with these concepts to arrive at a definition that works for all group members.

Finally, by way of introducing the concept of collaboration, you will want to make your expectations for collaborative activities clear—in terms of both process and product. For example, if collaboration involves give-and-take among all group members, how will you ensure that this actually occurs for students in their groups? An obvious strategy is to provide a guide for collaborative activities that details what group members need to do to contribute positively and productively to the group enterprise. (See sample guides on the website.) Another strategy is to model collaboration for students by, for example, sharing drafts of a collaborative project you have completed or asking some colleagues to help you demonstrate a truly collaborative discussion of an issue or problem. It will be important to highlight both points of consensus and points of discord or tension—places where you and a coauthor disagreed. Without a sense that disagreement is a natural part of many collaborations, students might back off from any potential conflict that arises during collaboration because working through discord can be challenging.

Along with clarifying expectations for the process, it's helpful to let students know what you expect in terms of the end result. If students don't have a clear understanding of what the goal of the collaboration is, they might not take the collaboration seriously. If you want students to break into groups to brainstorm possible research topics, for example, it can be helpful to ask the group to reserve some time at the end of their session to write a brief report on the ideas they generated. If you want students to collaborate on finding and evaluating sources, you might ask them to turn in a coauthored reflection on their process. And if you want to encourage students to actually write a research paper together, it would be helpful to negotiate with them a suitable scope for the paper, including length, and possible number of sources—criteria that reflect your (and, by now, their) understanding of the particular constraints and possibilities that collaborative ventures involve. Such negotiations can occur through a written assignment (e.g., students submit a research proposal and teacher responds in writing) or through a conference between the teacher and collaborators. Additionally (and in the interest of students taking collaboration seriously), you will want to make sure that all collaborative activities count toward students' course grade in some way—an issue we discuss more fully later.

Collaboration During the Invention Phase

Working together during the invention phase of the writing process is something that many composition teachers encourage throughout a semester, whether the assignment is research-oriented or not. It's typical for students to brainstorm topics on their own, for example, and then share possibilities with their peers in order to get more ideas for their papers. Such an activity can be especially helpful for research writing because of the fear students sometimes have about finding and claiming ownership of a topic. A group brainstorming session can help students approach their research feeling that they already have ideas or opinions that they will then work to support or complicate through their research. Another way to share during the invention phase is to publish a class list of topics that students are interested in researching. When Cindy does this, she simply has students go around the room and talk about what they're doing. She then compiles a list of students' names and topics that she copies for the entire class. When distributing the list to the class, she draws her students' attention to any topics that seem closely related, where it might make sense for students to pool their resources. Though, ultimately, you will want students to appreciate the difference between sharing and collaborating, sharing is often a helpful precursor to successful collaboration.

To move students from a simple sharing of ideas to real collaboration, you might ask them to identify a promising topic on their own and then meet with a small group to collaboratively develop research questions or potential sources for one another. You can support this kind of collaboration by holding the entire group accountable for completing the tasks for each group member. When Peggy uses this technique, she asks group members to report to the class on each other's research plan. This encourages group members to engage with and feel responsible for each other.

In first-year composition, a useful collaborative activity at the beginning of the research process is to break students into groups to explore and report on one aspect of the library (including electronic sources). For example, Peggy has used an assignment that required student groups to become "experts" on one library feature or resource and then present their findings to the rest of the class. Presentations included everything from handouts to how-to videos. (See the assignments on the website.) Students in this class actually did individual research projects later in the semester, but they collaborated on learning how to use the university library. Once the library research started, students with questions were directed to the appropriate "experts," so in many ways, the collaboration continued throughout the semester.

Invention for research assignments also includes doing research itself: interviewing, observing, reading articles and books, and surfing the Internet. Collaboration has many practical benefits here, too, especially for novice researchers. Students working on similar topics can explore different databases and compare results. Two people can split a list of interviews and compile notes or, better yet, both attend an interview and compare and analyze their notes. Last semester, for instance, two of Cindy's first-year composition students researched the campus parking problem collaboratively: designing a student survey, sharing responsibility for conducting the survey, and interviewing. Though they wrote two different reports, they used the same research—and in different ways, which made it even more interesting. One student used the research to illustrate the problem and discuss various solutions. The other student used it to make the point that the fees were too high and that money for parking permits and fines wasn't being funneled back into the parking budget, as she (and her classmates) had assumed.

Some teachers will invite students to collaborate as they learn to evaluate sources for credibility and reliability. One possible exercise is to ask students to break into groups and locate a source on a topic they are working on. Then, they are asked to read the source and evaluate it according to criteria, such as audience, purpose, reliability, relevancy, and documentation, before writing a single report for the instructor or class. This activity works especially well with websites because students seem less familiar with reading websites critically. Besides, because they can read websites from different locations and at different times, students often find them easier than print texts to access and review collaboratively. Peggy has used this activity in a networked classroom with each pair of students responsible for finding and evaluating one website to recommend to the rest of the class as a research source. The evaluations with links to the site were posted on the class website, creating a useful resource list for class research.

Another way for students to collaborate during the research-gathering process is through a dialogic journal. For this activity, based on Ann Berthoff's "dialectical notebook" (1988), students take notes individually and then trade journals and comment on each others' notes, asking questions, challenging assertions, and so on. As with any peer-response activity, teachers who wish to encourage dialogic journaling will want to be aware of the tendency for students to simply affirm one another's summaries and evaluations with comments like "Yes!" or "Good point!" instead of really reflecting on and conversing about the research findings.

Collaboration During Drafting and Revising

Working together during the drafting process can take many forms. It can involve a sharing of drafts—and peer response—similar to what happens typically with other papers in most writing classes, or students can actually draft a paper together. The benefits of peer response at the draft stage have been covered elsewhere, so we'd like to focus here on the benefits of drafting together. In our experience, topics that work well for collaborative drafting include those that are complex and often controversial, such as affirmative action in college admissions or same-sex marriages. By not only researching together but also writing together, students are forced to confront and incorporate different people's experiences and points of view, thus moving beyond simplistic pro/con thinking, especially if writing groups are designed to include students with diverse perspectives and opinions. In addition, by coauthoring a text on a sensitive or controversial topic, students can share responsibility for the ideas and opinions, encouraging them to step out of their comfort zone and take a risk by supporting a position or tackling an issue that may be unpopular. With these types of topics, instructors need to be sure that group members are respecting each other, valuing each other's diverse experiences and opinions, and contributing equally to the document's content. To establish coauthoring groups for controversial issues, an instructor can start by having students write independently about their views on several politically charged topics, then create groups based on these preliminary writings that include students with different perspectives.

As an alternative to coauthored texts on hot political topics, you can invite students to consider issues that are less controversial but similarly multifaceted, such as proposing a solution to a real-world problem, which requires the authors to synthesize a variety of information, address a variety of audiences, and write multisection texts. For example, a group of Peggy's students coresearched and wrote a proposal for a new online registration system for the college. The group had to investigate the different kinds of systems available; the needs of the registrar, students, and other interested segments of the campus; and the resources available. They had to identify multiple audiences—from faculty senate to the registrar to the chief financial officer—that would have a voice in the decision and figure out how to address these audiences in one document with multiple sections. Besides helping students appreciate the challenges and benefits of collaboration, tasks like this one introduce students to the kinds of writing required not only in many upper-level classes but also in most workplaces.

Requiring students to draft together can be very challenging—after all, most successful professional academic writers who collaborate often do so by choice, after getting to know one another. We only began collaborating on our research and writing, for example, after taking graduate courses together, working on committees together, and supporting each other through our early years as professors. Encouraging successful drafting collaborations among students is difficult to orchestrate because at the beginning of the semester they may not know each other at all, and at the end of ten or twelve weeks, when extensive research projects often start, they still may not know each other well. Peggy usually waits to assign a collaborative writing project until later in the semester, after students have had the chance to work with lots of different peers across different activities, and after she has a better sense of students' strengths and weaknesses. If you want to assign collaborative writing activities earlier in the semester, you can help students to identify their strengths and weaknesses, which can be valuable for matching students. In a series of quick-writes, students are asked to respond to different questions about their previous writing experiences and habits. It is useful to stress to students that everyone has weaknesses as well as strengths. The idea of the collaboration is to create research teams that can compensate for weaknesses and build on strengths so that the final product is better than if one individual wrote it. Of course, factors such as personality, attendance, and schedules can also be significant variables in creating groups.

In our experience as collaborators, we have found that drafting a piece of writing together—particularly writing that requires substantial research—helps us stay on track, improves the content and style of the final text, and makes the entire process more enjoyable. The process can seem to take more time, however, as we trade drafts, negotiate changes, and rethink ideas or approaches—especially since we work at different universities that are hundreds of miles apart. To facilitate the collaborative drafting process for a recent book-length project, we set deadlines. These deadlines seemed to take on greater import since we felt obligated to the other person to keep them. Our practice looked something like this: After talking or emailing about the topic several times, one of us (usually Peggy) would draft something quickly, and then the other would read it; respond to it; add, cut, rearrange; and then send it back for the other to do the same. We completed four or five rounds of drafting and revising before we worried about sentence style or word choice. This sort of process works really well for collaborators with different writing strengths. In our case, Peggy is generally better at generating ideas or content, while Cindy feels more comfortable dealing with the unity of ideas, organization, emphasis, and style. Both of us, however, are willing to negotiate instead of digging in if we disagree on something.

Other ways that students might approach the collaborative drafting/revising process include assigning parts of a draft to group members to complete individually. If students do this, they need to be sure to allow plenty of time for revising and working out differences in style, tone, voice, or other features of a written text that can be different across writers. Simply pasting together individually written texts doesn't result in a truly collaborative product. While a cut-and-paste effort might constitute an early draft, students need to revise and edit the work into a single text, which is a super way to teach about style, voice, tone, and other features of writing. When Peggy invites students to write this way, she discourages one person from becoming responsible for the editing and proofreading, instead encouraging students to work through the polishing phase together so that the entire group has the opportunity to learn more about concepts such as voice and sentence structure. By working together and negotiating the sentence-level concerns, students learn how to talk about language and appreciate how complicated issues of editing and proofreading can be. If one student is responsible for this phase of the process, the student is usually the strongest writer of the group, which means that the others don't realize the benefits that group writing offers. Besides, negotiations about what at first appear to be only surface-level concerns often lead to discussions about more substantive issues such as rhetorical context, content, and sources.

While we typically compose collaboratively by exchanging drafts and pieces of text electronically and talking on the phone about the text periodically, some students, especially those working in groups of two or three, might prefer to compose together, in real time. One person sits at the computer and the other(s) brainstorm ideas as the typist types. As writers who have tried this approach, too, we find that it works best when collaborators have similar writing processes and perspectives on effective writing. It can be maddening, for example, for someone who is comfortable freewriting during the draft stage to work with someone who must perfect the wording of each sentence before moving on to the next. Another consideration for this type of collaboration is scheduling. Meeting together physically requires that people are available to work at the same time and in the same location. Given their increasingly busy schedules (filled with school, work, and often family responsibilities), students sometimes find it difficult to coordinate schedules. One solution for this dilemma is to allocate class time for collaborative work, either scheduling a work day (no class) or reserving room in a computer lab for drafting.

Another approach to collaborative drafting involves one person writing a preliminary draft, getting responses from others, and then revising according to the responses. This method is very common in business settings. Both of us work this way in our administrative positions, for example, routinely drafting memos of reports, getting responses to them from colleagues, and then revising in terms of the responses.

Again, besides improving the quality of the written text, working with someone else can just make the whole process less daunting. During the process of drafting our book proposal, for instance, when one got tired and frustrated, the other cheered her up; just as one was losing steam, the other would generate a huge amount of material to get us going again. Students who may be learning how to do research at the same time they are learning how to integrate research findings effectively into an academic essay can be overwhelmed by the drafting process. Having someone who is equally responsible for getting the text drafted, revised, and polished can encourage students to take risks and try things they might not on their own. It can also discourage procrastination because students need to plan and schedule time for the collaborative writing. Finally, and perhaps most important, collaborative writing (which often involves meeting outside of school; taking breaks to socialize, laugh, eat, and drink good coffee; and, in the process, making new friends) can be fun.

Collaboration During the Presentation Phase

Although we discussed proofreading and editing in our section on drafting, they need to be emphasized as part of the final phase of the writing process when students are preparing documents for class presentation or instructor evaluation. In this phase, students are focused more on correcting for typos and errors as well as conventions of research writing such as documentation and formatting. Given that most writing classes include attention to peer editing throughout the semester, students should be accustomed to helping each other proofread and correct errors. One difference with research writing is that the collaborators need to pay special attention to citation and documentation. Since there is so much to consider in these areas, the collaborators might want to split up the work. For example, one writer might make sure that the in-text citations follow conventions while another handles the works cited pages. Alternately, a group might divide the proofreading by the kind of editing being done: one person could read for grammatical and mechanical errors, another for accuracy of quotations and paraphrases, and another for proper documentation style.

Another means of collaborating during the final stages of a research project involves preparing a presentation of research for the class. For first-year students, individual presentations can be intimidating, as often they are adjusting to an environment very different from that of their high schools, where they had friends who offered moral support. Group presentations in college-level writing courses can reduce the anxiety for shy students while providing valuable public speaking practice. In addition, students may be more willing to try something new—such as creating a PowerPoint presentation or webpage—if they have partners with whom they can share the perceived risk. Of course, collaborative presentations also provide opportunities for students to showcase strengths, such as artistic talent or technical skill, while downplaying (but still working to improve) weaknesses such as public speaking skills. Group presentations can also be a more efficient way to include oral communication skills as part of a class, because providing enough time for all students to present on their research can be difficult—and even unproductive—for the rest of the class.

Research texts can also be presented to the class through a class anthology—an edited collection of student research writing that brings the collaboration full circle because each student or research team contributes to the whole. A research anthology is a useful way to introduce students to the idea that, in the academy, doing research is not simply an exercise about how to find and document information, but an important part of participating in a community of scholars. A collection like this works especially well if the course has been designed around a theme, so that each individual essay contributes something to understanding the theme. The collection can then become part of the course materials, illustrating extended inquiry and emphasizing rhetorical issues of purpose and audience during the research and drafting processes for both current and future students. Peggy recently used a class anthology as a resource for the final essay in a course. After compiling the anthology of students' individually written researched essays, Peggy asked the class to read the anthology as a whole. She then led a brainstorming session in which the class came up with a long list of potential topics for their final essay assignment. Students chose their own topic, identified the purpose and audience for their essays, and used MLA documentation as they incorporated each others' work from the anthology into their own texts. In short, the students used their peers' work as the sources for an essay on a topic, issue, or theme of their choice. Finally, if students are assigned editorial roles (e.g., reviewer, copy editor, production manager), a class anthology offers a great way for them to further develop critical reading, proofreading, and organizational skills.

Evaluating Collaborative Work

Like any teaching approach or method, collaboration isn't without its potential pitfalls. The most obvious concern for teachers is that all collaborators do their fair share of the work—or, at least, feel as if everyone in the group has contributed equally. Ensuring equity can seem especially crucial with extended research projects because they take more time, require more work, and typically comprise a greater part of the course grade than other writing assignments. In addition to letting students choose whether they wish to collaborate, discussing what it means to really collaborate (and, perhaps, inviting students to read articles about successful collaboration), there are a few things you can do to make collaborations work well. In his eminently useful essay on peer-response groups, "Ensuring the Success of Peer Revision Groups," Edgar H. Thompson (1988) highlights the value of modeling and providing guidance during the first few weeks of class as well as "monitoring" group work throughout the rest of the semester. Such monitoring includes circulating among groups, noting questions and concerns; joining groups and participating in discussions (as a way to both assess group productivity and to model successful behaviors); inviting student assessments of "what worked or didn't work" in particular group sessions; and discussing these struggles and successes with students before they collaborate again.

As a way of monitoring longer-term, collaborative research-writing projects, some teachers require that students turn in weekly progress reports, in which they not only report on group progress, but also assess their own contributions to the project and the contributions of other group members. Besides helping to ensure that all group members are contributing equally, these periodic reports can assist you in identifying (and negotiating) personality conflicts among group members as well as writing/research-related questions that a group may need help answering. An alternative to requiring weekly reports or progress memos is to ask students to keep individual or group research logs that they turn in with their final project. These logs can be collected during the writing process to pin-point problems and again at the end to help you assign grades. Peggy has even used an electronic discussion board for logs so that she can check in periodically and see how groups are functioning. Finally, some teachers rely on group confer-ences to both monitor group progress and help students recognize the many benefits of collaborative work.

The assessment method you choose for collaborative work can also in-fluence how well individual members share responsibility. A group grade can motivate all students to work hard for the benefit of the group, but will only be successful if all of the group members really care about the others in their group. Assigning individual grades, based on group reports and self-evaluations, can motivate group members to fully participate, too, yet such a practice assumes that all students will be motivated to earn a high grade. As most seasoned teachers know, many students are perfectly content with a grade of "C" and will do only the amount of work needed to pass the course. Of course, students who are overly concerned with earning an "A"—and who don't think their peers have anything worthwhile to contribute—can also sabo-tage collaboration, since they can dominate the group and undermine peers' ef-forts. Aware of the problems associated with the two basic approaches to grading, many teachers choose a combination approach, assigning both an in-dividual and group grade for collaborative projects. Peggy has used both ap-proaches but typically assigns one grade to the entire group if students collaborate by choice. When she requires the collaboration, she usually in-cludes both individual and group grades. Whatever approach you choose, it can help to involve students in the evaluation process by negotiating grading criteria with them, encouraging them to discuss and specify expectations for themselves and other group members (in a manner akin to contract grading), and then reporting on their progress (mentioned earlier).

Even with preplanning, choice, and preparation, collaboration may not work out, at least not for all groups. Despite having the best initial intentions, students may find that their personal work styles aren't as flexible as they thought, personality conflicts arise that simply could not have been foreseen, or sometimes extenuating personal circumstances interfere in unexpected ways. Again, regular group reports to the instructor can highlight problems that the teacher can then help the group discuss and solve. If there seems to be no solution, then dissolving the group may be the only viable option. Some groups just can't work—at least, not within the parameters of a college semester. At this point, it might be useful to ask everyone to reflect on the process and what they might have done differently so that the experience isn't dismissed as just another bad encounter with group work. In fact, we suggest building in reflection at the end of the collaboration for you and your students, so that successes (as well as failures) are not attributed to luck or serendipity. Reflection provides participants with the opportunity to acknowledge the effort, commitment, and skills needed to accomplish a collaborative task and to identify their own strengths and weaknesses as participants in the collaborative process.

Notes

[1] See Howard (2001) for an overview of theoretical and pedagogical literature on collaboration in composition studies.

[2] See Day and Eodice (2001), Chapter 2, for an overview of the scholarship on collaborative writing in the academy.

Works Cited

Berthoff, Ann E. 1988. *Forming/Thinking/Writing*. 2nd ed. Portsmouth, NH: Boynton/Cook.

Brooke, Robert. 1994. "Invitations to a Writer's Life: Guidelines for Designing Small-Group Writing Classes." In *Small Groups in Writing Workshops: Invitations to a Writer's Life*, edited by Robert Brooke, Ruth Mirtz, and Rick Evans. Urbana, IL: NCTE.

Bruffee, Kenneth A. 1984. "Collaborative Learning and the 'Conversation of Mankind.'" *College English* 46 (7): 635–52. Rptd. in *Cross-Talk in Comp Theory: A Reader,* edited by Victor Villanueva, 393–414. Urbana, IL: NCTE, 1997.

———. 1999. *Collaborative Learning: Higher Education, Interdependence, and the Authority of Knowledge*. 2nd ed. Baltimore: Johns Hopkins University Press.

Cross, Geoffrey. 1994. *Collaboration and Conflict: A Contextual Exploration of Group Writing and Positive Emphasis*. Cresskill, NJ: Hampton Press.

Day, Kami, and Michele Eodice. 2001. *(First Person)2: A Study of Co-Authoring in the Academy*. Logan, UT: Utah State University Press.

Ede, Lisa, and Andrea Lunsford. 1990. *Singular Texts/Plural Authors: Perspectives on Collaborative Writing*. Carbondale, IL: Southern Illinois University Press.

Howard, Rebecca Moore. 2000. "Sexuality, Textuality: The Cultural Work of Plagiarism." *College English* 62 (4): 473–91.

———. 2001. "Collaborative Pedagogy." In *Guide to Composition Pedagogies*, edited by Gary Tate, Amy Rupiper, and Kurt Schick, 54–70. New York: Oxford University Press.

Locker, Kitty. 1992. "What Makes a Collaborative Writing Team Successful? A Case Study of Lawyers and Social Service Workers in a State Agency." In *New Visions of Collaborative Writing*, edited by Janis Forman, 37–62. Portsmouth, NH: Boynton/Cook.

Schleifer, Ronald. 1997. "Disciplinarity and Collaboration in the Sciences and Humanities." *College English* 59 (4): 141–48.

Thompson, Edgar H. 1988. "Ensuring the Success of Peer Revision Groups." In *Focus on Collaborative Learning*, edited by Jeff Golub and the Committee on Classroom Practices. Classroom Practices in Teaching English Series. Urbana, IL: NCTE.

13

Moving Writing Out of the Classroom
An Appeal for Community Literacy Composition Pedagogies

Kenneth R. Wright

In his dialog, *De Oratore,* Cicero describes his view of the "general education" curriculum necessary for producing the perfect orator:

> We must also read the poets, acquaint ourselves with histories, study and pe-
> ruse the masters and authors in every excellent art, and by way of practice
> praise, expound, emend, criticize, and confute them; we must argue every
> question on both sides, and bring out on every topic whatever points can be
> deemed plausible; besides this we must become learned in the common law
> and familiar with the statutes, and must contemplate all the olden times [i.e.,
> history], and investigate the ways of the senate, political philosophy, the
> rights of allies, the treaties and conventions, and the policy of empire; and
> lastly we have to cull from all the forms of pleasantry, a certain charm of
> humour, with which to give a sprinkle of salt, as it were, to all of our dis-
> course. (1970, I.xxxiv)

A demanding courseload, no doubt, and to top it off, a requirement to be hu-
morous. Of course, few in Cicero's time received any education, much less
such an extensive one; and few of today's students, in this era when college
costs and career imperatives require students to (over?) specialize, would be
willing to take on Cicero's version of general education. Also, most students,
and perhaps most university faculty, would likely find Cicero's implied
curricular hierarchy disturbing; for he places all other subjects in service to
rhetoric, the primary function of which is to prepare students for participatory

civic life. Well, Cicero wrote more than two thousand years ago, and, of course, things have changed. Colleges and universities now primarily prepare students for employment or for further schooling, with preparation for partici- patory citizenship being a distant secondary objective, if it exists as an objec- tive at all. Rhetoric, through college and university composition courses, now serves general education and upper-division courses as the site wherein stu- dents "learn" to write for college.

However, I am not about to suggest (at least not out loud) that we adopt Cicero's hierarchy. Cicero came from humble beginnings, but rhetorical educa- tion in his time was almost solely reserved for the male elite; it was used as a means of gaining and maintaining power, and was only slightly tinted with the Greek democratic (though patriarchal) ideals of rhetoric's origins. Therefore, it was not related to our society's shared belief, however poorly implemented, that each citizen has an equal say in how the society operates. What I would like to suggest, though, is that Cicero's concept of the proper education for an orator implies two important functions for rhetorical education that can inform modern composition pedagogy. First, because rhetorical education prepares students for civic life, it focuses on preparing students for agency in the nonacademic or civic community. Second, as Cicero implies through his suggestion about hu- mor, effective rhetorical practice requires a rhetor to suit his or her discourses to audience and occasion, to season them, so to speak, so that rhetor and audience achieve a reciprocal relationship. Or, in the words of Wayne Booth, "Rhetoric at its best has always been the art of revealing connections—'relevancies'—that other men [sic] have longed for but ignored" (1970, 46). Whether we call it achieving reciprocity or revealing relevancies, rhetoric is a communal art in which rhetor and audience mutually create a working literacy for application to questions that the community has a vested interest in answering.

In the next section of this essay, "Composition's Inward Focus," I will ask readers to consider developing community-literacy approaches to composition instruction that more nearly match Cicero's view of rhetorical education.[1] I will argue that this change is necessary because composition instruction, as it cur- rently operates, generally possesses an "inward" focus. What I mean by "in- ward" focus is that current composition pedagogies tend to serve the internal needs of the academy because they focus on teaching students to produce writ- ten discourse acceptable to the academy but not necessarily connected to stu- dents' pre- or postcollege lives. Following that, I will discuss the concept of community literacy in practice by exploring its use by myself and other practitio- ners in composition courses. What I hope to demonstrate is that community- literacy pedagogies can tie student research and writing to both the academic and civic realms.

Composition's Inward Focus

In their essay, "Service-Learning: Bridging the Gap Between the Real World and the Composition Classroom," Wade Dorman and Susann Fox Dorman

(1997) argue that current composition instruction alienates students from meaningful interaction with civic discourse because it "divorces the classroom from the real world" (120). Therefore, lacking reasons for writing other than that their teachers have given them assignments, students "give up being motivated by their own authentic needs and interests as individuals in the world, becoming consumers of learning predigested and packaged by well-intentioned experts" (120). What Dorman and Dorman expose is an education-as-product model encouraged by inwardly focused composition pedagogies. Composition provides a product, academic discourse, to its consumers, the students. As it is with all producers, composition attempts to form its consumers' values to make the product more appealing. Composition makes academic discourse appealing by claiming it is what students need to get through college (true enough if getting our students through college is our only goal), and it supports that claim through required writing courses. The problem with this structure is that academic discourse, if it can be taught at all, serves few rhetorical functions in the students' lives because it is only tenuously connected to the discourses they will use and experience once they leave college. Yet colleges evaluate students, sometimes denying them advancement, based on their abilities to meet discourse standards that most students can only view as artificial. It is no wonder, then, that Dorman and Dorman find students unmotivated by their own needs: instead of active composing in response to conditions arising in their lives, students write merely to fulfill assignments serving the academy's needs.

In the previous paragraph, I alluded to an exclusionary function residing in contemporary writing pedagogies. That function bears examination because when postsecondary schools developed writing courses near the end of the nineteenth century, they may have embedded exclusion into composition's practices, and that exclusion, as Sharon Crowley claims, still pervades those practices:

> This [nineteenth-century composition ethic] is the instrumental service ethic of the required composition course: to make student writing available for surveillance until it can be certified to conform to whatever standards are deemed to mark it, and its authors, as suitable for admission to the discourses of the academy. When the Harvard overseers instituted English A, the target language was that spoken by the genteel white male upper class. Today, the target language is called "academic discourse." (1998, 253)

To address these problems, Crowley suggests abolishing the universal writing requirement because it "has obscured the potential of composition instruction at the college level, and it has delayed the development of composition studies as well" (262). Moreover, Crowley claims that composition participates, through holding on to its traditional service ethic, in maintaining its low status within the academy "precisely because its work is perceived to be instrumental, even remedial" (254). First-year writing is the only course tasked by colleges and universities to perform the impossible: teach students a general written discourse that somehow encompasses the discourses of all academic fields so that they will be able to reproduce those field discourses when they write for their other college courses. The absurdity of composition's situation, when it is compared to other required courses such as mathematics, stands plain. Students are not required to take math so as to reproduce math in their, say, literature courses, but in order that they have the math skills necessary for them to succeed after college. It is true, of course, that many lower-level courses serve the needs of later courses, as with math, but their ultimate goals are to provide students with skills for postcollege life. Yet this untenable situation persists in composition pedagogies, in the only course students are likely to take that even touches upon rhetoric of the civic scope envisioned by Cicero.

Like Crowley, who asserts that "we have, in ancient rhetorics, model theories of composing" (263), I see a way for composition to gain the ability to operate in civic space through a return to many of the principles of Classical rhetoric. In fact, her curriculum (readings in the history and politics of education, literacy, and rhetoric) for upper-division elective courses is very similar to the curriculum I envision for first-year composition. However, to make rhetorical operations in civic space a topic for classroom discussion, I would require students to enter that space through volunteering some time each academic term to nonprofit organizations so that they, the students, might experience the rhetorics operating in off-campus communities. Where Crowley and I differ is in determining which students would receive instruction in rhetoric. I believe that students in first-year writing courses should study both rhetoric as a subject and the rhetorics operating in off-campus communities, and I think Crowley actually supports my approach when she states, "[T]he composing principles taught in ancient rhetorical theories were fully situated in public occasions" (263). If rhetoric is "fully situated in public occasions," then colleges and universities have a responsibility to teach students, through required writing courses, the rhetoric necessary for them to adequately participate in those occasions. Classroom instruction in the principles of Classical rhetoric will provide students with the tools necessary for them to produce and critique arguments in public space, and by adding community-literacy service requirements to composition pedagogies, students will gain practical experience applying their learning in the nonacademic community.

Community Literacy and Composition

I want to begin this section by defining *community literacy* as I use the term. Writ large, community literacy is the ability to adequately manage the discourses of the communities in which one works, plays, and lives. In other words, community literacy is the ability to understand, be understood in, and to analyze for clarification of misunderstandings the discourses tethered to one's communities. Understanding and analysis are dynamic cognitive functions. When focused on the discourses of one's communities they become socially dynamic operatives that, drawing on the work of Wayne Campbell Peck, Linda Flower, and Loraine Higgins, function to "yoke community action with intercultural education, strategic thinking and problem solving, and with observation-based research and theory building" (1995, 200). Community literacy seeks to familiarize students with the intercultural rhetorical structures that lead both to conflict and cooperation among our society's diverse communities and to encourage students to participate in the rhetorical practices of the communities they will encounter and join during their lives. Literacy, as Richard Ohmann contends, is an activity "of social groups, and a necessary feature of some kinds of social organizations. Like every other human activity or product, it embeds social relations within it" (1987, 226). Peck, Flower, and Higgins foreground these social relations through "the work of a community/university collaborative whose home base is a settlement house and whose mission entails collaborative problem solving in the community" (1995, 201). The Center's clients (hereafter called Writers) live in the neighborhood. They come to the Center because they want assistance in forming discourses or literacies that those in city government or on school boards or in the business community can hear. Carnegie Mellon students (hereafter called Mentors) volunteer through the university to aid the Writers in these endeavors. The Mentors and the Writers share the experience of participating in "a community discourse in the making that they [all] struggle to enter" (200). The mutual struggle to enter that "community discourse" requires Writers and Mentors to negotiate its structure. That negotiation demands that all parties risk moving away from their familiar discourse structures. However, from taking that risk, the community becomes more cohesive through the reciprocal relationship the Writers and Mentors have created.

According to Peck, Flower, and Higgins, community literacy has four aims: "first and foremost, community literacy supports *social change*" (205, emphasis in original). It is a "problem solving" literacy in that the community members "use writing not as an end in itself, but literally to compose themselves for action" (205). Community literacy's second aim "is to support genuine, intercultural conversation" (205). Carnegie Mellon students foster this conversation by moving "out of their own comfort zone of academic practice and campus realities" (200) to socialize their orientations in relation to the Community House Writers. Third, community literacy should "bring a strategic approach to this conversation and to support people in developing new strategies for decision-making" (205). This aim may be the most difficult to achieve, for it depends on both the Mentors and the Writers' identifying with each other's discourses. Nevertheless, when the connection occurs, it empowers *both* Writers and Mentors.

Empowerment, as defined by Ellen Cushman, is enabling another to reach his or her goals (1996, 14). She found, while working as a literacy tutor, that empowerment through reciprocity can occur between university students and community members:

> As I write my dissertation, they [the neighborhood residents] add, clarify, and question. In some very important ways, we collaborate in this research. [. . .] They have given me the right to represent them to you and have facilitated my work in doing so. They've also lent me their status. They've legitimized my presence in their neighborhood. [. . .] Through reciprocity, they enabled me to come closer to achieving my goal every day. (17)

Without reciprocal empowerment, students participating in community literacy programs may come to perceive themselves as bearers of knowledge to the less fortunate, making the community a site from which students mine essay topics for their writing classes. I cannot overestimate the importance to our students and our communities of this reciprocity. From it community members and students gain new perspectives on how their discourses operate to help or inhibit them in attaining their goals. In addition, attending to reciprocity is another way that composition can connect with the larger community. For providing the community with volunteers trained in the effective use of language, while relaxing its grip on student discourse to facilitate a faithfully negotiated community/university discourse, composition would receive back students who have experienced rhetoric in its civic applications. In other words, composition would receive students who bring community rhetorics back to their classrooms to enrich composition theory and to expand our understanding of society's rhetorical operations.

Community literacy's fourth aim turns it toward the academy because it is based on reflection, analysis, and research. The fourth aim is "to openly acknowledge not only the difficulty of empathy and the history of failed conversations, but to purposefully examine the genuine conflicts, assumptions, and practices we bring to these new partnerships" (Peck, Flower, and Higgins 1995, 205). In addition, this aim combines scholarship with community service, through analyses of "conflicts, assumptions, and practices," to encourage the Mentors to critique social conditions through their writing instead of focusing on the Writers' individual situations.

Explaining how to combine academic "reflection, analysis, and research" with community service is problematic, for local distinctions (the curricular and administrative structures of a particular college or university plus the specific service needs of its surrounding community) make all such explanations site specific, and, therefore, of limited usefulness. However, examining how teachers have incorporated community literacy or service learning into their classroom practices can inform our pedagogical choices. At James Madison University in Harrisonburg, Virginia, where I work, community literacy in writing classes is in its infancy. I have twice taught a writing course that incorporated community service with academic work, one each during the past two fall semesters. The JMU administration strongly supports service learning, a must for any college or university faculty member thinking of incorporating service into his or her courses, but because Harrisonburg is relatively small (population 30,000) and because first-year students are not allowed to have automobiles, finding service opportunities and getting students to service sites proved difficult.

The first semester, I had my students tutor elementary school children for a local migrant worker education program, and while my students enjoyed it, it put quite a strain on the organization and the parents because the children had to be brought to their tutors rather than the tutors traveling to them, as is normally the case. I have no doubt my students gained an understanding of the value of a literacy that they take for granted, and I believe that the children were helped to some extent, but it does not help an organization assist its clients if I add scheduling and travel hassles to the clients' already difficult lives just so my students can experience "helping." Also, I discovered that I, as a member of the university community, had a limited understanding of the non-academic community in which I live and into which I sent my students. Harrisonburg and JMU exist in a wide "town/gown" separation, as is the case in many places, and I learned during the course of the semester that my students (and I) gave somewhat the impression that we were "missionaries" come to enlighten those living in darkness. Also, nearly all my students are not from Harrisonburg (going to college in one's hometown appears to be anathema these days), so my students were being thrust into service and civic environments that were totally new to them.

Therefore, for the second semester I had my students enter the community in a less obtrusive manner by performing service containing elements very familiar to them. They were required to visit a number of the local high school's senior English classes (the high school is within walking distance of JMU's residence halls) to give presentations on applying for college (at the semester's beginning) and what being in college is like (at the semester's end). But before sending them off to the high school, I developed a relationship with two high school English teachers in order to diminish the "missionary effect." Now I admit that giving advice to high school students about college has far less social significance than tutoring the children of migrant workers, but this first entry into the community by doing something familiar, and relatively easy, has led many of my students to continue their service into the next semester, doing what one might call more socially valuable work with organizations such as a local food bank and women's center. Also, visiting the high school informed the course readings, and subsequent research-based writings, on education, the general topic for the essay unit.

This structure reverses the traditional receive-assignment-go-to-library pattern for composition courses because my students' initial research occurred off campus during their hour or so in the high school. I asked them to pay attention to what went on in the high school both outside the classroom as we waited in the hall and inside when they were, more or less, in the teacher's position. Knowing that at some future point my students are likely to be sending their own children to high school, I wanted them to note verbal and nonverbal communication activities within the high school and consider what they thought about them from an observer's rather than student's position. Then, during the classroom meeting following their presentation at the high school, we discussed how they believed their audience had responded to their presentations as well as their observations during their visit at the high school. We also discussed the similarities and differences between their high school experiences and the experiences, briefly observed, of the local students—even going so far as to touch upon the social hierarchies within high schools and the use of slang among young people. Part of my reason for holding these discussions was to encourage my students to reflect upon the rhetorical effectiveness of their presentations, of course, but the main reason for the discussions was to help my students choose an education-related issue on which to research and write. Their issues, however, did not come from a list of topics prepared by me, but rather from the students themselves, based on present and past experiences in the off-campus community; and through "batting around" their ideas during our discussion, they began to modify and develop support for their ideas before starting formal academic research. I have found that when students move through such a process, they are more likely to write on issues important to them, more likely to use research materials to support their arguments rather than "make" their arguments for them, and more likely to produce well-reasoned arguments because they have a personal investment in the issues.

For example, during our discussion class member Stephanie Trilling discovered the germ-idea for her essay when we touched on the way high school students today use the word *gay* to mean "'dumb' or 'stupid'" (Trilling 2002, 2). She chose to open her essay with a personal anecdote describing an act of "gay bashing" by a young man with whom she worked in her part-time job during her final year of high school. However, her essay quickly shifts in tone from the personal to the academic when she begins to incorporate her research into her writing, and Stephanie's final version became a fairly compelling examination of how language usage may contribute to homophobia and heterosexism. J. R. Slosson, a student in the same class as Stephanie, followed a similar path to his essay's final version. After considering the educational environment he might wish for his children, he began to wonder about the ethics of place-based advertising in public schools. J. R.'s starting point was his personal opinion that there is something "not quite right" about advertising in schools, and he began to formulate support for his opinion during our in-class discussions. Then, through his research into the perhaps not so "philanthropic motives" of "place-based" advertisers like Channel One and the Scholastic Teen Network (2002, 1), he discovered that children may be emotionally harmed from the social pressure to possess the products advertised and the materialist ideology that the ads, often disguised as news, promote. (Stephanie's and J. R.'s essays may be viewed at this volume's companion website.)

J. R.'s essay differs from Stephanie's in voice and structure in that J. R. choose to write in the academic third person and to employ a generally syllogistic progression of assertions followed by proofs. However, I would claim that both essays make strong, research-supported arguments appropriate to academia and society. As mentioned, Stephanie chose to open with a personal anecdote informally delivered, and while her writing's formality does increase somewhat when she begins to incorporate sources into her writing, she never fully moves away from directly addressing her readers, and she recalls the opening anecdote in her conclusion. I believe this approach works well for her argument because, unlike J. R. who is attempting to demonstrate to his readers that place-based advertising is harmful to children, Stephanie must convince her readers that their unexamined use of language and acceptance of stereotypes contribute to homophobia, thus requiring Stephanie to employ a more "comradely" ethos than J. R. What is most important, pedagogically speaking, for writing teachers is not that Stephanie and J. R. successfully composed academic essays incorporating research, though I am pleased about that; rather, it is the paths they followed during their composing processes. The issues both writers chose to tackle arose from their experiences outside academia, from something they observed in the world, so to speak; and, recalling Dorman and Dorman, they were "motivated by their own authentic needs and interests as individuals in the world" (1997, 120) to respond to these issues in hopes of changing the world.

In constructing the community-literacy curriculum for the course in which Stephanie and J. R. were enrolled, I was guided by the following three questions and by a service-learning program at Michigan State University (described later). The first guiding question is, Will the pedagogy give students, through volunteer work, experience interacting with the rhetorics of various extra-academic communities? From this volunteer work, I want students to learn how communities make decisions, set policies, and negotiate interactions with other communities. If, as Kurt Spellmeyer claims, composition in "the university fails to promote an awareness of the human 'world' as a common historical *project* and not simply as a state of nature to which we must adjust ourselves" (1991, 73, emphasis in original), then volunteer work can foreground in the students' experiences an understanding that cultural structures are not inevitable but created through the social and political acts of their fellow humans.

The second guiding question is, Will the pedagogy foster democratic social change? The responsibility for promoting said change, as implied by John Dewey, indeed lies with the culture's educational system: "The moral responsibility of the school, and of those who conduct it, is to society. The school is fundamentally an institution erected by society to do a certain specific work— to exercise a certain specific function in maintaining life and advancing the welfare of society" (1909/1975, 7). Community-literacy pedagogies would meet that responsibility because participating students and community members would combine the rhetoric of the academy with community rhetorics to advance society's welfare by solving local problems. One reciprocity derived from this cooperation includes an increase in the rhetorical effectiveness of the nonacademic community's discourse through its members learning to engage in rhetorical acts that consider audience and occasion. In addition, students experience the active application of their individual and academic literacies as they work within those communities.

In their essay, "The Write for Your Life Project: Learning to Serve by Serving to Learn," Patricia Lambert Stock and Janet Swenson provide an example of reciprocal community literacy from their work at Michigan State University. The Write for Your Life Project, state Stock and Swenson, was designed to keep the maxim "literacy is learned through use across cultural contexts and over a lifetime" (1997, 153) foregrounded as the project's guiding statement. The project's mission includes "working to improve the quality of literacy in MSU, to developing new knowledge, and to serving the public good [by reaching] out to involve itself in the teaching and uses of literacy in both the communities and schools from which MSU students come" (153). Students involved in the Write for Your Life Project "define issues that concern them," and through "this process, students transform their preoccupations into the occupation of their studies" (154). Student writing in the Write for Your Life Project takes narrative form initially (153), but it becomes academic research writing when teachers assign, among other texts, "media reports, medical reports, and sociological studies" (155) as source texts for the students' writing. This results in the students becoming "local 'experts,' capable of informing their peers about their expertise" (155). In addition, "the MSU Writing Center publishes these writings and distributes them in students' home communities and across Write for Your Life classrooms" (155). (The Write for Your Life Project has collaborative projects operating on university campuses in eleven states besides Michigan.)

The effect of student research followed by publication is to connect learning with social action to create a community literacy through which students and community members operate together to solve local problems. An example of this connection's realization was the publication and distribution in her doctor's waiting room of an MSU student's research into the causes of anorexia (155). Stock and Swenson "recognize this student's writing not only as evidence of the student's learning and literacy development but also as a service to others who might benefit from her experience and her learning" (155). She, through combining her academic work with service, contributed to the community literacy surrounding the problem of anorexia by adding her learning to that of others seeking solutions to this problem. Students in the Write for Your Life Project typically become deeply involved in their local communities, with some even serving on "community foundation boards" (156), and the connections between their academic and civic work have effected tangible positive changes in the students' local communities. In 1995 and 1996, no fewer than ten grant proposals—from recycling programs to graffiti-reduction programs—were funded in the communities participating in the MSU Write for Your Life Project (158). Each grant proposal started as a student narrative about an issue in which the student was interested, and, through research combined with community service, these proposals evolved into reciprocal community literacies in which both students and communities empowered one another toward reaching their respective goals.

The third guiding question is, Will the pedagogy require sufficient scholarly writing from the students? My personal approach is to teach writing by teaching critical analyses of community discourses *and* of class readings in the history and politics of rhetoric, literacy, and education. This closely resembles Crowley's proposal for upper-division courses in composing. The difference, stated previously, is that I place this pedagogy in required, lower-division writing classes because colleges and universities have a responsibility to train all students to communicate well with nonacademic communities. In modifying and redirecting Crowley's curriculum, I part company with some applications of the service-learning model for composition. Service-learning practitioners usually require their students to volunteer time to off-campus organizations, and my pedagogy includes that component as well but shies away from writing assignments that are, under some service-learning approaches, often not much more than the students' impressions about the organizations in which they work. As Bruce Herzberg states, "[T]he connection [of volunteer work] to composition is by no means obvious. It is all too easy to ask students to write journal entries and reaction papers, to assign narratives and extort confessions ['I never knew the homeless were just like me!'], and to let it go at that" (1994, 309). Without practice in critical analysis or the experience of using language to act in the world, students will not learn how social structures and ideologies lead to conditions like homelessness or illiteracy. Nor will they learn that they can actively use language to do something about those and similar conditions.

In addition to the concerns just mentioned, I am also concerned that service-learning approaches that do not balance service with critical analyses of social structures can lead students to adopt classist attitudes. It is all too easy for students to "attribute all attitudes, behavior, and material conditions to an individual rather than [a] social source" (312). I chose the concept of community literacy to alleviate this problem because, as mentioned before, community literacy is a dynamic social process encompassing all public discourse. And, as C. H. Knoblauch reminds us, literacy "is always literacy for something—for professional competence in a technological world, for civic responsibility and the preservation of heritage, for personal growth and self-fulfillment, for social and political change" (1990, 75–76). Therefore, literacy within any one community is always contingent upon that community's discourse and its social aims, thus making literacy an act of continual negotiation between members within communities and between communities themselves.

Conclusion

I want to return briefly to Cicero's "gen ed" curriculum, specifically to what he does not mention: that a rhetorical education encourages civic participation. Cicero said nothing about civic participation because it was a given. Roman students studied rhetoric and the subjects supporting it because such schooling was necessary "in order to play a significant role in Roman society" (Herrick 2001, 92). That is not to say that today's college graduates do not play significant roles in our society, nor is it to ignore the fact that Roman students' motives for studying rhetoric included elements of elitism and a desire for political power. Nevertheless, the roles for which we prepare our students generally consist of economic roles, workplace roles, and not the role of citizens who participate in the decision-making processes of our society (one need only check voter turnout statistics to see evidence of the preceding); and while colleges and universities do have the responsibility to prepare students to succeed in their chosen fields, I would argue that they also have the responsibility to train them, and encourage them, to be participatory citizens. Because they combine academic reading and research with community service, community literacy composition pedagogies can help colleges and universities meet both responsibilities.

Note

[1]What I call "community literacy" is called "service learning" by many. While deciding between the terms, I was influenced by the word *service* and the implications using that term might have when connected to the field of composition, already considered a field that provides service courses to the academy. However, in choosing "community literacy," I risk confusion later in this work when I reference essays describing specific service-learning projects. Therefore, unless I expressly contrast them, the two terms should be considered interchangeable.

Works Cited

Booth, W. C. 1970. *Now Don't Try to Reason with Me: Essays and Ironies for a Credulous Age.* Chicago: University of Chicago Press.

Cicero. 1970. *Cicero on Oratory and Orators*, edited and translated by J. S. Watson. Carbondale, IL: Southern Illinois University Press.

Crowley, S. 1998. *Composition in the University: Historical and Polemical Essays.* Pittsburgh: University of Pittsburgh Press.

Cushman, E. 1996. "The Rhetorician as an Agent of Social Change." *College Composition and Communication* 47 (1): 7–28.

Dewey, J. 1909/1975. *Moral Principles in Education.* Carbondale, IL: Southern Illinois University Press.

Dorman, W., and S. F. Dorman. 1997. "Service-Learning: Bridging the Gap Between the Real World and the Composition Classroom." In *Writing the Community: Concepts of Service-Learning in Composition*, edited by L. Adler-Kassner, R. Crooks, and A. Watters, 119–32. Urbana, IL: NCTE.

Herrick, J. A. 2001. *The History and Theory of Rhetoric.* 2nd ed. Boston: Allyn and Bacon.

Herzberg, B. 1994. "Community Service and Critical Teaching." *College Composition and Communication* 45: 307–19.

Knoblauch, C. H. 1990. "Literacy and the Politics of Education." In *The Right to Literacy*, edited by A. A. Lunsford, H. Moglen, and J. Slevin, 74–80. New York: MLA.

Ohmann, R. 1987. *The Politics of Letters.* Middleton, CT: Wesleyan University Press.

Peck, W., L. Flower, and L. Higgins. 1995. "Community Literacy." *College Composition and Communication* 4 (2): 199–222.

Slosson, J. R. 2002. "Unethical Advertising in America's Schools." (Student paper for Critical Reading and Writing course at James Madison University. See companion website.)

Spellmeyer, K. 1991. "Knowledge Against 'Knowledge.'" In *Composition and Resistance*, edited by M. Hurlbert and M. Blitz, 70–80. Portsmouth, NH: Heinemann.

Stock, P. L., and J. Swenson. 1997. "The Write for Your Life Project: Learning to Serve by Serving to Learn." In *Writing the Community: Concepts of Service-Learning in Composition*, edited by L. Adler-Kassner, R. Crooks, and A. Watters, 153–66. Urbana, IL: NCTE.

Trilling, S. 2002. "This Essay Is So Gay." (Student paper for Critical Reading and Writing course at James Madison University. See companion website.)

14

The Half-Life of the Classroom
Students as Public Agents
Lisa Bickmore and Stephen Ruffus

Sidney Dobrin and Christian Weisser, in their article "Breaking Ground in Ecocomposition: Exploring Relationships Between Discourse and Environment," describe a "discursive ecology pedagogy" as involving the notion of "words, language, and writing [as] themselves parts of ecosystems" (2002, 584). Such a pedagogy, they argue, asks that

> . . . we, as teachers, conceptualize writing not as an individual activity, separating the author from the world, but as an activity of the world; that we step beyond examining the processes of individual writers to examining larger environmental forces on those writers; that in addition to the ideological, cultural contexts in which we have situated writers in recent times, we look to physical environments, textual relationships, and the locations from which language and discourse arises. It asks us to see writing as an activity of relationships. (584)

As Dobrin and Weisser suggest, the activity of writing is a worldly one, always situated in and among others—other individuals, but also more corporate entities, such as agencies and institutions—as well as among physical environments, relationships among texts, and diverse locations. While Dobrin and Weisser's chosen metaphor is ecological, we might also fruitfully elect other metaphors of sociality and relationship, such as Richard E. Miller's bureaucracy—what he calls "the fraught, compromised world where all our classes are actually convened" (1998, 23). In our classrooms, writing and its actual effects disappear if students cannot in some sense realize that, as an activity of the world, writing has constitutive power within its surrounding environment, whether that environment is conceived bureaucratically or ecologically.

In an assignment developed over a number of years and by a number of faculty members[1] at Salt Lake Community College, called a "Collaborative Community Writing Campaign," students work with peers to produce several coordinated pieces of writing on a topic of their own choosing, writing that could potentially have a place within a public setting (see companion website). We take many of our premises for the assignment from John Trimbur's work in *The Call to Write* (2002), most particularly from that book's attention to genre and public writing. In the preface to that work, Trimbur notes that writing is "not just . . . a skill to master but . . . a means to participate meaningfully in the common life" (xxxv). We believe making assignments that are likely to give students a more fully articulated sense of what participation "in the common life" might mean entails complex rhetorical play in a multitude of genres and modalities, with an emphasis on writing and research that are contingent in nature. By contingency, we suggest two things: first, that knowledge itself is contingent and contextual; and second, that students can, in their writing courses, explore their knowledge, which is for the most part not viewed as expert, as a means of discovering the several possible subjectivities and positions they may occupy in re/constructing the rhetorical economy, and in entering it.

Any understanding of contemporary public life must take into account its institutions and their bureaucracies. Writers in the public sphere must take such bureaucratic environments into account in any attempt to enter their discourses in some productive way. Writers in the public sphere must also become more aware of their own subjectivities, which will enable new strategies to theorize and adapt the versions of themselves they present as they write. Every act of writing involves to some extent an act of reassembly on the part of the writer, always in response to a particular situation or location, to public environments. A more attentive understanding of any situation—which we take to be part of the heuristic enterprise of research—allows also for a more strategic and calibrated understanding of the self as a part of the web of relationships involved in any act of writing.

We might borrow again from Richard E. Miller, saying that what we are after in assigning writing for the public sphere is something like "discursive versatility," which he defines as "the ability to speak, read, and write persuasively across a wide range of social contexts" (23). He notes that he's interested in "promoting a fluency in the languages of the bureaucratic systems that regulate all our lives; a familiarity with the logics, styles of argumentation, repositories of evidence deployed by these organizational bodies; a fuller understanding of what can and cannot be gained through discursive exchanges, with a concomitant recalibration of the horizon of expectations" (23). To these fluencies, we might add an initiation into the ways that genres function in different public settings. Charles Bazerman (1997) suggests that "Genre is a tool for getting at the resources the students bring with them, the genres they carry from their educations and their experiences in society, and it is a tool for framing challenges that bring students into new domains that are as yet for them unexplored, but not so different from what they know as to be unintelligible" (24). Embodied within genres is another means of exploring various discursive landscapes, both for terrain students know very well, as well as for less familiar territory. The versatility Miller envisions, then, would allow student writers to develop a more adaptable sense of themselves as agents within a public setting.

Writing as oneself in a public setting means adapting that self to be its most persuasive. Moreover, we cannot conceive of the available forms of public writing for student writers in a way that limits their thinking. For instance, in the letter to the editor, now apparently the default genre for public writing, students are unlikely to engage with writing as an activity of relationships, which will always mean more than expressing one's opinion. In *Moving Beyond Academic Discourse: Composition Studies and the Public Sphere*, Christian Weisser critiques the "letter to the editor" assignment by noting the ahistorical version of "the public" that it invokes:

> Letters to the editor are one-way assignments; students put effort into writing them but get little subsequent response. As a result, these types of assignments are often counterproductive. Students come to feel that participating in "public discourse," if letters to the editor are indeed public discourse, has little effect on what happens in the world. They surmise that the public sphere is a realm where nothing actually gets accomplished—at least not by them. (2002, 94)

If we want students to develop strategic knowledge and flexibility as writers in public contexts, teachers must shape public writing assignments to do more than enable students merely to choose an issue and express a view. Public writing assignments must provide students multiple opportunities to frame, and frame again, the working version of the worldly environments their writing might approach, opportunities to put that knowledge into calculated use, and opportunities, finally, to assess the results of their attempts, so that they can try again.

The Assignment and Its Locale

The centerpiece of the assignment is the work students do, in their collaborative groups, in a variety of genres for the public setting(s) of their community writing campaign. At the same time, students write a rhetorical analysis of sources they identify through their research, as well as an annotated bibliography. These pieces, which are recognizable in their own right as academic genres, also serve a heuristic purpose. Each collaborative group also makes a presentation to the class on a genre in which they're working. The assignment unfolds over a period of five or six weeks, and it is the culminating assignment of the course. Students sort themselves into their collaborative groups by common interests.

The project begins with the rhetorical analysis, which asks students to use the occasion of researching and selecting sources to construct a working version of the rhetorical context in which they might write. The rhetorical analysis fits the genre of academic essay, but it also serves a heuristic purpose. Their work on this piece helps them to generate ideas for pieces of public writing, the genres of which they choose based on their working understandings of the rhetorical context, as well as on their sense of themselves as potential participants in the public settings they've identified. The annotated bibliography is, like the rhetorical analysis, a typical genre of academia and of research; however, students often identify a public setting in which an annotated bibliography might serve as a knowledge resource for audiences other than academic ones. The presentation of a genre in which students are working offers the class a window into the work other students are doing. The presentations also extend the class conversation about genre as it functions in particular contexts, as students show their ongoing and developing conceptions of the sites in which their writing might potentially play a role.

Even though the assignment unfolds over the course of several weeks, practically speaking, students will be writing the various pieces of the assignment virtually simultaneously. This means that, at any given time, most pieces will be in an ongoing state of development. For instance, students begin by quickly producing a draft of the rhetorical analysis. This early draft, in our conception of the assignment, is designed to get them mobilized by assembling a preliminary version of the rhetorical field. Eventually, as with all the pieces the students produce, the rhetorical analysis will be finished, but at the outset, its destiny as a finished essay is not its purpose. Rather, its initial purpose is heuristic, exploratory. Since students in their collaborative settings are always working on more than one piece at a time, the more academic pieces are thus in a productive relationship with the publicly oriented pieces. The very fact of multiple pieces being produced at the same time means that the notion of recursivity—always allowing for the possibility of invention and revision—plays out in complex and potentially profitable ways.

We should say a word about the particular environment for this assignment, since it comes in response to our students and our institution, as we understand them. Salt Lake Community College is a large, multicampus site in an urban setting. It is a comprehensive community college; students at our college study in a variety of programs and for a variety of aims, including vocational training and certification, as well as in transfer-oriented programs. Many of the students are older; most of the students work either full- or part-time; many students bring working-class backgrounds and values to their academic work. These facets of their identities play into the work they do in this writing course. Often, their focus in this particular assignment draws upon their interests and affiliations deriving from their positions as workers, as consumers, as community participants, and even as clients of community agencies. In this sense, we might say that their knowledge and experiences give them a kind of adjunct status as participants in the course, many students bringing significant knowledge to bear on these writing projects. Thus, they contribute to a sense of the material nature of writing, awareness of which is one of the goals of the course.

The Emergency Preparedness Project: An Example

One group of student writers and their project for a community writing campaign gives an illustrative case for looking at the workings-out of the various components of the assignment. This group of students, prompted by the onset of the war in Iraq, came together by virtue of a shared interest in emergency preparedness. Initial conversations with the group about their early thinking suggested that they took the notion of a "call to write" in a very concrete way. Their intent as they approached the assignment was to see how their work might make a material difference, and how its circulation might improve people's lives.

At the outset, one member of the group, Elizabeth, said she thought that the group should approach an agency, Community Action, that she was familiar with as a client; the group had decided to focus on helping people on the economic margins to become better prepared for disasters. They spent some time looking at the websites of this and other community agencies to get a better sense of the ways that their own purposes might match or overlap with the missions of these agencies. Over the next week, they contacted several, including Community Action, as well as WIC and the American Red Cross. These contacts constituted one form of their research: through their investigations and conversations, they assembled a working knowledge of the environments where their work might potentially come into circulation and become socially useful.

They began writing their rhetorical analysis. This part of the assignment asks students to analyze several of their sources with an eye toward sizing up the rhetorical features, as well as the implications of the sources for their project. The aim of this piece of the overall assignment is to focus from the beginning on the way these texts might, taken together, create an initial representation of an environment into which their writing might enter. In other words, students construct a working fiction of the discursive situation, and then test it by trying things out. This can happen as a result of ongoing conversations between the collaborative groups and the instructor; it can also happen as a result of their conversations with one another. As an academic genre, the analysis allows for developing fluency in the vocabulary, intellectual strategies, and acceptable evidences of academia, but also suggests some of the ways that these fluencies might become a working part of a worldly writer's battery of tools.

This group's draft of the analysis began with a description of the circumstances that led them to write about emergency preparedness. They explained their purpose as follows: "This rhetorical analysis is a conglomerate action on the part of our group to sort through the many Internet sites available to the public and find the information we can use to inform low-income families and individuals. We wish to make it feasible for an average person to become well prepared for natural or man-made and terrorist disasters." Their introduction also outlined their method both of composition and of research: "Our group split this assignment by having each member look into their area, pick two web sites and write a rhetorical analysis for each site. As a group we edited and wrote beginning and ending paragraphs. Each individual gives his interpretation of the information and analyzes the source of the information so we can give an idea of the context of the web sites and convey the importance of this subject matter for our project and our intended audience." This approach shows, even at this early point in the collaboration, a working assumption about where they will get the most useful entry points, both as gatherers of information, readily available on the Web, and as rhetorical strategists. For instance, in the analysis of a website linked to the FEMA site, "Talking About Disasters," the writers say, "We found many web sites that talked about general supplies and their lists were atrocious, but what we were looking for was a kit that had full purpose and that could be grabbed quickly, effortlessly, in case an evacuation was necessary. The article did just that." Here we see the students, in response to what they see in their research, refining their purpose in response to the websites they've seen ("atrocious"); sizing up the source for what it yields ("The article did just that."). They also imagine the usefulness of this site for their own readers: "We feel the writers of this article made this useful for readers of every audience. . . . This site is a place that is designed to hit home for everyone who is interested in this subject."

At the same time students were preparing the draft of the rhetorical analysis, they also engage in the conversations and negotiations that result in the choices they make for the community writing campaign. Much of the classroom time for the duration of this assignment is given over to student collaborative work. Their discussions suggest that the ideas they have for the community writing campaign at the outset of the project often take many turns after investigation and discussion. For instance, while students may start out with a desire to play with a particular genre—a brochure, for instance—their research into the environments in which their writing would presumably circulate subsequently suggests to them that production of a brochure would be infeasible or cost-prohibitive; that an agency they had believed might be interested in using the brochure would be unlikely to reproduce it; that instead, some other activity of writing will prove more likely, for them as the writers they are and for the agencies, institutions, or individuals that would receive and potentially use the writing.

The group working on emergency preparedness for people on the economic margins began with the notion of a series of documents—fact sheets, possibly distributed or posted as flyers—to be strategically placed in retail establishments such as Sam's Club, places where supplies could be purchased more cheaply in bulk. However, as they began drafting these documents, they began to feel that the fact sheet might be too limiting a discursive space. Jennifer, a member of the group, said she felt that as she worked on her document that she needed more explanatory room, and that the document might end up being several pages, which then made its portability and reproducibility more problematic. The group was already discussing a packet of documents. Their research suggested that, while there was a great deal of Web-based information about emergency preparedness procedures and supplies, that most sites' focuses were too limited. They wanted their work to be comprehensive, a one-stop compendium of useful material, arranged in such a way that the user would be able to assess her needs without having to do additional research.

At the same time, their research showed them another possibility—of putting their work in the form of curriculum that WIC might be able to use in classes it offers to its clients. However, if the students were to act on this possibility, they would need to put their research into a readily available presentation format, such as PowerPoint. Moreover, as their work progressed, they obtained a booklet on earthquakes, which caused them to consider again the most usable form for the documents they wanted to put in the hands of people who might need them.

The students, in their research and deliberations, made ongoing, practical judgments about the institutional environment where their writing might have a life. As they've identified a need that they believe is genuine, they hope to persuade an agency with access to the readers they see as needing their knowledge to validate their belief by taking on their research and their writing—by using it. Here again, Charles Bazerman (1997) helps us to see what is at stake as we ask students to consider genre in sizing up the worldly environments where their writing might circulate:

> Genre is a rich multidimensional resource that helps us locate our discursive action in relation to highly structured situations. . . . In understanding what is afoot in the genre, why the genre is what it is, we become aware of the multiple social and psychological factors our utterance needs to speak to in order to be most effective. Once we understand the dynamics and factors, we may have a range of choices available to us, including choices that are far from traditional in appearance, but which nonetheless speak to the circumstances. (23)

The deliberations of the students working on the emergency preparedness project are an example, perhaps, of the understanding Bazerman speaks of, of "dynamics and factors," which in turn present certain choices to the writer. These deliberations also represent a form of research—finding out what the particular exigencies of a communication situation are, and responding to them. In this sense, the research is contingent—what is necessary, exigent, in a given situation to approximate a successful performance in that situation.

As these students made their genre presentation to the class, they had begun to solidify their plans. They decided to make a proposal to WIC that their research, in the form of a PowerPoint presentation supported by an extensive collection of fact sheets gathered as a booklet, be used as the core of a new training course on emergency preparedness for WIC clients. In addition, they were in the process of preparing a commentary on the need for emergency preparedness, especially for people who were operating on the economic margins; the group was debating whether this commentary might serve as a preface to the booklet, or whether they might send it to a newspaper's opinion pages. The presentation foregrounded the proposal and PowerPoint slides.

These choices represented decisions that the group had made as a result of their deliberations about the project, and the place in the public sphere where they thought their work had the best chance of causing change. The group was only able to arrive at these decisions by virtue of their research, which entailed a serious consideration and reconsideration, not only of subject matter but of contexts and environments, not only of possible statements and their genres but of potential points of contact. The assessment they made of these things represents what we think is a considerably sophisticated and nuanced understanding of the public sphere into which they hope their writing will enter.

Weisser (2002) again helps us to see why this level of sophistication and nuance is critical for any adequately theorized understanding of public writing as it is assigned in composition classrooms. "Public" is not an easy category; any useful conception of the public requires complex analysis:

> Effective public writing must account for the degree to which public writing exists in a historically textured sphere that is the product of innumerable social and political forces. These forces have long histories and are in a constant state of flux. If we are to fully and cogently theorize public writing, we must begin by establishing it as a complex historical category. (95)

Students working through a complex assignment such as this one will have many opportunities to engage with the issues Weisser nominates. Their genre presentations offer a window into that engagement. It's clear, for instance, that many students will still be working with a notion of genres as somewhat fixed forms and formats, rather than as socially marked forms of writerly activity; yet they mostly at least begin to connect the ways that a certain social situation as they understand it calls more for one sort of writing act than for another. Their understandings may in many cases retain a nascent quality, but it seems clear that they understand the connection between the writing environment, the social needs they identify, and the particular shape that the writing takes in response, at least on something like a symbolic level. And why should this surprise us? As a field, we may not yet have identified the methods by which we may construct the history of certain genres. It seems clear, too, that working through the analytic and heuristic tasks of the assignment helps students to begin sorting out the differences between understanding an issue and understanding the *discourse* of the issue. Again, this understanding may be more nascent than explicit. However, traditional ideas about research—collecting sources and citations—may prove to be singularly unhelpful on this point; but public writing assignments of a complex and situated nature can create the environment where significant discoveries about the relation between texts and the world can happen on a surprisingly regular basis for students.

"The Productive Means to Name the World"

The public writing assignment, in order to do the work we claim for it, must foreground research as knowledge making on several fronts. Of course, our students develop knowledge of their public topics. More than that, though, they develop knowledge about the sorts of writing produced within particular locales; knowledge about how particular sorts of writing, produced within specific locations, fit with the representations that institutions and agencies make of themselves; and knowledge about the ways their own aims for writing might mesh with, or fit within, the missions of such institutions or agencies. Students also come away from this assignment with a more sophisticated and more fully articulated sense of the ways genres function in multiple settings, and the ways that their acts as writers might effectively exploit those functions and settings.

Moreover, we see some evidence that students move toward a conception of writing as socially useful knowledge. The boundary between the classroom world, academic sources of knowledge and knowledge making, and the world outside the classroom, is less rigid than we think—more permeable. We draw this conclusion from our observations of our students, who traverse this permeable boundary with more regularity than we would have predicted. They do this both to find and make knowledge about sites outside the classroom, but also to approach those sites with their writing. When students make strategic knowledge about sites outside the classroom, what they have potentially created for themselves is the ability to have a hand in how a problem gets named; in how a social need is defined, or as Trimbur (2000) puts it in "Composition and the Circulation of Writing," "the productive means to name the world" (209).

The notion that we must find ethical ways to negotiate our authority in the classroom is almost a given in our field. One avenue for this continual investigation is to interrogate the subject positions that our classroom environments and assignments construct for our students. Here, what is at issue is student knowledge. How well are our courses and assignments designed to uncover—to make evident—that knowledge, and the investments of our students? Positioned as arbiters of knowledge in the classroom, we can be lulled through our academic and critical traditions into a sense that we know what counts as knowledge. But knowledge, or what counts for it, is always negotiable and contingent, as is expertise; for our students can sometimes leverage enough authority and know-how to create performances that make things happen, or have the potential to make things happen, in environments other than our classrooms. In terms of writing as knowledge making, then, our classrooms can exist in a curious half-life. We as teachers have the authority to bring categories and forms to bear that can enable more capable performances on the part of our students. However, traditional research assignments often don't make evident, let alone activate, what students already know by virtue of their experience in other environments. Nor do public writing assignments, such as letters to the editor, which are not fully historicized or contextualized. With such assignments we risk, despite our best intentions, eliciting from our students either essays addressed to the academic world that at best are apprentice work, or pieces nominally addressed to the public sphere that do not fully participate, even imaginatively, in a thoroughly conceived approximation of that environment.

Situated public writing assignments may have a better chance at enabling student writing that creates meaningful effects in the world, and can help us as teachers to "locate the kinds of writing [students] will want to work hard at, the kinds of writing problems they will want to solve," as Bazerman puts it (1997, 24). We see a great strength in enlisting the category of genre. Amy Devitt (1993) argues that the genres "help us to see how individual writers and individual texts work . . . by removing us one level from the individual and particular" (580). Thus, genre "mediates between text and context . . . between form and content" (580). Public writing assignments such as the one we've described, premised on heuristic inquiry into sites and subjects that matter to students, with the concept of genre as a mediating framework, will help students to construct discursive intelligence. The practical result of such discursive intelligence would mean student writing that has the potential to succeed on its own terms in environments other than our classrooms. In this context, having enough knowledge to write may mean something different than our commonplace assumptions about academic authority. "Enough knowledge" here may mean that students can put it to use for purposes they assign themselves. If legitimate knowledge is also contingent knowledge, we may concede that we do not have the sole authority to certify it; students themselves participate in assigning this value, as they no doubt always have.

We are grateful for the participation of our students Jennifer Bradbury, Joshua Jaimez, Elizabeth Terpening, and Ruth White for their conversations with us and for giving us permission to present their work in progress.

Note

[1] We acknowledge the important work of our colleagues Allison Fernley, Tiffany Rousculp, and Craig Smith in the development of this assignment.

Works Cited

Bazerman, Charles. 1997. "The Life of Genre, the Life in the Classroom." In *Genre and Writing: Issues, Arguments, Alternatives,* edited by Wendy Bishop and Hans Ostrom, 19–26. Portsmouth, NH: Boynton/Cook.

Devitt, Amy J. 1993. "Generalizing About Genre: New Conceptions of an Old Concept." *College Composition and Communication* 44 (4) 573–86.

Dobrin, Sidney, and Christian Weisser. 2002. "Breaking Ground in Ecocomposition: Exploring Relationships Between Discourse and Environment." *College English* 64 (5): 566–89.

Miller, Richard E. 1998. "The Arts of Complicity: Pragmatism and the Culture of Schooling." *College English* 61 (1): 10–28.

Trimbur, John. 2000. *College Composition and Communication* "Composition and the Circulation of Writing." 52 (2): 188–219.

———. 2002. *The Call to Write.* 2nd ed. New York: Addison Wesley Longman.

Weisser, Christian. 2002. *Moving Beyond Academic Discourse: Composition Studies and the Public Sphere.* Carbondale, IL: Southern Illinois University Press.

PART V

Research as Process

15

Responding to Research Writing

Dan Melzer

In this chapter, I offer some suggestions for responding to research writing based on theories of response in composition studies and my own experiences teaching research writing. Since research writing is the most complex piece of writing my students undertake—and since it's the genre of writing that my students come to with the most baggage—I think it's important to devote an extensive amount of response time to assignments that require research. In this chapter I'll discuss the importance of responding throughout the writing and researching process and give practical advice about responding to research writing. To make this advice concrete, I'll draw on examples from a six-week-long research project in a freshman composition course I taught in the spring of 2001, ENC102: Public Discourse. I hope that some of the approaches I took to responding to my students' research writing will help you think about—or rethink—how you respond to your own students' research writing.

The Theory and Practice of Response: A Brief Overview

Before I get into specifics about how I responded to my students' research writing, I want to discuss some of the theories that guide my approach to response. Compositionists who have influenced my approach to responding to student writing include Lil Brannon and C. H. Knoblauch, Peter Elbow, and Donald Daiker. Although these compositionists don't necessarily focus on responding to research writing, the general advice they give about response is in many ways even more important to consider when we respond to research writing, since it's usually the most involved piece of writing instructors assign.

Each of the theorists I mentioned has a different approach to responding, but they agree on certain general principles we would do well to keep in mind as we respond to student writing:

- Responding requires a dialogue between teacher and student. Response that is overly directive appropriates the student's text.

  Brannon and Knoblauch (1982) argue that we reduce students' incentive to write when we project an "Ideal Text" on a student essay rather than paying careful attention to the writer's purposes and choices. Rather than instructor response that wrests control of a text, Brannon and Knoblauch call for instructor response that engages students in a dialogue. Both instructors and students may have stereotypical notions of what ideal research writing should look like, and as I will discuss in the next section, I think the most successful research assignments leave choices about purpose and audience up to the student.

- Writers need feedback throughout the writing process, and not just on a final draft.

  Brannon and Knoblauch suggest that the best way to create a dialogue between instructor and student is to respond to multiple drafts of student writing. They encourage instructors to respond to early drafts in one-on-one conferences, and to give students an opportunity to revise after receiving written comments on a draft. Response theorists also recommend peer response workshops as another method of giving writers the chance to receive feedback throughout the writing process. This kind of feedback is especially important with assignments that require research, since they usually involve a lengthy process of researching and writing.

- Not all response should be tied to a grade. Students need opportunities for evaluation-free writing.

  Peter Elbow (1993) recommends "evaluation-free zones": assignments or series of assignments that are not evaluated. Elbow also encourages instructors to try portfolio evaluation, since the portfolio approach helps instructors avoid frequent ranking and grading and instead emphasizes response throughout the writing process. Rather than just evaluating students on a final draft of a research assignment, I give response throughout the process that is not tied to a grade, and collect a final research paper portfolio—a way of responding I discuss in detail in the next section.

- Since writing is to a large degree an act of confidence, instructors should be generous with praise as well as constructive criticism.

  Donald Daiker (1989) argues that too often in our response to student writing, we fail to praise what students are doing well. Daiker feels that praise is the main tool we have as responders to lessen student apprehension and increase motivation. This is especially important to keep in mind with assignments that require research, since the thought of research writing causes anxiety for so many of our students.

ENC102 Spring 2001: A Narrative of Responding to Research Writing

In this section of the chapter, I'm going to discuss how I responded to research writing in one of my second-semester composition courses, ENC102. The focus of my ENC102 course was public discourse, and students explored everything from community discourse to university discourse to the discourse of popular culture. Their final project was a research-writing assignment that expanded on one of the themes they explored in their previous essays or in class discussions. As you read about the ways I responded to my students' research writing, keep in mind the bulleted list of advice in the previous section. As you'll see, I tried to use the best of current theories of response as I gave my students feedback on their research writing. Hopefully the examples I discuss will give you some new ideas for responding to research writing in your own courses.

Calming Research Paper Anxiety

The research assignment is the major project in all ENC102 courses, and I devoted six weeks of a fourteen-week course to it. Because students were aware, even before they registered for the course, that the focus of ENC102 is the research assignment, I knew there would be quite a bit of fear and apprehension when I handed out the research project assignment sheet. Because of this, I began our discussion of research writing even before I handed out the description of the assignment. In a sense, then, I began responding to their research writing before I even gave them the assignment. I asked students to share some of their previous experiences with research writing, and a number of them recalled with horror instructors who marked them down ten points each time they put the period in the wrong place in their citations or indented incorrectly in the works cited page. One student even shared a story about an instructor who gave her a "C" instead of a "B" because she spelled the instructor's name wrong on the title page. Not all of my students' high school instructors responded this harshly, but whether it was an English, history, or science class, most students had at least one story of a bad experience with research writing.

After hearing these tales of research writing pain and woe, I quickly emphasized to students that I would be responding to the content of their ideas, and that I was much more interested in their ability to support arguments and engage in conversation with outside sources than I was with correct, to-the-letter MLA style. I assured them that they would be choosing their own topics, and I let them know we'd be doing in-class exercises that would help them find an original topic they were truly interested in. Before they even got the research project assignment, then, students had a sense of what I would value in my response, and what they would be focusing on in peer response.

When it did come time to hand out the assignment description for the research project, I made sure to remind students that I was going to focus my response on content rather than format. Here's the assignment sheet I handed out to students:

Public Discourse Research Project

For the next six weeks, you will explore in more depth one of the themes that interested you from previous essays, class discussions, or response journals. In your previous essays and journals you've been responding to the readings in *Presence of Others*, and now you will engage in a larger conversation by arguing, exploring, and evaluating ideas with a variety of other authors.

Although this is a research project, this is not a traditional "term paper." I encourage you to think creatively about the audience, purpose, and form of the research project. For example, you might study the discourse of a subculture in an ethnography, create a 'zine about your favorite music group or television show, or research the discourse of your major and create a brochure about it for the Writing Center.

You will do some research on your topic and find five or more sources, but this is not a "report," and you should go beyond just a "collage of sources." You should engage in a thoughtful conversation with your sources, and your own ideas and arguments should dominate. You will cite your sources in MLA style, and you should look to collect a variety of sources: journal articles, Internet sites, interviews, surveys, etc.

Early in the process you will turn in a research proposal to get feedback on your ideas. We will go through a research and writing process, where we will brainstorm, collect sources, draft, discuss our topics, workshop, revise, have one-on-one conferences, and edit. You will turn in the proposal, drafts of the project, a final draft, and a process note in a final research portfolio.

In this assignment sheet, I tried to give students a clear sense of how I would respond to their research projects. I emphasized that I would value content more than correct MLA style, and I let students know that they would be receiving responses from both me and their peers throughout the research and writing process. I also included a grading rubric that described the qualities of "A," "B," "C," "D," and "F" research projects (see the companion website). My goal was to give students a sense of how I would respond to their research writing—and how my response might differ from responses they received to research writing in the past.

Responding Early in the Process: The Research Proposal

A common complaint my students had about their prior experiences with research writing is that they received no feedback until after the final draft was turned in. In order to emphasize that research writing is a process, and to provide students with some response very early in the process, I have them write a research proposal. In the proposal students write about what they know about a topic, what questions they might explore, what audience they have in mind, and where they might go for sources. Here is the proposal assignment I gave students:

> The research proposal is a chance for you to start thinking about your topic before you collect sources and begin drafting. The goal of the proposal is to explore what you know about your topic before you begin to research.
>
> In the proposal, discuss the following questions:
>
> 1. What topic do you have in mind? Are there related topics that also interest you?
> 2. What do you already know about the topic? Why are you interested in the topic?
> 3. What questions do you have about the topic? What aspects of the topic are you interested in knowing more about?
> 4. What audiences might be interested in your topic?
> 5. What kinds of sources might be helpful to you as you research your topic (books, newspapers, magazines, websites, interviews, etc.)?

Before turning their proposals in to me for an ungraded response, students brought in rough drafts for responses from peers. Just as Brannon and Knoblauch warn against responding to student writing based on an "Ideal Text," I would warn against responding to students' research-writing ideas based on an "Ideal Topic," and peer response is one way to take the emphasis off the instructor "approving" topics with a rubber stamp. During this small-group work, students helped each other choose target audiences, suggested research resources, and provided feedback on research topics. When they responded to their peers' proposals, students got ideas for their own research projects and had a chance to see examples of particularly strong proposals. We also began to develop a community of responders beyond just the teacher.

After the peer-response workshop, I gave a written response to my students' proposals. Because I responded so early in the research-writing process, I was able to assist students as they began to shape their topics. I helped a student who wanted to write about slang narrow her topic down to a more manageable size; I praised students who were coming up with especially original topics, such as the student who was going to study his own family's discourse and the student who planned on creating a website comparing the lyrics of female and male rappers; and I suggested some ways that a student writing about the public rhetoric over the death penalty could make his topic more original when I discovered in his proposal that he was inspired by the film *Dead Man Walking* (I suggested writing a story or screenplay about the issue after doing some research). This response was not quite "evaluation free," since the proposals were part of the research portfolio. But I didn't put a letter

grade on the proposals, and I assured students that this was a low-stakes, informal assignment. The research proposal was a way to combine the early response that Brannon and Knoblauch suggest with the evaluation-free writing
that Elbow recommends.

Drafting, Revising, Responding

Another effective way to provide feedback to the writer early in the process is
to share rough drafts as a class, in peer-response groups, and in one-on-one
conferences. I often begin this process by bringing in a draft of something I'm
working on that involves research, such as an article for a book or journal. In
my ENC102 course, I brought in a draft of an article I planned on submitting
to a journal. We discussed whether or not I supported my assertions with
enough evidence from outside sources and my own research, whether my interview questions were appropriate, and whether my voice and tone would ap-
peal to my audience. In their peer-response workshops, I had students fill out
a response journal that asks four questions about their peers' research paper
drafts, and we practiced these questions on my article:

1. What was working best in the essay and why?
2. What did you want to know more about?
3. Did the writer incorporate sources effectively? Why or why not?
4. What other revision strategies do you have for the writer? (You might comment on organization, development, style, voice, audience, etc.)

We had a total of four peer-response workshops over the course of the six
weeks I devoted to the research paper. In addition to the research proposal
conference, we workshopped an early draft, a late-stage draft, and had one final peer-editing workshop when the final drafts were finished. I also met one-
on-one with students after they'd received some feedback from their peers.
My goal was to follow Brannon and Knoblauch's advice that both instructors
and peers should respond to multiple drafts; advice that is especially important for writing as challenging as research writing.

After the one-on-one conferences but before the final draft, I offered students one more chance to receive feedback. I asked students to print or email
me a copy of their most current draft, and I gave each student a written response. I also asked students to reflect on what they wrote and direct my response by asking questions—students included with their drafts questions they
wanted me to address and a brief discussion of what they thought were the
strengths and the weaknesses of their papers in a process memo. In my responses I praised the students for what they were doing well and suggested
ways they could build on those strengths, and I also tried to find two or three
areas of the paper that I had questions about or that I felt could be developed.
If students had a target audience in mind, I role-played this audience when I

responded. At that point I didn't respond to grammar, and I didn't overwhelm the students by trying to respond to every strength or weakness in the paper. Since I knew students would continue to revise for the final portfolio, I was able to talk about the research projects in terms of what students might work on for the next draft, rather than just responding in order to justify a grade. Since the response was ungraded, there was no ranking involved. Here's an example of one of my responses to my students' drafts:

> David,
>
> As I mentioned in your proposal, I think the idea of analyzing the discourse of your own family is a creative and original topic. You do an effective job of quoting family arguments and discussions and then analyzing them closely. It also helps when you cite linguists and psychologists as you analyze your family's conversations, and I think it would strengthen the paper to have even more support from these outside sources (I pointed out places in your paper where I think your readers will be looking for more support). I agree with your comment on your process memo that since your audience is your family, you need to be careful about not taking sides, and I think you've done a good job of being fair. At the same time, I think you were a little too fair to yourself! You include a little bit of your own "family discourse," but you don't analyze your own conversation nearly as much as your mother, father, and sister's (which is a point that I noticed some folks in your peer-response group mentioned). I'm looking forward to reading the final draft.

In this response, I follow Daiker's advice and begin by praising what I liked best about the essay. I mention what I've looked at early in the writing process (the proposal) and make suggestions for the next draft based in part on the concerns that David has expressed about the essay in his process memo. As Brannon and Knoblauch suggest, I'm establishing a dialogue rather than merely justifying a grade.

I believe responding to our students' writing is the most important thing we do as teachers, but I understand that not every instructor has as much time to devote to responding as I do. ENC102 is capped at twenty-five students, but what about responding to research writing in larger courses? There are a variety of strategies instructors can use to provide students with a thorough response throughout the research and writing process without feeling overwhelmed. For example, the kind of peer-response workshops I've been discussing not only help students to become better readers of their own writing by teaching them to respond to their peers' writing, but they also translate to less responding for the instructor. Whether you're teaching a large or small class, it's a good idea to stagger written response by asking students to turn in drafts at different times. When you do collect drafts and respond, focus on two or three of the major strengths and weaknesses of the essay, rather than trying to respond to every detail and every error in grammar. Assigning collaborative research projects, where students write and research in small groups, is

another way to save time when responding. Collaborative research assignments give students valuable practice writing and researching in groups, and
the instructor will have fewer projects to respond to. For strategies on responding to collaborative research projects, see the Chapter 12 by Moore and
O'Neill in this collection. One final time-saver is a response rubric, which I
often use when I respond to a final portfolio. I discuss response rubrics in the
next section of this chapter, portfolio evaluation.

Portfolio Evaluation and the Research Paper

At the end of the research and writing process, my ENC102 students turned in
a research project portfolio. This portfolio contained a final draft, peer-
response workshop and conference drafts, and a process memo that asked students to reflect on the entire six-week process. Asking students to turn in a
research portfolio, rather than just one final draft, gave both them and me a
sense of their growth as writers and researchers. It also allowed me to respond
to their research projects holistically. I evaluated them on their growth as writers, the effort they put into the revision process, and the quality of the final
product. Since I'd already responded to students in one-on-one conferences
and in a written response, I didn't feel obligated to give a detailed response to
the portfolio. I wrote just a brief paragraph, keeping in mind what they'd said
in their process memos. I mentioned the major strengths of the portfolio, and
also pointed out areas that were not as developed. Since students no longer
had a chance to revise their research projects, I tried to connect this research
project with future research writing students might encounter in other courses.
Here's an example of one of my portfolio responses:

> Tina,
> Excellent job on the research portfolio. I enjoyed your essay on the Ebonics
> controversy, and I think it was thoughtful and well-written, with a careful
> consideration of both sides of the issue and great examples from personal
> experience as well as examples from Smitherman and Gilyard. You really
> did a lot of rethinking and revising from your original topic of slang, and I
> think you came up with a good focus as you drafted. I agree with you in your
> process memo that the "riskiest" part of the essay is the section that you
> write in vernacular, and it's true that some college teachers wouldn't be as
> persuaded as I am by the creative way you include the vernacular to make
> your point. But I'm glad you took some risks and came up with an original
> style for this research project.

Another technique for responding to final research portfolios that I've
used in large classes is a response rubric. Assignments that require research
tend to be the lengthiest piece of writing in any course, and response rubrics
are a way to save time but still provide students with a clear sense of what you
are valuing in their writing. Response rubrics list the criteria for an essay and

provide a checklist and a space for a brief comment. If I had used a rubric to respond to the ENC102 research projects, it would have looked something like this:

	Excellent	Above Average	Average	Below Average
Support and development				
Use of sources				
Organization of ideas				
Use of personal argument and experience				
Audience awareness				
Comments:				

Whether it's the use of response rubrics, peer response, or research proposals, hopefully my discussion of theories of response and the example of my ENC102 course has given you some new ideas and approaches for responding to research writing. Teaching students to evaluate and integrate outside sources is important, and our students' research writing deserves thoughtful, thorough response. If we respond only to a final draft of their research writing, or focus our response on correct MLA style rather than the content of the research writing, we do our students a disservice that is only magnified by the amount of time they've devoted to writing the paper and we've devoted to initiating students to academic research.

Works Cited

Anson, Chris. 1989. *Writing and Response: Theory, Practice, Research.* Urbana, IL: NCTE.

Brannon, Lil, and Cy Knoblauch. 1982. "On Students' Rights to Their Own Texts: A Model of Teacher Response." *College Composition and Communication* 33 (May): 157–66.

Daiker, Donald. 1989. "Learning to Praise." In *Writing and Response: Theory, Practice, Research*, edited by Chris Anson, 103–13. Urbana, IL: NCTE.

Elbow, Peter. 1993. "Ranking, Evaluating, Liking: Sorting Out Three Forms of Judgment." *College English* 55 (Feb): 187–206.

Straub, Richard. 1996. "The Concept of Control in Teacher Response: Defining the Varieties of 'Directive' and 'Facilitative' Commentary." *College Composition and Communication* 47 (May): 223–51.

16

Editing
Students' (and Teachers') Least-Favorite Part of the Research Writing Process

Deborah Coxwell Teague

Your students have almost completed their research writing projects. You've spent weeks working with them as they decided on topics they truly want to learn more about, conducted research about the topics they decided on, and thought about how they might approach their topics. You've given them guidance and feedback as they considered how to organize their projects and worked on interweaving their own ideas with those from outside sources. You've guided them as they decided which sources to include and which to leave out. From the very beginning of the research writing process you've stressed the absolute necessity of avoiding plagiarism, and you've provided instruction to help your students learn how to correctly document their sources both within their texts and in their list of works cited. You've made sure they understand the difference between summarizing and paraphrasing, and you've taught them when and how to use quotes effectively. You've even taught them how to correctly incorporate and document extended quotes. And while you know they were supposed to have learned all of this in high school where writing a research paper is almost always a required component of the curriculum, you took the time to teach it all again—just in case they forgot what they were supposed to have learned. So now all of the hard work is done, for both you and your students. All that's left is the editing, and surely after years of writing and editing papers, your students know how to polish their final projects before submitting them to you. Yeah, right—in your dreams. They need your guidance now just as much or perhaps even more than while they were working on their drafts.

Editing is almost never the most fun part of a writing project—not for many of us, not for many of our students. And the main reason most of us think of editing as far from exciting is because by the time a piece of writing is ready for the final polishing, we feel as if we are all done. We expect to read over what we've written one last time, find no more than a few mistakes we didn't see while drafting and revising—make a few little changes so that our writing will be the best we can make it at this point—and bring the project to completion. After all, we've probably read and reread the paper and/or the PowerPoint presentation or the website we created over and over as we composed, and we've made changes and corrections as we drafted. We've taken the time and put forth the energy to figure out what we want to say and how we want to say it; we've worked long and hard on the project and now the time has come to finish it.

If we, as teachers of writing, as individuals who are intrigued by and love playing with words, have this attitude about editing, think of how our students must approach this part of the writing process. Editing is not only unexciting for them, it's downright difficult for the student writer whose editing skills might not be as advanced as we, their teachers, would like them to be. It's usually easy for us to spot misspelled words, mistakes in subject-verb agreement, comma splices, and misused apostrophes—especially in others' writing—but it's highly likely that spotting these and a host of other potential errors is not so easy for many of our students. And when the papers our students are editing include outside sources, a whole new set of possible mistakes to watch out for comes into play. Many of our students are overwhelmed, and often with good reason. Unless we, their teachers, carefully guide them through this final stage of the research writing process, their grades will suffer, and so will we as we read and respond to their final drafts.

I learned these lessons the hard way. When I first began teaching college-level writing classes close to twenty years ago, after eight years of teaching high school English, I assumed my students knew how to write research papers. After all, I knew that as a high school teacher I had been required to teach both my juniors and seniors how to conduct research and write research papers; I assumed that my college students would not need to be retaught what they already knew. I assumed incorrectly. And even after I figured out my mistake and began actually teaching them how to go about conducting research and including outside sources in their writing, it took a while before I realized that I had not adequately prepared them for the final stage—editing. They turned in final drafts riddled with errors, and I had difficulty responding to the content of their research projects because their mistakes got in the way. The misused and misspelled words along with the comma splices and unintentional fragments jumped out at me and interfered with the communication of ideas. I found myself focusing on their errors instead of keeping my focus where it should have been: on the content of their writing. Now, I take the time to teach my students editing skills, and while the final drafts of their research projects are seldom error free, they are much more polished and readable than my students' writing used to be. With hopes that your students' final drafts will be more polished and that you, their teachers, will be able to concentrate on the ideas they are trying to communicate as you read and respond, I offer the following tips.

Writers Need to Distance Themselves Before Editing

When we first read over something we've written, we don't see what's actually on the page or on the screen in front of us. We see what we think is there—what we thought we wrote—what we meant to write. More times than I can count or remember—in fact, almost every time I have ever written anything, whether it's been an essay for a class, an article for a journal, or an email to a colleague—I've finished my writing, read back over what I wrote, and never seen some of the glaring mistakes I made. They were right there in front of me, waiting to be corrected, but I was blind to them. I needed to wait a while, to distance myself from my writing, to get away from the text for a while, to get it out of my head, before I tried to edit. While I hate to admit it since I definitely know better, on occasion—more often than I wish to recall, and for a variety of reasons, some good, some not so good—I did not make or take the time to achieve that distance, and I went ahead and turned in the essay or mailed the journal article or pressed "Send Mail" without waiting a while and *then* reading over what I'd written. And almost every time, I regretted my haste. When the teacher returned the essay to me with my careless errors circled, I felt like an idiot. *How could I possibly have not seen those mistakes?* I asked myself. When my rejected article was mailed back to me with a note about the essay needing to be more polished to be suitable for publication, I felt as if I had been slapped—and for good reason. And when I saw my hastily sent email printed out and stapled to a bulletin board for all to see, *then* I saw the silly mistakes—the "to" where I meant "too" and the "than" instead of "then." As an English teacher—a writing teacher, for goodness' sake—I am not supposed to make these mistakes, but I do when I don't take the time to gain distance from my writing before I edit, and so do my students.

Writers Need to Be Aware of the Limits of Technology

Many of our students seem to think they can rely on "spell-check" and "grammar-check" to do their editing for them. They should know better. After all, we aren't the first teachers who have returned papers to them that were supposed to be final drafts but still contained glaring errors—glaring to us, anyway. Maybe it all comes down to wishful thinking. Our students seem to keep hoping that their word processing programs were somehow mysteriously updated and are suddenly capable of catching and correcting all of their mistakes. We have to remind them that it just ain't so—that in spite of all that technology does to make our lives easier, writers must still carefully read and edit what they've written. We need to make sure they understand that while word processing tools can help them spot misspelled words, faulty subject-verb agreement, fragments, run-ons, and problems with punctuation, students who rely on their computers to spot all of their errors will end up with writing that does not communicate effectively. Our students need to realize that final editing is important because grammatical and mechanical mistakes, along with errors in documenting and citing sources, interfere with the effective communication of ideas between the writer and the reader.

Writers Should Listen to Their Own Words

As the mother of four children, one of my greatest joys was watching and helping each of my children learn to read. At first they could only read out loud; they needed to hear each syllable in order to make sense of the group of letters in front of them. But as their reading skills developed, they became silent readers. As teachers, we need to explain to our students that even though it's been many years since they progressed from oral to silent reading, there are times when they still need to sound out each word. As they edit their researched writing, they are much more likely to spot errors if they take the time to listen to each word they have written. If they try to edit by reading silently, they will probably read what they think they wrote—what they meant to write—instead of what is actually on the screen or paper in front of them. Reading aloud helps them hear where they left out a needed word, where they included a comma when one wasn't needed, or where they needed a comma to let the reader know to pause. Reading their papers aloud encourages students to slow down a bit so that they are more likely to see that they typed "there" when they meant to type "their." Listening to their own words can help them remember that once upon a time a teacher told them to use "me" after "between"—not "I." Actually, the teacher probably told them to use the objective case after a preposition, not the subjective case, but what the student remembers is that the teacher said "between you and I" is incorrect, so as she reads her paper aloud, she changes the phrase to "between you and me." *Not a big deal,* you might be thinking. And part of me agrees. But another voice says, *Hey, these are college students and you are their writing teacher. You should be encouraging correct usage in a final draft.* And while your students will probably feel silly reading their drafts aloud, hearing their words will help them spot mistakes that can interfere with communication.

Writers Often Edit Hard Copy More Thoroughly

There's something about reading from a piece of paper that allows many of us to see errors we miss when reading from the computer screen. When I want to make sure my final draft is the very best I can make it, I always edit carefully while reading my words onscreen, and then for the final editing I print out my entire paper and start over. Almost every time, I find careless errors that I somehow did not see on the screen. The same will hold true for many of your students.

Several of my colleagues have recently shared with me that they have made the switch to paperless classrooms. The rooms in which they teach writing include a computer for each of their eighteen students, along with one for the teacher, and my colleagues make it clear to their students from Day 1 of the term that no paper will be passed out or collected over the course of the semester. Even the course syllabus is available online only; there are no "handouts" in their classes. No drafts are submitted in print form, and all responding to writing, both by peers and the teacher, is done online. And while part of me thinks this is wonderful—after all, why waste trees?—another side of me shouts, *I want my paper!* Part of me rejects the idea of not printing out my writing and holding it in my hands. Perhaps I will one day get to the point where I am more comfortable with the idea of a paperless classroom, but for now, I'll hang on to my printed close-to-final draft and read from it as I do my final editing, and I'll encourage my students to do the same.

Writers Are Often Blind to Their Own Mistakes

Many parts of the writing process are more than a bit mysterious to me. For example, I don't understand why it is that sometimes the ideas and words flow smoothly and with little effort, almost as if they simply pour forth from our fingers, and other times, even when we're rested and not stressed and we're engaged with our subject and think we know what we want to say, the words absolutely refuse to come in any halfway intelligible form. Another aspect of the writing process that puzzles me is that while many of us can easily and quickly spot the mistakes others make—especially those made by our students—we often absolutely do not see some of our own. We gain distance from our writing by letting it sit a while, and when we return to our writing, yes, we do see problems we didn't see earlier. We read over our writing, perhaps first onscreen where changes are easy to make and then from a print copy when we see other changes we want to make, and while we catch most of our careless errors, others that we should easily spot absolutely evade us. And because of this, when a piece of writing is especially important to us, many of us ask someone to help us spot those pesky errors that hide from us. Sharing these kinds of experiences with our students allows them to see us, their teachers, as fellow writers while we also help them strengthen their repertoire of effective editing strategies they can use in our classrooms and beyond. We can set aside class time for editing workshops in which students exchange papers and help each other spot problem areas they might not see in their own writing.

Writers of Research Projects Need to Do Extra Editing

One thing I've learned over the years is that when it's time for students to edit research projects, they are often overwhelmed if they are expected to do all of their editing at once. This is an especially challenging task for students because in addition to trying to spot and correct their grammatical and mechanical errors, they have to try to find the mistakes they might have made in referring to their sources.

Before we ask our students to focus on editing their research projects, we've provided instruction in citing and documenting sources. Many of us make this instruction part of the research-writing process from the very beginning. We expect our students to become familiar with their sources and refer to them even in early drafts. But still, correctly citing and documenting sources is often quite problematic for students because they have had little experience in this area. In fact, some of my first-year students swear to me they've never before been required to correctly cite or document sources, so I'm hardly surprised when they are less than adept at spotting their errors.

To make the editing process a bit less challenging and almost certainly more effective, I first have students edit their own and their classmates' projects for the kinds of errors they are used to looking for: misspelled and misused words, faulty subject-verb agreement, comma splices, misplaced modifiers, and so on. I tell them to try to ignore mistakes with citation and documentation—that we'll get to that later, and we do, sometimes during the same class or perhaps the next time we meet. We bring our handbooks to class and briefly review the rules we've already studied and discussed regarding in-text citations and works cited entries. Then on their own, perhaps in class, perhaps outside of class, they read through their own writing and double check to make sure they've followed the appropriate guidelines. I ask them to look closely at each place in their text where they've referred to a source and make sure they've used quotation marks around any words not their own. Students carefully look at each spot where they've included parenthetical documentation to make certain they made no mistakes. They look over their quotes again and make sure they've followed the rules for incorporating extended quotes if they've included any quotes over four lines long. They identify each work listed on their works cited page in the actual text of their writing, and they also make sure each source they mentioned in their writing is listed on the page of works cited. Many of them have a little trouble understanding that if they list a work on that page, they had to have referred to it in their text, and if they referred to a source in their writing, they have to list it on the works cited page. Obvious to us, I know—but not necessarily to them. And after students go through all of this with their own research projects, they exchange and repeat the process with each other's projects. I can't promise you that following this procedure will enable your students to spot all of their errors, but it certainly helps. For discussion of the rhetoric of citing and documenting sources, see Chapter 17 by Chris Anson in this volume.

Writers Benefit from Seeing the Editing Process Modeled

One of the most effective ways I've found to help students learn to edit their research projects is to first edit sample projects with them. The university at which I teach and direct the first-year writing program has an online collection of selected essays written by our own students—thus the title: *Our Own Words*—and these serve as a valuable source of sample student writing. While these selections are generally well written, they aren't perfect and could benefit from additional editing. Our site includes samples of a wide variety of types of writing, and several of the samples are researched essays. I frequently use these pieces in class to teach editing skills to my students. Perhaps your school has a similar collection of your own students' writing, or maybe you keep copies of writings from your former students to use in your class as samples (with written permission from the students, of course). Or you may use a research text such as Bishop and Zemliansky's *The Subject Is Research* (2002) or Ballenger's *The Curious Researcher* (2003), or a handbook that includes sample student research projects. Whatever your source of samples, the point I'm trying to make is that as teachers we need to teach our students *how* to edit by modeling for them using sample papers. Read the researched writing aloud to your students or ask for volunteers to read various sections. Read slowly and carefully, showing your students exactly what you expect them to do as they edit their own and each other's papers. First model for them how to edit for mechanical and grammatical errors, and then demonstrate for them the process you go through to make sure you clear up any problems with documentation and citation of sources. Explain to your students *why* we edit—that cleaning up errors in their writing leads to more effective communication of ideas, and that communication between a writer and a reader is what writing is all about.

Writers Need to Remember That Once Is Not Enough

Make sure your students clearly understand that reading through a close-to-final draft once to check for problems with grammar, mechanics, punctuation, and incorrect or incomplete documentation and citation of sources simply won't cut it. Making their writing the best it can be requires time—time for thinking and talking, time for exploring ideas through invention, time for researching, drafting, revising, editing—and not in that linear order but in a recursive fashion. They'll think and talk and explore ideas throughout the writing process, just as they will continue to draft, research, and revise until they submit the final project. And while they'll edit some as they write, even though we encourage them to turn off their internal editor until they figure out what they want to say and how they want to say it, they'll need to make time to edit and edit again—to edit their onscreen version when they finish writing, to let their writing sit a while and then edit the onscreen version again, to edit a print version, to have a classmate edit for them, and then to edit one last time. I suppose we could go on editing the same project forever, but most of us come to a point when we either have to let go or we are ready to bring the writing to closure and move on.

Editing might not be especially exciting for many of us or for many of our students, but it is a vitally important part of the writing process for all writers. We need to take time to allow our students to see us as fellow writers and to share with them the kinds of editing skills we have learned over the years. After all, our goal is to help them grow and develop as writers, and unfortunately, if their writing includes more than a few errors, many readers will lose sight of the ideas being communicated.

Works Cited

Ballenger, Bruce. 2003. *The Curious Researcher*. New York: Longman.

Bishop, Wendy, and Pavel Zemliansky, eds. 2002. *The Subject Is Research*. Portsmouth, NH: Heinemann.

Our Own Words. 2003. Florida State University First-Year Writing Program, *http://writing.fsu.edu/oow/*.

17

Citation as Speech Act
Exploring the Pragmatics of Reference

Chris M. Anson

Author's note: At several decision points in the first part of this chapter, I stopped to take notes in a separate file in order to explore my referencing decisions and reflect on the differences between what we do in professional practice and what students do to display their learning. These notes will appear throughout the first several pages, designated by numbers in small raised circles (e.g., ⑩).

Most college-level instruction in how to incorporate outside sources into an original paper focuses on concerns that lie at the surface of the writer's text: deciding whether to quote material directly, paraphrase it, or summarize it; knowing when to use block quotations; choosing the appropriate reference style and following its conventions for source attribution.❶ Although these general skills are important for much documented writing, they are also insufficient. Students need experience with the more complex "deep structures" of source work—including its rhetorical and informational purposes.❷ Such work involves judging the worth and effectiveness of a source; weighing the sophistication and relevance of a source against the emerging text; estimating whether an intended audience will know (and find unimportant) a potential source; deciding how many sources to cite and what effect source density has on the writer's persona and level of projected security as a researcher or scholar; and negotiating the line between "common knowledge" and attributable information. In this chapter, I will first explore source work from a pragmatic perspective, illustrating its complexities with analyses of an "emerging text" (that text being the present chapter).

The Pragmatics of Reference

In the teaching of writing, source work tends to be reduced to a set of text-based skills that prepares students to follow the conventions of various research genres in different disciplines. This is perhaps why instruction in source work has focused so relentlessly on the surface mechanics of quotation, citation format, and reference style.❸ While we can't deny the importance of these skills for successful academic and professional writing, students need to be taught other, more complex strategies for working with sources. Among the most important of these is an ability to judge the value, placement, and purpose of a source relative to the writers text—to answer the question, What is this source really doing here? Most of the time, this question is answered from an ideational perspective (Halliday 1973)❹: writers draw on outside sources to add to or support their ideas and contribute to the information flow of their paper. But within this general ideational category, more complex purposes for referencing shape and give meaning to a text—purposes that students must understand if they are to write successful research-based papers. We can become more thoughtful about teaching the process of source work by examining these different pragmatic functions of citations in academic writing.

Basic, informational purposes for referencing are like speech acts. In speech-act theory, all utterances are not only locutions (verbal acts) but also illocutions, involving authorial intention. When I say to my son, "I promise I'll play basketball with you after dinner," my words don't just *mean*, they also perform an *act*—a commitment to behave in a certain way in the future (see Austin 1962; Searle 1969). In speech-act terms, I haven't only uttered words with meaning, I have created a "commissive" act through those words, indexed by the performative verb in the utterance ("promise"). Because theoretically all verbal utterances serve a purpose, even just representing a state of affairs ("It's ten o'clock"), speech-act classifications include many categories such as verdictives (pronouncing, decreeing, sentencing), directives (excusing, forbidding, ordering), or constatives (reporting, attributing, or denying; see Bach and Harnish 1979).❺ Of course, the purpose of outside sources in a written text is less clearly marked, pragmatically, than speech acts; whereas many speech acts such as the common example "I hereby pronounce you husband and wife" are obvious, reference acts are less explicit ("Jones 1977" may mean "I hereby support the validity of my claim by citing Jones 1977"). We usually infer the pragmatic force of such references from their surrounding context.

One common pragmatic purpose for referencing, for example, is *evidential*; the source is used to support an assertion or claim. If a student writes, "Practicing religion makes people healthier and causes them to live longer," teachers are likely to ask the student to support the assertion with reference to some well-conducted research published in reputable sources. The more controversial or opinion-based the assertion, the more likely that, at least in some expository genres, teachers will expect references that serve an evidential function.

Yet even in what seems to be unambiguous pedagogical advice ("Support your assertions with reference to the literature"), we run into problems when we consider finer judgments about the nature of an assertion and how likely readers are to take issue with it. The assertion that precedes my decision point #1 on page 203 makes a claim about "most instruction" that begs for an evidential use of reference. Yet, as my notes explain, I opted against it:

> *Although there's clearly a call for a reference here, I'm resisting one. A handful of references to cases demonstrating the assertion would provide support for it, but the benefit of digging them up doesn't seem to be worth the effort. I'm relying on two likely conditions: first, that most readers will understand and agree with the point, and second, that two or three parenthetical references would create a subargument—that these cases are representative of "most instruction" when some readers might think they aren't. Diverting the reader's attention this early in the text could be frustrating and stall the advance my line of thought. There's also a slight convenience factor—this wouldn't involve tossing in a reference but investigating a handful of popular textbooks, say. Yet if I were worried about my authority in making such a claim, I might be compelled to spend a lot of time working out the delicate issue of citation choice in support of this claim. Instead, I risk its absence.*

My decision not to include a reference here was based partly on my appraisal of my readers and their tolerance for my assertion, and their willingness to suspend judgment at the start of the essay.

The third decision point, on page 204, repeats and elaborates on the assertion. Again, I opted not to include a reference:

> *I'm torn here; I know of no literature that shows, e.g., that American composition textbooks focus on these issues predominantly. I really want to cite the study by Thompson and Tribble, who examined British textbooks and found that they focus overwhelmingly on surface features of citation (quotation, summary, paraphrase). But it's about schooling in Britain, and again, I'm not sure that very many readers would disagree with what seems like common sense. So I'm leaving that reference out.*

As these decisions show, the evidential function of sources is influenced by other pragmatic and rhetorical factors such as the predicted knowledge of an audience (based on the assumed or planned context of the writing) and the distance between the original source's focus and the focus of the text at hand.

Helping students with the evidential function is complicated by their rhetorical situation, in which they address expert readers (teachers) by feigning a certain degree of expertise as writer-researchers in a context that already defines them as apprentice-novices, all while trying to inform peers and being admonished to "write to a general academic audience." They are also trying to emulate professional or academic writing, which has useful purposes in a field, while knowing that none of their actual readers in the class will be likely to look up their references for further edification, or use their writing to further the knowledge base of a field of topic. For students, the evidential function is also developmental, a way to practice supporting claims with reference to authoritative work. Explaining and demonstrating such a use for reference, and distinguishing it from its use in other academic and professional contexts, can help students to be clearer about why and how they are using references to back up or document their ideas.

Another important pragmatic function of referencing is the *preparatory* function—to provide a context for an argument or lay the groundwork for a research study or analysis. Consider the opening paragraph from a research study on overpopulation, published in the journal *Population and Development Review* (Goldstein and Schlag 1999).

> Recent successes in prolonging the life spans of laboratory animals have raised the possibility of large increases in human longevity (Carey et al. 1998; Lin et al. 1997; Biddle et al. 1997). The prospect of longer life is often greeted by fears of overpopulation (Kevles 1999; Kolata 1999; Gavrilov and Gavrilova 1991; Bova 1998). Kevles's concerns, which appeared on the opinion page of the *New York Times*, are typical. He wrote that "forestalling death would inevitably worsen many of the social crises that we already see looming. It would increase population, further burdening the planet—and might well create a generation gap of gigantic proportions." In this article, we use a simple mathematical model to show that longer life need not—and, if current trends continue, will not—lead to population growth. (741)

The rest of the article explores mathematically and statistically whether population growth increases when members of the population live longer. The authors claim that when increased longevity results in postponing childbearing until later in life, population does not increase as might be expected. Notice the preparatory function of the two opening lines. The authors begin with a reference to three research projects that successfully extended the life spans of fruit flies (Carey et al.), mice (Biddle et al.), and nematode worms (Lin et al.), and each study raises the possibility of overpopulation. These three references to controlled studies yield the central question: will human longevity lead to increased population? Increased population is then tied to social and environmental fears in a second string of references. The seven references included in the opening paragraph, then, strategically establish the background for the authors' claims and subsequent model. Interestingly, the second string of references represents a mix of scholarly and popular-press publications (Gavrilov and Gavrilova is a book-length academic study; Bova is a mass-market paperback; and the other references are to articles published in the *New York Times*). This mixture of general and academic work serves a more refined preparatory function: to imply that this isn't just an arcane, academic issue, it's an issue that folks are worried about "out there" as well (which justifies and fortifies what the authors are about to say). In a student paper, we might think that this mixture of popular and academic sources reveals not conscious strategy but a lack of ability to distinguish between intended audiences or domains of publication (commonly seen when students use a hodge-podge reference method or dump many references into a paper without critically analyzing their function, source, or intended audience).

The strategic mixture of lay and scholarly references in the population article suggests that, like the evidentiary function, the preparatory function is also influenced by other pragmatic and rhetorical factors. For example, in decision point #2 on page 203, I have invoked a historically important term ("deep structures") from linguistics, one usually associated with the work of Noam Chomsky. Yet I didn't cite Chomsky to serve what would have been a preparatory reference function. My notes explored this exclusion:

> *I'm leaving Chomsky out. At this decision point, I'm relying on readers' common knowledge of the concept of "deep structure," which has entered the general academic lexicon familiar to readers of this essay. From an interpersonal perspective, I'm also sensitive to condescension. The alternative (putting "see Chomsky 1961" at the end of the line) may seem unnecessary or trivial to those in the know. Some others would, however, interpret my reference as assistance to less informed readers. But, as placed, it also suggests that Chomsky said something about the pragmatic and rhetorical purposes of source work (which he didn't). Placing the parenthetical reference just after "deep structures" and removing "see" helps: now the reference notes that there's an association between the term and the person cited. But even though the concept of deep structure is convenient for my purposes, why would I want to send someone uninformed about Chomsky, in the context of this essay, into formal linguistic theory of the 1960s and '70s? The reference really doesn't serve a useful purpose.*

My decision, then, involved considering readers' knowledge, my own persona, and the "distance" of the concept's initial context (Chomsky, formal linguistics) from its context of use in my own text.

For students writing research papers, it may be very difficult to assess a "general academic reader's" knowledge of concepts they might cite, in part because they may have encountered these concepts themselves for the first time. As a result, they may make decisions about documentation "egocentrically," based not on what they believe an audience knows or can bring to a text, but on their own recently acquired knowledge of the researched subject. I can generally predict what readers of this volume know about Chomsky and deep structure. A student writer who learns about deep structure while completing a research project may believe that all readers share his or her naiveté about the concept, and include the reference where I omit it. Teachers, for their part, may *demand* the reference, distrusting the student's prior knowledge of Chomsky (and even suspecting plagiarism). In the professional case, the reference is redundant, risks condescension, or adds nothing; in the student case—assuming similar content—the reference is "required." Rhetorically, this is an astonishingly complex situation for students, but they often receive little guidance in how to negotiate it.

A third informational function of referencing might be called *terministic*, a way of invoking or incorporating another author's use of a specific term (or concept) into a text, often for purposes marginally related to those of the term's author. This is an especially interesting function because of the complexities of deciding whether to cite the term's originator. Consider a review in the *Journal of Political Ecology* of a book by Lesley Gill, *Teetering on the Rim: Global Restructuring, Daily Life, and the Armed Retreat of the Bolivian State* (Albro 2001). The reviewer, Robert Albro, uses the term "thick description" three times in reference to the author's ethnographic study of El Alto, Bolivia. The following excerpt contains two of those three references:

> With such a multi-sited, if occasionally scattershot, approach, one can wonder what happens to ethnographic thick description under a neoliberal regime. If Gill's work suggests anything, thick description is easily victimized in the "displacement" of ethnography both by the multi-sited technique itself and by the destabilizing effects of the structural adjustment process, the very object of Gill's analysis here.

In no case does Albro attribute the term "thick description" to Clifford Geertz, whose widely known and highly acclaimed *The Interpretation of Cultures* is the source to which the term is most often attributed. Compare the following excerpt from an article titled "The Thick Description of Law: An Introduction to Niklas Luhmann's Theory of Operatively Closed Systems." The purpose of this essay, author Klaus Ziegert tells us in its first paragraph, is to "give an overview of the guiding concepts and objectives of a particular methodology, namely Niklas Luhmann's theory of social systems" (Ziegert 2001, 1). This except contains Ziegert's first use of the term "thick description" beyond the title of the article:

> Evidently, Luhmann offers more than just a general theory in the conventional deductionist natural science paradigm. In a very particular way he moves on to what amounts—in methodological terms—to a thick description of society[27], including its law. Such a thick description of society is complex because society is complex and it is "thick" because it follows up conceptually and situationally every detail that happened or happens in society as it happens. (12)

As preserved in the excerpt, Ziegert's twenty-seventh footnote provides direct attribution to Geertz:

> See C. Geertz, 'Thick Description: Toward an Interpretive Theory of Culture', in C. Geertz, *The Interpretation of Culture* (New York: Basic Books, 1973), pp. 3–30.

In both cases, authors are discussing or reviewing other writers' works; one review is in an area of political theory heavily influenced by anthropology (the reviewer is a professor in the department of sociology and anthropology at Wheaton College, and the journal is sponsored by the Bureau of Applied Research in Anthropology); the other is in the field of legal theory and political philosophy. Both use the term "thick description" in their analyses. But why, with overlapping interdisciplinary audiences, does one author provide a full citation to Geertz's work while the other doesn't? The answer almost certainly lies in decisions made by the reviewers relative to their readers' familiarity with the term. Few undergraduate anthropology majors have not heard of "thick description," while it's likely that the term will be unfamiliar to many scholars of legal and political theory. In citing Geertz, one author does his readers a favor through a terministic reference—pointing to a perspective essential to his analysis—while the other only invokes a concept that has a solid foundation in his field (and his readers' minds). Because these journals admit to some degree of interdisciplinarity, these reference decisions are not simple but fine-grained, more like theories or estimates than absolutes.

In deciding to cite the work of Michael Halliday (decision point #4, page 204) to serve a terministic function, I noted the following:

> Halliday's functional approach to language had a strong influence in my thinking and played a role in some of my earlier work. His ideas are very relevant here, but I guess I also really like citing him and think that others should know his work. That seems like a strange reason for referencing someone, but there it is. But I'm wrestling a bit with this because I'm only using one of his functional categories, and it may not mean a whole lot to readers who don't know his stuff. But the alternative—just using the word ideational—doesn't help much. It's the kind of term that if used alone will bring an editor's query ("explain?"), and I don't really want to go into all that much detail. Referencing Halliday is probably a bit about just forestalling questions or puzzlement. Those who don't know his work will think, "OK, that term means something," and move on and maybe look into Halliday later. Without the reference, they might think, "What the heck does this mean, anyway?" Those who do know his work may think, "Hmmm . . . that raises the question of whether references can serve others of Halliday's functions, such as the interpersonal." And that's a good thing.

My use of the terministic purpose of referencing, then, was influenced by other complicated factors: my own preferences for certain scholars' work, and my concern about forestalling the possible puzzlement of readers who would otherwise feel confused by the term or want my own definition of it. Such rhetorical decisions are also based on the nature of the term itself—how commonplace it is, and how easily a reader who does not know its source can at least understand how it's being used. Teachers and scholars of composition, for example, use the term "freewriting" all the time without referencing Peter

Elbow. Although Elbow meant something specific by the term, most readers, even in other disciplines, can guess what the term means when it's used in context. Compare another term popular in composition studies, Paulo Freire's "conscientization." The rarity of the term makes it beg for a definition—and reference—in almost any conceivable text, even one aimed at teachers and scholars of composition.

Students often use the terministic function erratically. Having seen a specialized term in one of their sources, some will misjudge their audience's knowledge (blaming themselves for not recognizing it), and place it into their own papers without reference. Others will overreference terms, not knowing which are familiar to their audience and which are not, or they will overgeneralize their instructor's admonition to "cite your sources." Classroom strategies that make use of groups to gauge the familiarity of a term can help writers to make more accurate decisions about terministic reference.

Many other informational functions for sources can be hypothesized and described: a *speculative* function, for example, which is often used at the end of paper or in the discussion section of research article; a *concessional* function, strategically allowing in work opposed to a point or conclusion; a *facilitative* function, pointing readers to work that provides essential background information about an idea so that they can learn more; or a *contestatory* function, common when writers want to cite previous literature or opinion in order to disagree with it. My brief analysis of the evidential, preparatory, and terministic functions suggests that many other factors and motives are at work, influencing more fine-tuned decisions within these functions. But ideational functions aren't the only ones that motivate writers' reference practices; to explore the full spectrum of functions, we need to move beyond the text to consider what else writers are trying to do.

Digging Deeper

As further analyses explored the nature of speech acts, theorists became aware that some utterances carry a surface illocutionary force (usually marked by their verbs) but are actually intended to perform a different speech act (Brown and Levinson 1987; Grice 1975). These are said to be "indirect speech acts." Their underlying or "deep-structure" intent is usually recoverable and interpretable by a listener. When my sons were babies and my wife would sometimes wake me in the middle of the night with the utterance, "The baby's crying," she was literally—on the surface—describing a state of affairs (such as "Today is Tuesday," or "It's raining outside"). But from the surface form I interpreted this to have the intent of a directive (a request or demand that I get up and tend to the baby). My context gave me enough clues about her speech act to interpret its indirectness, since she wouldn't otherwise tell me something in the middle of the night that I already knew or that would have been irrelevant to me if she intended to take care of the baby herself, which she often did.

Although the speech-act analogy is imperfect, we can gain some insight into the nature of reference by examining the different "indirect" functions that citations serve in academic writing. Unlike indirect speech acts, in most cases indirect reference functions are not recoverable, at least not without some way to tap into writers' more concealed motivations. Some of my decision-point notes suggest these motivations, such as my preference for citing a certain scholar, my concern about seeming condescending, and the like. Understanding the deeper layers of motivation can help us to work with students as they struggle to meet the demands of their research assignments without always having sufficient resources for elegant reference practices.

Consider, for example, decision point #5 on page 204. There, I have referenced one article, by Bach and Harnish, to document the idea that speech acts can be multiply classified. My notes:

> *Most readers who want to learn more about speech-act classification will find as much as they need, at least for starters, in this piece, and its own references will link them to other work should they want to study it more extensively. After the general references to Austin and Searle a bit earlier, there's no reason to cite more than this piece.*

But consider the same piece of text followed by many references—to many scholars who named or categorized types of speech acts. Because the surface pragmatic function of this reference *(facilitative)* is amply realized in a single reference, the presence of so many other references begins to reveal something deeper, a motivation relating more to the writer's ethos or projected persona than to helping readers. We can more easily imagine this function if we absurdly extend the reference list to, say, thirty works, strung together like beads. The "indirect" speech act here can be seen from Halliday's interpersonal perspective. It serves a kind of "positioning" function, the equivalent of, "Look at this wealth of information I'm aware of and can cite; I'm showing you my expertise and extensive knowledge, so you can certainly trust my words and opinions." Interestingly, novice readers or those outside the field may be seduced by this kind of indirect purpose, while it may backfire with experts, who interpret insecurity instead of authority.

The positioning function is especially important in teaching because it often powerfully influences students' referencing decisions. When students' audiences are teachers in the role of "examiner" (Britton et al. 1975)—and that's most of the time—they often use references to show that they have met certain expectations ("Look at all the research I did," or "Here are the eight to ten references you asked for—count 'em"). When pedagogical and teacher-based functions for referencing dominate, they subvert students' learning of strategies for more diverse audience-based research writing and for the strategic, ideational use of sources in their work.

In academic writing, references can serve a *broadening* function, showing how some idea, concept, or conclusion is relevant to another, related area. In a study of the relationship between children's cruelty to animals and the presence of corporal punishment in their homes, author Clifton Flynn (1999) includes the following reference in the discussion section of the article:

> Discovering the mechanisms by which this association [between corporal punishment and child cruelty to animals] operates would be a fruitful area of investigation. Research on corporal punishment has revealed negative psychological and behavioral consequences, including greater likelihood of both approving of and engaging in interpersonal violence (Straus, 1994).

Until this point, Flynn's study has focused sharply on the relationship between two variables—the presence of corporal punishment in subjects' experiences and their tendency to abuse or be cruel to animals. Coming at the end of the study, this reference to a more general 1994 book, *Beating the Devil Out of Them: Corporal Punishment in American Families,* connects Flynn's analysis to broader social, interpersonal concerns (such as family violence). Given the context of his essay (the *Journal of Marriage and the Family*), its purpose is likely to create links and associations in a heuristic way that can lead to further research studies or encourage different research communities to communicate with each other.

Students often begin their research by digging up bits and pieces of information, and then use those pieces to structure their papers—the research drives their writing, not the reverse. When we scrutinize their references, their inexperience is sometimes betrayed by their inability to manipulate their source material to fit specific rhetorical and information functions. What appears to be, say, a broadening function really serves to display the research process: "Here's another reference that fits, as the title shows," or "This article also deals with the topic of X." But without a clearly defined context—such as the *Journal of Marriage and the Family,* or a collection of articles marketed to composition experts—they have a hard time judging whether a source broadens or narrows their ideas. All relevant references are relevant to them at the same level. A pragmatics of reference—constantly asking what purpose a reference serves—can help students to move beyond what they believe are arbitrary and school-based requirements and into more purposeful scholarly writing. But to do so, they also need more clearly defined contexts, audiences, and purposes for their writing.

Strategic Instruction: Student Learning and "Deep" Source Work

As these brief examples suggest, source work requires deep, strategic knowledge and a keen awareness of the pragmatics of referencing. Research papers of all kinds—I-Search, traditional, and short documented papers alike—provide excellent opportunities for students to learn such strategies. The companion website to this volume provides teaching materials and classroom strategies to help students begin that journey.

Works Cited

Albro, Robert. 2001. "Review of Teetering on the Rim: Global Restructuring, Daily Life, and the Armed Retreat of the Bolivian State." *Journal of Political Ecology* 8.

Austin, John. 1962. *How to Do Things with Words.* Cambridge, MA: MIT Press.

Bach, K., and R. M. Harnish. 1979. *Linguistic Communication and Speech Acts.* Cambridge, MA: MIT Press.

Britton, James, Tony Burgess, Nancy Martin, Alex McLeod, and Harold Rosen. 1975. *Development of Writing Abilities* (11–18). London: Macmillan.

Brown, Penelope, and Stephen C. Levinson. 1987. *Politeness: Some Universals in Language Usage.* Cambridge: Cambridge University Press.

Flynn, Clifton P. 1999. "Exploring the Link Between Corporal Punishment and Children's Cruelty to Animals." *Journal of Marriage and the Family* 61 (4): 971–81.

Goldstein, Joshua R., and Wilhelm Schlag. 1999. "Longer Life and Population Growth." *Population and Development Review* 25 (4): 741–47.

Grice, Herbert P. 1975. "Logic and Conversation." In *Syntax and Semantics, 3: Speech Acts,* edited by Peter Cole and Jerry L. Morgan. New York: Academic Press.

Halliday, Michael A. K. 1973. *Explorations in the Functions of Language.* London: Arnold.

Searle, John R. 1969. *Speech Acts: An Essay in the Philosophy of Language.* Cambridge: Cambridge University Press.

Thompson, Paul. 2001. "Looking at Citations: Using Corpora in English for Academic Purposes." *Language Learning & Technology* 5 (3): 91–105.

Ziegert, Klaus A. 2001. "The Thick Description of Law: An Introduction to Niklas Luhmann's Theory of Operatively Closed Systems." *Vienna Papers in Legal Theory, Political Philosophy, and Applied Ethics,* No. 25, edited by Nikolaus Forgó, Dennis Patterson, Alexander Somek, and Klaus A. Ziegert. Vienna *www.univie.ac.at/juridicum/ forschung/wp25.pdf*

18

Walking the Fine Line
Balancing Assessment Politics with Writing Pedagogy

Traci Pipkins and Jim Zimmerman

Assessment defines goals and expresses values more clearly than
do any number of mission statements. When our students ask us
whether a class topic will be on the test, they express the same view:
if you really value it, you will assess it. The converse is also true:
what you assess is what you value, whatever you assert.
—Edward White, William Lutz, and Sandra Kamusikiri (1996)

On balance, the faults of performance funding can be ascribed
primarily to overly detailed prescriptions, inadequate consultation,
poor design, hurried implementation, and either too little or too much
funding. But the potentially fatal flaw is the reluctance of the
academic community to identify and assess learning outcomes.
—J. C. Burke, S. Modarresi, and A. M. Serban (1999)

Writing assessment is nothing new to writing teachers. The process of commenting on papers and assigning grades is an integral, often controversial, part
of writing instruction. But increasingly, writing assessment is being required on
state and national levels, to measure writing competencies and to evaluate the
efficacy of writing programs. It is this category of assessment—assessment beyond the classroom, beyond the contract between teacher and student, beyond
the local control of a department or program—that demands more and more of

our attention these days. With this shift in audience and purpose comes a need for a clear understanding of why such assessment is mandated or whom it will serve. Without such understanding, assessment can distort writing pedagogy and tacitly define what a program's values should be, rather than accurately measure what is valued in student writing. On the other hand, the presence of external pressures may help us redefine and rededicate ourselves to the "learning outcomes" a writing course should provide for its students.

We believe that one of the newer responsibilities of all writing teachers, but especially those who model the intellectual practice of research writing, is to work to ensure that assessment practices serve the teaching of writing and not the other way around. Rather than passively submit to relatively new assessment traditions, routines, habits, rules, and regulations, faculty members must actively interrogate these practices with the intention of preserving pedagogical principles and eliminating even the most benign forms of misrepresentation of the teaching of writing in the academy.

One of the best ways to begin such an interrogation is to look carefully at the language with which the assessment process is narrated to members of the academic community. The epigraph from Burke, Modarresi, and Serban labels as a "flaw" the "reluctance" of the academic community to get behind the efforts to "identify and assess learning outcomes." But part of this reluctance stems from what White et al. identify in the first epigraph as the inherent power of assessment: the fact that it inevitably communicates a value system that may or may not accurately represent what is actually valued. Adding to this conflict is the fact that the things we value as teachers of writing are difficult to assess by a quantitative scale, so we are forced into uncomfortable compromises. But in order to understand the reasons behind the "reluctance" to acquiesce to outside assessment forces, it is necessary to look at the process from the inside out, with a careful eye to assessment at all levels.

Assessment Intersections and Outcomes

For practical purposes, from the point of view of the writing teacher, "assessment" can be identified at three intersections: teacher-student, teacher-program, and program-and-beyond. Viewed simply, teachers assess students, programs assess teachers, and "higher powers," including other units within the institution and agencies outside the institution, assess programs.

At the first intersection—teacher-student—it is critical that the writing teacher perform assessment in a meaningful way so as not to contribute to a climate in which the teaching of writing is seen as irrelevant, trivial, relativistic, or mysterious. When writing is viewed in this way, it becomes easy for students to characterize their instructors in one-dimensional ways, for example as an overbearing "grammar cop," a "format freak" who takes off points if the title page or the works cited aren't just right, or a "disciplinarian" whose chief emphasis is order in the classroom. As teachers, we need to fight for assessment of student writing that is significant and meaningful, assessment that helps us communicate and reinforce our core principles in a lasting way.

Similarly, writing programs must assess their teaching faculty in relevant, meaningful ways, whether through student evaluations, peer evaluations, or observations and reviews by administrators. If student evaluations are designed that emphasize knee-jerk reactions (like whether or not the teacher was "boring" or "awesome"), or comparatively superficial issues (like whether the teacher canceled classes or ended late), meaningful assessment of the teaching of writing is missing. Finally, quantitative results of assessment activities that purport to measure the effectiveness of a writing program may not be of any real use if what is being observed and judged is limited to easy-to-count elements such as errors in grammar or inconsistencies in documentation format.

Thus, in order to "actively interrogate" overall writing assessment practice, we must begin by questioning our own classroom assessment practices. The grading of student papers is the first place that we, as teachers of writing, assert and reinforce what we most value. As such, the purposeful assessment of student papers by writing teachers is the first line of defense against irrelevant or trivialized assessment at other levels. For at each assessment intersection, the larger question remains the same: "Is what we are assessing what we most value?"

It behooves every teacher of writing to continually rethink how the syllabus and assignments are constructed, what is being emphasized, and what is capable of being quantified in points or grades. A writing teacher's personal assessment philosophy must be both consistent with the program in which the teacher is employed and readily communicated to students. Where there is conflict between program goals and personal assessment philosophies, writing teachers are better off being conscious of the areas of conflict and how they negotiate them.

Writing teachers must carefully navigate the tricky terrain of student writing so as to consistently emphasize what is stated in their syllabus, which presumably embodies both their program's goals and their individual pedagogy. Grammar is easily quantifiable; errors, in general, are. Students have "been taught," perhaps inadvertently, that good grammar *is* good writing, though most writing teachers would agree that this is not necessarily true. What is important is understanding where that idea comes from. In the face of large stacks of student work, teachers can use grammar mistakes, marked in red, as quantifiable data for the ultimate assessment; teachers can readily point to these errors when students ask why they didn't get a better grade. It is more difficult to generate the same number of substantive comments about content, given the volume of papers teachers face.

All writing, student research writing included, is definitely greater than the sum of its parts. Our methods of assessing such writing have to reflect this.

If our comments are weighted disproportionately—that is, if we spend more ink on marking commas than on marking content—then our students will understand that imbalance as a reflection of what is valued. Students then tend to internalize and perpetuate that value system, worrying more about structure than substance. In this way, students are a valuable resource for locating discrepancies between theory and practice by challenging us to articulate what matters. We advocate inviting students to question our evaluation of their papers in follow-up conferences. That way, students have the opportunity to interrogate our assessment of them, which mirrors what we advocate at every level of the assessment process: that the assessed should have a role in the assessment. Equally important is the way this process encourages students to cooperate in and even construct—rather than complacently consume—the assessment process.

In much the same way, all writing teachers should be encouraged to actively participate in the construction of a program-wide philosophy of valuing writing. As members of the Writing Program faculty at James Madison University (JMU), we've witnessed an effort toward inclusiveness when it comes to growing the program philosophy. This is especially fitting and important for a program that is barely five years old and the only one of its kind in our state.

When our program separated from the English department, there were two fairly standard, traditional composition courses required of most freshmen. In the past few years, those courses have evolved, and when our most recent program assessment was conducted (May 2003), the course we focused on (GWRIT 102) had the following description:

> Building on the experience of GWRIT 101, 102 continues the development of the critical mind by introducing the writer to the methods of research-based writing. Writers should learn to build and defend reasonable, intellectual positions based upon close readings of texts. The course reinforces the understanding of writing as a process, including the practices of invention, arrangement, and revision; refines the writer's awareness of audience, occasion, organization, and style; strengthens the ability to craft a defensible argumentative thesis and to develop a thorough, logically organized, and well-supported essay; develops the ability to use research (variously defined) to inform and advance a thesis; and refines the ability to edit for clarity and grammatical/mechanical correctness.

What is immediately striking is how much was promised. Imagine trying to measure success in critical thinking, critical reading, thesis construction, argument, research, clarity, correctness, and components of classical rhetoric. Should each component be weighted equally? Part of the difficulty in assessing these components is in discerning the boundaries between such things as argument and thesis or clarity and correctness; these are neither mutually exclusive categories nor the sole lynchpins upon which good writing can be based.

The reason for creating such a course description was to provide for a common philosophical foundation upon which every individual writing teacher in our program was expected to construct a syllabus. The course description was also required to pass muster with the General Education Program and various faculty committees in that program. As such, this course description not only functioned as an important guide for writing program faculty but also as a statement to the university community of the significance of research writing in the college curriculum. Obviously, too, it tried to be all things to all people, speaking to various constituencies using multiple voices. Not incidentally, and largely at the urging of the Dean of General Education, we have since implemented a single freshman composition course with, we hope, a more focused purpose.

It is easy to see the ways in which program goals and individual pedagogy can (and need) to inform and support one another. This is an important base to have before beginning a large-scale program assessment as it provides a kind of "check and balance" between what we *say* we value with what we actually evaluate.

The Why Behind the How: Identifying the Motivations Behind the Urge to Assess

Teachers of writing are accustomed to the requirement to grade students and have, more recently, grown accustomed to pressure from administrators to resist "grade inflation" in the midst of a student culture that increasingly presses for high grades. To set up a syllabus with weighted assignments, to allow for participation points or extra credit, or to build in mechanisms that credit students for effort and improvement are familiar components in the experience of teaching writing. So, too, is the student evaluation of faculty and the practice of having a colleague or supervisor observe a class. But lately assessment has gone off in new directions.

In 1999, the State Council for Higher Education in Virginia (SCHEV) created a new accountability tool called the "Reports of Institutional Effectiveness" (ROIE). This tool was informed implicitly by SCHEV's mission: "To promote the development and operation of an educationally and economically sound, vigorous, progressive, and coordinated system of higher education"—-and addressed explicitly in "Item 9" of SCHEV's "Roles and Responsibilities"—"To develop in cooperation with institutions of higher education guidelines for the assessment of student achievement."

These annual reports were designed to provide evidence of institutional effectiveness as well as to provide "meaningful information on the academic quality and operational efficiency of Virginia's public institutions of higher education." An integral part of these reports is the "Core Competency Report," which focuses on "general education" assessments in written communication and technology and information literacy. And it is the Core Competency Report that we are most interested in, as it was (and continues to be) the motivating force behind our Writing Program's establishment of a program-wide, quantitative writing assessment for our first-year writing course.

White, Lutz, and Kamusikiri (1996) write that the politics of writing assessment is a central concern

> because assessment is unavoidably a political act. All authoritative decisions that affect the lives and conduct of individuals and groups, such as the decisions made in writing assessment, are political. Assessment expresses a hierarchy of values and those who control assessment determine the values that prevail. Assessment results identify those who most fully internalize and support the prevailing values and who thus are most entitled to the best rewards. Such is the nature of assessing writing: whether its purpose is formative or summative, whether it decides placement or measures achievement, or whether it is carried out in the classroom or statewide—it is political. (1–2)

Indeed the whole enterprise is a political one. A second look at SCHEV's rationale for conducting "Reports of Institutional Effectiveness" shows a motivation that is far removed from merely wanting to document the "quality" of higher education in Virginia. They also look for "operational efficiency" and the "value added" by the programs offered by Virginia colleges. Of most concern is the rather unclear language used to describe the use to which these studies will be put. They write that the reports, "though not formally linked to any future funding model for higher education," are intended to "provide evidence of the value added by our colleges and universities to the Commonwealth of Virginia." They go on to contend that "by design, the Reports of Institutional Effectiveness will not be directly related to funding" but follow that assertion with an entirely opposite sentiment:

> however, since the information contained in the Reports will reflect institutions' actual performance in meeting and fulfilling institution-specific goals and missions, it naturally follows that the Reports likely will prove to be a useful source of information for those making budget requests as well as those considering and making decisions about such requests.

What is difficult to discern from these descriptions is the extent to which these reports can and will be used to determine funding for each institution. We can learn from such an example that the "why" needs to be put before the "how"; that is, before undertaking an assessment project initiated from an outside agency, those participating in assessment need to learn more about the uses to which such data will be put. White et al. echo this sentiment: "Crucial is the issue of who determines the policies that control any writing assessment and who defines the uses to which the results of the assessment are put" (2).

Case in Point—Case in Progress:
Addressing the "Why?"

The Writing Program at JMU became a stand-alone program in the fall of 1998. No longer housed in the English department, the program was encouraged to enhance the professional status of the writing curriculum and to "grow" the rich field of rhetoric and composition (this "growth" would take root three years later in the formation of a writing minor). But a great deal of our work in the program is centered on the delivery of first-year composition, work that we as a faculty take very seriously as it is often the only instruction in writing that students will receive while at JMU.

Still a brand-new program with (mostly) brand-new faculty in the fall of 1999, we had not yet formulated a program mission or articulated our own sense of writing pedagogy when we were asked by JMU's General Education program to prepare guidelines for assessing our first-year students. Working closely with the Center for Assessment and Research Studies at JMU and assessment expert Edward White, the Writing Program's newly formed assessment committee developed an assessment plan.

As a new program, we were already struggling with how best to refine and revise (and, now, review) our writing instruction. After all, there were two freshman composition courses (101 and 102), and the second one, GWRIT 102, was divided into four different "packages" (A, B, D, and E), which corresponded to different focuses within possible major concentrations (philosophy, business, history, and technology, respectively; a "C" package was developed but not implemented). This division made it particularly difficult to establish a stable mode of assessment, as each class had a different textbook, employed different writing assignments, and endorsed different critical modes of thinking about writing.

After surveying numerous approaches (standardized writing "test," writer survey, entry/exit writing sample), we decided that the best course of action would be a portfolio assessment because it would allow for a small cross-section of the writing done in our classes to be looked at in a more holistic way. The actual portfolios contained three student essays: one cover essay that was written as a summative "Myself as a Writer" self-assessment, and two other essays that were representative of the students' best work in the class. In our eagerness to be thorough and cooperative, we collected portfolios from every GWRIT 102 student, and three of four portfolios were randomly selected for evaluation (a sample of 1,108 portfolios, or 3,324 essays, or over 15,000 pages of student writing). Understandably, the final sample was subsequently reduced to 478, given rating time. The seventeen raters recruited from JMU included five permanent faculty, two adjunct instructors, and three graduate teaching assistants from the Writing Program, as well as five instructors (three permanent and two adjunct) from related fields (e.g., School of

Communication Studies) plus an assessment graduate student and our consultant Edward White.

A four-point holistic rubric was created to rate the portfolios; this rubric
was based on the course guidelines for GWRIT 102, as developed by the
Writing Program. There were two four-hour norming sessions to train raters in
how to apply the rubric. Writing Program faculty who recognized an essay as
being from one of their own students were asked to mark it with an asterisk,
rate it, then pass it on to the next rater. Only 23 such instances actually occurred in the total of 478 portolios that were subsequently rated. Portfolios receiving rankings with greater than a one-point discrepancy were rated by the
consultant and his rating was the final rating.

An informal benchmark mean score of 2.5 was agreed upon by the group
as what the "average student" should be expected to receive on the portfolio.
The mean for this initial portfolio rating session was 2.36. What this rating
meant to the program was that the writing samples, on average, were below
what we would have wanted/expected for someone leaving our 102 courses.
What this rating did not tell us was what to do about it. Furthermore, the "Rating Results" section of the report—written by the Center for Assessment
Studies—detailed some other limitations of the study and offered some rather
reductive conclusions.

The results note that "inter-rater reliability"—that is, the extent to which
each rater agreed with the second rater—was not high. The cause of this was
not made clear in this initial report, but was later explored in a paper written
by two of the outside representatives from the Assessment Office, Kathleen
Haley and John Willse. This paper, titled "Issues in Assessing Writing: Rater
Influences," was presented at the 2001 American Educational Research Association (AERA) Conference and explored the low reliability numbers. What is
rather shocking about the existence of this report is that the authors neither
received permission from the raters to use them as "human subjects" for such
a study, nor did they inform the raters that they were thinking about writing
such a report. The report itself is largely anecdotal, not informed by any studies on the assessment of writing practices, and, we believe, misleading in its
conclusions: for they conclude that writing faculty are biased in writing assessment because their scores were higher than those outside raters, thus prov-
ing that "raters will rate their own students' work higher than will outside
raters." The flaw in this conclusion lies in the question that produced it. They
investigated a question that arose from their very limited observations of our
handling of our (very new) writing assessment procedures: "Do raters rate
work produced by their own students higher than do other raters?" The flaw in
this question lies in the fact that it is less a question of *writing* assessment than
it is a question of *rater* assessment; that is, the study spends more time examining variations in rater performance than in assessing writing, which is the
raison d'etre for the study itself.

Haley and Willse's implicit assumption that all of the writing would be
largely the same fuels the drive and the justification for a quantitative analysis

of such writing and denies the fact that each instructor could choose his or her own textbook, could advance very different writing assignments, and endorse very different (but equally valuable) critical modes of thinking about writing. Certainly, this kind of an example points to the fact that we, as teachers of writing, need to carefully assess the assessors; we need to ask, at the very least, "To what ends will this research be used?" In this case, the writing faculty at JMU were portrayed in a rather negative light, but more than that, the implication from this study is that we are not qualified to assess the writing coming out of our own program. The loss of sovereignty here is significant, for it suggests that in order to validate our work as teachers of writing we must surrender our expertise and fragment our process into easily measurable components.

Despite all of the conclusions formulated from our initial portfolio assessment, the actual results speak to a very different problem: no conclusions about writing can really be offered from quantitative writing assessment. The results from the summer 2000 Writing Portfolio Assessment Report, also written by Haley and Willse, read as follows:

> Because there is no pre-measure of writing ability taken before students have the class, there is no way to know how the class affects students. Students' portfolios could contain writings that are the same, worse, or better than their writings were before the class. So data from this assessment can speak to the quality of student writing after GWRIT 102, but the data cannot provide information about how the class contributed to this writing. Also, because the data is only in terms of holistic scores, there is no empirical indication of what aspects of students' writing are meeting or failing to meet expectations. (6)

Essentially, this data points to the fact that it can neither measure the degree to which the course affected student writing nor the ways in which the program can respond to the deficiencies noted in the portfolios. Over the next three years, along with the holistic scores, the program would be asked to begin assessing two "trait scores" that would look closely at specific elements of student writing and measure them with a separate four-point scale.

The idea behind developing such a measurement tool is that trait scoring, because of its limited and specific nature, would allow us as a faculty to better identify the weaknesses in student writing and, thus, be able to address those weaknesses in our classes. But what trait scoring really does is divide the whole of the writing process into manageable, measurable pieces, which is great for generating data, but unthinkable for teachers of writing who espouse a philosophy based on the idea that "writing and its pedagogy is exceedingly complex, that ever shifting individual and group contexts govern effective communication" (White et al. 1996, 14).

Beyond the logistics of conducting a study with so many mitigating factors, came a larger, more important question: Why conduct such a study at all?

In that question alone, we realized that we had put the "how" before the "why"; now, we are trying to design a method of assessment that would best address our needs as a program, so we begin with the end in mind. More than just providing data about which of our four packages were the strongest and which the weakest, we wanted the assessment to help us address how to make improvements to our existing method of delivering freshman composition and, more important, we wanted our assessment structure to help us address exactly where those improvements needed to take place. In other words, we wanted assessment to help us, not for us to help assessment.

The impetus to develop a mode of assessment that dealt in percentages and means and averages came from without. Now, as we prepare for program review and launch our new writing course, we very much need a mode of assessment developed from within.

Do we want to be accountable for our classes? Of course. But to whom?

"Are You Afraid to Be Held Accountable?"

As a writing faculty member, you have limited power, but you can always ask questions. If you're new to a program or interviewing for a job, don't hesitate to ask about assessment early on. But don't stop with the answer. Follow up and find out how your courses will be assessed, what you have to provide, how your assignments may be affected (or even limited and regulated), and what duties you will have—or what pressures to participate—in terms of the actual assessment procedures.

Ultimately, these questions will lead you back to your own attitudes toward evaluation, accountability, and authority. These are important questions because they affect the way you choose textbooks; create a syllabus; run a classroom; interact with your colleagues and the administrators of programs, colleges, and universities and funding agencies, whether grant-giving foundations or state legislatures.

It's up to you to come to your own conclusions about accountability and evaluation, but remember that what is now called assessment is likely to move you in a certain direction without your full awareness unless you aggressively seek to understand the current process, its history, and the forces that are molding it. As a teacher, you assess individual student writers in various ways. For any given assignment, you not only attach a grade but also make remarks, orally and in written form. Ultimately, at the end of the course, you assign a final grade, which permanently represents the credit earned by the student in your course at your institution. It goes on the transcript as if it is a clear indication of ability and accomplishment in writing, when in fact it is possible that a student who has earned a "B" doesn't "write better" (whatever that may mean) than a student who got a "C." Frequently, course grades are determined by negatives: absences, missed assignments, uncharacteristically poor performances. And, just as frequently, grades are "inflated" by "participation" and "bonus points," components that have almost nothing to do with the quality of the student's writing. We simply do not assess individual students in the same way that an outside agency assesses an individual program.

Finally, almost the worst thing you can say about an intellectual worker is, "You don't know what you're talking about." Unfortunately, in the case of assessment, this is understandably all too true. We have neither the statistical expertise nor the political awareness to fully comprehend the forces at work. We had better at least ask a lot of questions in order to educate ourselves, while adapting to rapidly changing funding and regulatory environments.

Given the realities of politics and higher education in the public sector, one of the better questions is, "What can a program possibly learn from the best possible assessment, and how can we negotiate to make sure that the best possible assessment is what happens?" If we as faculty members bring to the assessment process the same good faith and conscientious desire to help students that we bring into the classroom, we certainly contribute to clarifying and improving assessment in our programs.

So is writing assessment something to be avoided? No. It is, ironically, something to be vigorously assessed; teachers of writing need to carefully question and investigate the motivations of those who initiate such assessment and to be ever aware that these results can be used in the service of political bodies to determine funding, in the service of assessment offices to develop instruments to test and sell to other institutions, or as food for reports that may not be reliable indicators. Teachers of writing need to take an active role in the shaping of assessment. At the very least, we should "expect our assessment theory to be consistent with our theories of reading, writing, and pedagogy" (White et al. 1996, 17).

Nancy Wood wrote that "argument is everywhere." We think the same can be said of assessment. (And wherever there is assessment, there is bound to be more argument.) But the urge for writing assessment can be used in a valuable way:

> Writing assessment does not exist in its own sphere, as a simple instrument of educational or public policy, but rather is an integral part of the field of composition. We cannot assess writing unless we know what we mean by writing, what it is we are trying to assess. (White et al. 1996, 4)

In short, White et al. point out a simple but powerful way that assessment can be made meaningful: it forces discussion about what it is we really *do* in our writing classes, what we value, how we reinforce it. And indeed, we found this to be true in our writing assessments at JMU. While the data was not meaningful to us, the discussions we had while rating the portfolios, talking (and disagreeing) about the items on the rubric, and commenting on the types and styles of writing we encountered in the portfolios were the most valuable feedback we received. From these conversations, we were able to generate new course guidelines, institute training seminars and workshop discussions, and begin to articulate a writing philosophy that informs our teaching in our new first-year course. Assessment can be used to merely regulate and narrate progress, or it can be used to stimulate and create it. It is this creative potential that we are most interested in as we turn a careful eye to the future.

Works Cited

Burke, J. C., S. Modarresi, and A. M. Serban. 1999. "Performance: Shouldn't It Count for Something in State Budgeting?" *Change: The Magazine of Higher Learning.* November, Heldref Publications, 1999; Gale Group Copyright 2000.

Haley, Kathleen, and John Willse. 2001. "Issues in Assessing Writing: Rater Influences." Paper presented at the annual meeting of the American Educational Research Association (AERA), Seattle.

State Council of Higher Education in Virginia (SCHEV). 1999. *www.schev.edu/ SCHEVs/SCHEVs.asp?from=schevs* Accessed 11 October 2003.

White, Edward M., William D. Lutz, and Sandra Kamusikiri. 1996. *Assessment of Writing: Politics, Policies, Practices.* New York: The Modern Language Association of America.

Wilse, John, and Kathleen Haley. 2000. "Cluster 1 Writing Portfolio Assessment Report." Summer (Unpublished Report).

Wood, Nancy. 1997. *Perspectives on Argument.* 2nd ed. Englewood Cliffs, NJ: Prentice Hall.

Contributors' Notes

Shelley Aley is associate professor in the James Madison University Writing Program, where she serves as the director of composition. She teaches composition and courses in rhetoric and writing. She has presented papers and published articles and book chapters on the history of rhetoric, composition studies, technology and writing, popular culture, and literature. Her current writing projects focus on the history and future development of independent writing programs.

Sarah Allen comes from a literature and creative writing background. She started writing exploratory essays five years ago and now devotes much of her work to scholarship on the essay. Sarah is a rhetoric and composition PhD student at the University of South Carolina at Columbia, where she teaches composition courses and is the assistant director of the first-year English program.

Chris Anson is professor of English and director of the Campus Writing and Speaking Program at North Carolina State University, where he helps faculty in nine colleges to use writing and speaking in the service of students' learning and improved communication. Before joining NC State in 1999, he spent fifteen years at the University of Minnesota, where he directed the program in composition from 1988 to 1996 and was Morse-Alumni Distinguished Teaching Professor. He has published and spoken widely on writing, teaching, and literacy development. He is the president of the Council of Writing Program Administrators. His professional summary may be found at *www.home. earthlink.net/~theansons/Portcover.html.*

Lisa Bickmore has taught writing at Salt Lake Community College for twelve years. Her current research focuses on the rhetorical economy of poetry. Her book of poems, *Haste,* was published in 1994 (Signature Press).

Wendy Bishop, former Kellogg W. Hunt Professor of English, taught writing at Florida State University. She was the author or editor of a number of books, including *Ethnographic Writing Research*; *Teaching Lives*; *Thirteen Ways of Looking for a Poem*; *The Subject Is Research* (with Pavel Zemliansky); *In Praise of Pedagogy*; *On Writing, A Process Reader*; *Acts of Revision*: *A Guide for Writers;* and several chapbooks of poetry.

Elizabeth Chiseri-Strater teaches composition, literacy, and research methods at the University of North Carolina at Greensboro, where she has worked with the freshman English, English education, and women's and gender studies programs. She is the author of *Academic Literacies* (Boynton/Cook, 1991) and coauthor with Bonnie Sunstein of *FieldWorking: Reading and Writing Research* (Bedford/St. Martin's, 2002). Together they teach at Northeastern University's Martha's Vineyard Summer Institute on Writing, Reading, and Teaching.

Deborah Coxwell-Teague is director of the first-year writing program at Florida State University. She trains and supervises the more than 130 graduate teaching assistants who teach FSU's two hundred-plus sections of first-year writing each semester, and she enjoys working with students of all ages. Deborah loves spending time with her four children—ages eight, nine, twenty-seven, and twenty nine—and her nine-year-old grandchild. She also enjoys working in her yard and taking long walks on the beach. Her current research interests include seldom-discussed yet crucial issues for new teachers of writing along with exploring resistance to technology.

Robert Davis is an associate professor of English-writing at Eastern Oregon University, where he directs the Cornerstone Program that combines research, practice, community service, and intercultural learning. He is also the university's director of strategic planning and the former chair of the Division of Arts and Letters, as well as a past chair of the Oregon Writing and English Advisory Committee. He teaches courses for students on campus and at a distance in research writing, rhetoric, the essay, discourse theory, and writing in electronic culture.

Catherine Gabor is an assistant professor at California State University at Sacramento, where she teaches undergraduate and graduate courses in composition and helps administer the writing program.

Maureen Daly Goggin is associate professor of rhetoric in the English department at Arizona State University, where she teaches courses in the history and theories of rhetoric, composition, and writing. She is author of *Authoring a Discipline: Scholarly Journals and the Post–World War II Emergence of Rhetoric and Composition* and editor of *Inventing a Discipline: Rhetoric Scholarship in Honor of Richard E. Young.* Her publications on the history of rhetoric and composition as well as on visual and material rhetoric appear in *Rhetoric Review, Rhetoric Society Quarterly, Composition Studies,* and various edited collections.

Paul Heilker teaches courses in writing, rhetoric, composition pedagogy, and literary nonfiction at Virginia Tech, where he serves as coordinator of the university writing program and director of first-year composition. He is the author of *The Essay: Theory and Pedagogy for an Active Form* (NCTE, 1996) and coeditor (with Peter Vandenberg) of *Keywords in Composition Studies* (Heinemann, 1996). His work has appeared in *Rhetoric Review, Composition Studies, Computers and Composition, Teaching English in the Two-Year College, The Writing Instructor*, and *Writing on the Edge.*

Carrie Leverenz is associate professor of English and director of composition at Texas Christian University, where she teaches courses in writing, cyberliteracy, and composition theory. She is currently at work on a book,

Doing the Right Thing: Ethical Issues in Institutionalized Writing Instruction, which uses ethics theory to understand the complex work of writing programs. With her colleague Ann George, she edits the journal *Composition Studies.*

Emily L. Sewall received her Master's degree in English from Virginia Tech in 2003. During her time at Tech, her research and scholarship focused on composition studies, specifically in the area of one-on-one conferencing pedagogy. She currently teaches first-year writing and technical writing at the Virginia Military Institute in Lexington, Virginia.

Janette Martin, assistant professor in the McIntire School of Commerce at the University of Virginia, teaches courses in business communication and managerial writing. Her scholarly work has appeared in *INTERFACES: A French/English Journal of the Humanities, The Academic Exchange Quarterly, World Literature Written in English,* and others. Her research interests include persuasive writing and audience, rhetoric and corporate communication, culture and communication, and ethics and communication.

Dan Melzer is the reading and writing coordinator at California State University at Sacramento. He teaches a variety of composition courses and runs the Writing Across the Curriculum program at CSUS.

Cindy Moore directs the composition program at St. Cloud State University, where she also teaches courses in writing and writing theory. She is a strong advocate of collaborative scholarship—an attitude that is reflected in her two coedited books (*Practice in Context: Situating the Work of Writing Teachers* [NCTE] and *The Dissertation and the Discipline: Reinventing Composition Studies* [Boynton/Cook]), coauthored articles that have appeared in such places as *CCC* and this volume, and collaborative conference presentations.

Joyce Magnotto Neff is associate chair and associate professor of English at Old Dominion University, where she teaches in the professional writing program. Previously, she served as chair of the writing department at Prince George's Community College and worked as a writing consultant for the U.S. General Accounting Office. She is coauthor of *Professional Writing in Context* and has published numerous articles and chapters on writing across the curriculum, writing centers, grounded theory, and workplace writing. Her current research includes a longitudinal study of writing and distance education. Neff also serves as secretary of the Conference on College Composition and Communication.

Georgia A. Newman has taught writing-intensive English courses for three decades, first at Polk Community College (Winter Haven, FL) and, more recently, at Georgia College & State University (Milledgeville). Authoring many articles and conference presentations on composition pedagogy, Newman also writes on literary topics, especially the work of writer Flannery O'Connor.

Peggy O'Neill teaches writing and directs the composition program at Loyola College in Maryland. Her scholarship, which includes writing assessment theory and practice, composition pedagogy, and teacher preparation, has been published in a variety of journals and edited collections. She is a dedicated collaborative writer and researcher, a habit formed during graduate school. Recent collaborative projects include *Practice in Context: Situating the Work of Writing Teachers* (2002, coedited with Cindy Moore) and *A Field of Dreams: Independent Writing Programs and the Future of Composition Studies* (2002).

Traci Pipkins is assistant professor of writing at James Madison University. For the past two years, she has served as the chair of the Writing Program's Assessment Committee and has revisited and re-visioned the program's measurement tools at all stages: course assessment, teacher evaluations, and program review. She has presented papers on assessment at several conferences and looks to find ways to combine writing process with assessment practice. Her current research is grounded in the rise of the reader in the early modern period.

Tom Reigstad is professor of English at Buffalo State College, where he teaches writing and American literature. He has directed the freshman writing program and pioneered the college's writing portfolio assessment program. He is coauthor of *Tutoring Writing* and has published numerous articles and chapters on writing pedagogy and Mark Twain studies. He was awarded a researcher-in-residence at the Elmira College Center for Mark Twain studies and is currently writing a book on Twain's Buffalo period.

Duane Roen, professor of English at Arizona State University, performed duties as director of composition before assuming his current job of directing ASU's Center for Learning and Teaching Excellence (*http://clte.asu.edu*). In addition to more than 140 articles, chapters, and conference papers, Duane has completed the following book projects: *Strategies for Teaching First-Year Composition* (with Veronica Pantoja, Lauren Yena, Susan K. Miller, and Eric Waggoner); *Composing Our Lives in Rhetoric and Composition: Stories About the Growth of a Discipline* (with Theresa Enos and Stuart Brown); *The Writer's Toolbox* (with Stuart Brown and Bob Mittan); *A Sense of Audience in Written Discourse* (with Gesa Kirsch); *Becoming Expert: Writing and Learning Across the Disciplines* (with Stuart Brown and Bob Mittan); and *Richness in Writing: Empowering ESL Students* (with the late Donna Johnson). His current book project, with Greg Glau and Barry Maid, is *Writing for College, Writing for Life*, under contract with McGraw-Hill.

Stephen Ruffus is in his fifteenth year teaching at Salt Lake Community College, where he formerly directed the writing program and founded a student writing center and community writing center. He has also taught writing and literature at the University of Utah. He serves on the editorial board for *Teaching English in the Two-Year College* and is a past member of the *CCC* editorial board. Professor Ruffus is a coauthor of *The Mercury Reader* (Pearson 1999). He is about to complete his term as a member of the CCCC Executive Committee.

Mark Shadle is professor of English-writing at Eastern Oregon University in La Grande, Oregon. His current teaching on campus and through distance education are specializations in writing and discourse theory, exploratory writing, multicuitura! iiterature, detective fiction, travel writing, and the literature and rhetoric of place. Past president of the Pacific Coast Writing Centers Association, he has also been a member of the National Writing Centers Association and Chair of the Oregon Rhetoric and Composition Conference. He has published on writing centers, writing across the curriculum, teaching in the Oregon Writing Project, Wendell Berry, Ishmael Reed, contemporary African literature, and blues/jazz. With coauthor Rob Davis, he has published articles, book chapters, and two forthcoming books on multiwriting in multiple genres, disciplines, media, and cultures.

Bonnie Sunstein is professor of English and education at the University of Iowa in Iowa City, where she directs both undergraduate writing and English education and teaches nonfiction writing, ethnographic research, folklore, and English. She has taught English in public schools and colleges throughout New England, and at professional development institutes across the country. In 2000, she received an "Imagining America" grant from the Woodrow Wilson Foundation for the website "FieldWorking Online" (*www.fieldworking.com*) now a virtual community for student and faculty researchers. A Trustee of the National Council of Teachers of English's Research Foundation, she has co-edited three widely read collections of articles about portfolios—*Portfolio Portraits* (Heinemann, 1992), *Assessing Portfolios: A Portfolio* (NCTE, 1996), and *The Portfolio Standard* (Heinemann, 2000). Her chapters, articles, and poems appear in many professional journals and books.

Kenneth R. Wright is an assistant professor in the Writing Program at James Madison University. His current research involves exploring academia's perceptions of independent writing programs through Kenneth Burke's concept of "trained incapacity."

Pavel Zemliansky is assistant professor of rhetoric and writing at James Madison University, where he teaches courses in composition and rhetoric. His publications include *The Subject Is Research* (coedited with Wendy Bishop, Heinemann) as well as articles in *Kairos* and *Composition Forum*. His scholarly interests include research-writing pedagogy and computers and writing.

Jim Zimmerman, assistant professor in James Madison University's Writing Program, first became involved in assessment in 1970–71 as an undergraduate at The University of Michigan when he chaired the Association for Course Evaluation and administered the undergraduate course evaluation, sponsored by the Student Government Council. As a journalist, he has written about alternative grading systems. He has taught college writing and coached leaders of large organizations for the past twenty-five years, continually confronting issues of grading, faculty evaluation, performance reviews, and other forms of quantitative and qualitative evaluation. At JMU, he served on the Writing Program's Assessment Committee in 2001–02 and participated in the annual writing assessment in 2001 and 2002.